WHOSE RIGHTS?

WHOSE RIGHTS?

COUNTERTERRORISM AND THE DARK SIDE OF AMERICAN PUBLIC OPINION

CLEM BROOKS AND JEFF MANZA

Russell Sage Foundation • New York

The Russell Sage Foundation

The Russell Sage Foundation, one of the oldest of America's general purpose foundations, was established in 1907 by Mrs. Margaret Olivia Sage for "the improvement of social and living conditions in the United States." The Foundation seeks to fulfill this mandate by fostering the development and dissemination of knowledge about the country's political, social, and economic problems. While the Foundation endeavors to assure the accuracy and objectivity of each book it publishes, the conclusions and interpretations in Russell Sage Foundation publications are those of the authors and not of the Foundation, its Trustees, or its staff. Publication by Russell Sage, therefore, does not imply Foundation endorsement.

Library of Congress Cataloging-in-Publication Data

Brooks, Clem.
  Whose rights? : counterterrorism and the dark side of American public opinion / Clem Brooks and Jeff Manza.
    pages cm
  Includes bibliographical references and index.
  ISBN 978-0-87154-058-4 (pbk. : alk. paper) 1. Terrorism—United States—Prevention. 2. Public opinion--United States. I. Manza, Jeff. II. Title.
    HV6432.B76 2013
    363.325'170973--dc23   2012032508

Text design by Suzanne Nichols.

RUSSELL SAGE FOUNDATION
112 East 64th Street, New York, New York 10065

10 9 8 7 6 5 4 3 2 1

Contents

Figures and Tables

About the Authors

Clem Brooks is Rudy Professor of Sociology at Indiana University, Bloomington.

Jeff Manza is professor of sociology at New York University.

Preface

THE ORIGINS of this project go back seven years. We were beginning a new collaboration that sought to apply experimental survey research techniques to examine how Americans form policy attitudes in the contemporary era, especially on issues relating to rising economic inequality and social policies that might redistribute the benefits of economic growth more widely. But as our work unfolded, with the collection of initial survey data from a couple of national surveys we conducted in 2005 and 2007, we were bowled over by results that had nothing to do with inequality or domestic social policy. Instead, something that was initially a small part of our data collection—some experiments on attitudes relating to the war on terror—produced unexpected results that we found riveting.

This initial interest in Americans' responses to the war on terror emerged just as some of the most important revelations about the Bush administration's departures from international law and established civil liberties protections were coming to light. We wondered whether and to what extent Americans would continue to support war on terror policies. Survey experiments, we thought, would be ideal to get more detail as to how far Americans were willing to go in support of post-9/11 counterterrorism.

The kinds of issues invoked by national security policies relating to rights and terrorism have wide-ranging and troubling implications. For one thing, they put to the test the view that Americans' willingness to extend civil liberties protections to unpopular groups has changed since the 1940s (when Japanese Americans were rounded up and interned during World War II on the basis of ethnicity) or since the 1960s, after which Americans moved closer to embracing the principle of equality under the law for African Americans and women, and arguably moving in recent years closer to such a posture toward gays and lesbians. Because the threat of terrorist attacks came from Islamic radicals from the Middle East, we wondered what carefully designed experiments might show about Americans' attitudes toward people of Middle Eastern descent or more generally to foreign nationals.

In 2008, the election of Democrat Barack Obama, a frequent critic of many Bush administration policies, seemed to usher in a new era of respect for Constitutional limits on surveillance and international law regarding the treatment of enemy combatants. It also provided us with a "natural experiment" in which the pivot of political and policy rhetoric coming out of the White House would shift dramatically. We wondered if this shift would move mass opinion away from policy positions supported before Obama's election, as well as whether the same framing experiments used earlier might now have different impacts.

We had the good fortune to be able to conduct two additional national surveys, in 2009 and 2010, that included an expanded battery of survey items that would allow us to see how much regime change at home might impact the way Americans thought about these issues. The results of these surveys, as well as the 2007 survey, are presented in this book. We think the results provide a new picture, one benefiting from experiments that uncover novel dynamics as well as some of the complexities of Americans' attitudes towards counterterrorism policies pursued by the U.S. government since 9/11. Our results also speak to some important and long-standing scholarly debates in public opinion research, political sociology, and American politics, and we also draw connections to the broader historical and cultural contexts in which our results are situated.

Acknowledgments

W<small>E HAVE</small> had support from three wonderful institutions—the Russell Sage Foundation (RSF), the National Science Foundation (NSF), the Department of Sociology and Center for Survey Research (CSR) at Indiana University—that have provided the funding and in the CSR's case, survey expertise, that allowed us to design and conduct our surveys. We first began the project when Manza was a fellow at Russell Sage in New York in 2005–2006, where he benefited immensely from a superb collection of social scientists and the warm support and intellectual guidance of RSF president Eric Wanner. We later received an RSF grant, as well as two NSF grants, that enabled us to continue our work and conduct the 2009 and 2010 surveys we draw upon in the book.

We have also had the good fortune to call on friends and colleagues for guidance and assistance, as well as the opportunity to present our work to a variety of scholarly audiences. We would like to thank Fernández Albertos, Arthur Alderson, Robert Andersen, Stephen Benard, David Brady, Paul Burstein, Ines Calzada, Kyle Dodson, Jamie Druckman, David Grusky, Timothy Hallett, Nikole Hotchkiss, Michael Hout, Koen Jonkers, John Levi Martin, Joe Margulies, Javier Moreno, Patricia McManus, Sigrun Olafsdottir, Robert Robinson, Stefan Svallfors, John Torpey, and especially Paul Sniderman for comments and help with the project. We also benefited from suggestions provided by two RSF reviewers. We presented parts of this project at annual meetings of the American Sociological Association, the CUNY Graduate Center, Florida State University, Princeton University, Rutgers University, the University of Toronto, and the University of Washington, where we benefited from feedback and discussion with seminar participants.

Clem Brooks
Bloomington, Ind.

Jeff Manza
New York City

Introduction

THE TERRORIST attacks on the World Trade Center and the Pentagon carried out by al-Qaeda operatives on September 11, 2001, were shattering events. They fueled widespread anger, a desire for revenge, and a new sense of threat and vulnerability among most Americans. Powerful and deep-seated responses coincided with unprecedented, blanket media coverage of the attacks in the days following 9/11. This coverage featured seemingly endless loops of planes crashing into buildings, speculation about the source of the attacks and the possibility of further terrorist activity, and news conferences in which political leaders vowed revenge. One day after the attacks, a *New York Times* editorial referred to the specter of "more lethal nuclear, biological or chemical attacks by terrorists," arguing that "this cannot be just another moment when the president declares that the United States is unbreakable. . . . It must be the occasion for a fundamental reassessment of intelligence and defense activities" ("The War Against America: The National Defense," September 12, 2001).

The response of the Bush administration and Congress was rapid and far-reaching. At a press conference just days after 9/11, President George W. Bush announced that America was facing "a new kind of evil," and CNN reported that the administration anticipated a new war on terror that could "take years" ("Administration Predicts the Fight Will Take Years," *CNN Online*, September 16, 2001). Referring to the American public, a *Time* magazine article proclaimed that "if ever there was a time when they might be receptive to trimming their accustomed freedoms, that time is now. And whether they are receptive or not, the changes have already begun" (Richard Lacayo, Andrew Goldstein, Chris Taylor, and Elizabeth Bland, "Terrorizing Ourselves," September 24, 2001). Under the leadership of Vice President Dick Cheney and Defense Secretary Donald Rumsfeld, the Bush administration began preparations for war, first in Afghanistan and later in Iraq.

On the home front, a wide-ranging policy response to the attacks

1

quickly unfolded. Measures such as the Patriot Act, in conjunction with newly implemented electronic intelligence-gathering and surveillance programs, vastly expanded the domestic reach of the Central Intelligence Agency (CIA) and the National Security Agency (NSA). Abroad, a dramatic increase in military special operations and covert CIA actions included the seizure—or "rendition"—of terrorism suspects without due process, the use of torture to extract information, and targeted killings of specific individuals.

There can be no question that the new counterterrorism laws and policies adopted by the federal government in the wake of the September 11 attacks had major impacts on American society and politics. Legal scholars have noted that these policies altered long-standing interpretations of the Constitution, generating new debates surrounding America's relationship to international human rights agreements (American Bar Association 2003; Cole and Dempsey 2006). To this point, post-9/11 counterterrorism policies have largely survived the transition from Republican congressional majorities during the presidency of George W. Bush to Democratic congressional majorities established after 2006 through 2010, and the presidency of Barack Obama. They appear poised to become lasting institutional features of American government.

A quick examination of the most important of these policies attests to their importance. Consider first the 2001 Patriot Act. Signed into law forty-five days after the attacks, the Patriot Act enables law enforcement agencies to more readily obtain phone, email, and financial data. In doing so, the act significantly weakens the protections created by the Fourth Amendment's prohibition on unlawful search. Before its passage, for instance, agencies such as the Federal Bureau of Investigation were required to obtain court warrants for searches and provide documentation to the accused. The Patriot Act's "sneak and peak" provisions dispensed with this protection, making it unnecessary to establish probable cause as a precondition to the surveillance of individual suspects.

The Patriot Act presents a new trade-off on a second constitutional protection. The act's broad definition of terrorism appears to have unintentionally facilitated the wider use of ethnic profiling. After the 9/11 attacks, the mere suspicion of a connection to terrorism, or even immigration violations, was enough to prompt interviews and aggressive requests for information by law enforcement agencies. In this way, the Patriot Act butts up against the Fourteenth Amendment's guarantee of equal protection. According to some observers, traveling, studying, or doing a charitable activity while Arab or Muslim has become a new source of discrimination and political suspicion.

Also emerging in the wake of the 9/11 attacks were contentious, de facto practices adopted by the CIA that departed from international agreements and laws. Stung by sharp criticism from government officials of having failed to anticipate the threat posed by Osama bin Laden and his al-Qaeda organization, the CIA embarked on a broad new course of paramilitary activities. Terrorism suspects numbering in the thousands were apprehended by U.S. operatives in a manner that bracketed the array of established international legal protections. By circumventing due process rights to hear charges and have access to legal representation, the CIA's new practice of rendition bypassed United States, European Union, and international law. Some terrorism suspects were transferred to third-party country governments, some of which were known to routinely torture political prisoners. More frequently, they were detained indefinitely in a network of secret prisons located outside the United States and operated by the CIA. The largest facilities were located at Bagram Air Base in Kabul, Afghanistan, and at Guantanamo Bay, Cuba. But other detention centers, including a number of more secret "black sites," were also created for special "high-value" targets.

In 2004, journalists unearthed evidence of the use by American government operatives at the Abu Ghraib prison facility in Iraq of what was euphemistically described as enhanced interrogation techniques. These included the use of repeated beatings, exposure to extreme cold and sleep deprivation, and the near-death experience induced by waterboarding. The release of photographs highlighting the treatment and torture of detainees at the Abu Ghraib prison provided a visual record of some of these practices, and others were recorded on videotapes that would later be—illegally—destroyed.

Other contentious counterterrorism policies and practices continued to emerge well after the initial shock of the 9/11 attacks. The Bush administration decided soon after 9/11 that many detainees would be tried in military courts, a decision that the Supreme Court would strike down in 2006, on grounds that the use of those courts had not been authorized by Congress. Shortly thereafter, however, the Congress passed, and President Bush signed into law, the Military Commissions Act. This act authorized the use of military courts for trying accused terrorism suspects, effectively limiting Sixth Amendment rights to a jury trial for individuals classified as "enemy combatants," and gave a degree of after-the-fact legalization to the due process and habeas corpus violations associated with the CIA's rendition and detention activities. It also codified the power of the government to try terrorism suspects in secret courts not subject to normal rules of evidence and procedure.

A different and particularly wide-ranging counterterrorism activity involves the growing use of electronic surveillance. After President Bush secretly lifted a ban on domestic spying, the National Security Agency moved swiftly to collect millions of electronic communications involving American citizens as well as foreign nationals. NSA spying within the United States was initially warrantless, bypassing a 1978 law requiring government operatives to apply for court approval. These surveillance activities would later be given retroactive authorization by the passage of the 2008 Foreign Intelligence Surveillance Amendments Act. According to a variety of investigative reports, email and phone communications, banking, even web browsing have become far more subject to collection by government agencies (Bamford 2008; Lichtblau 2008; Risen and Lichtblau 2009).

On their own, each of these new policies and government actions related to the war on terror have been important. Collectively, they have spiraled into an open-ended search for terrorism suspects, directly affecting the lives and liberties of thousands, and even millions in the case of electronic surveillance. Remarkably, however, few viable suspects have been unearthed through these searches. As we note in more detail in chapter 1, evidence indicates that when plots have been uncovered and convictions obtained, they appear to have resulted from traditional law enforcement methods. In an era of large government budget deficits, the economic costs of these programs also appear to be substantial.[1]

To put the issues into sharper focus, the results of scholarship and reporting concerning the risks posed by terrorism are useful. According to this literature, war on terror policies appear to be premised on an exaggerated view of threat. Surprisingly, the evidence suggests that terrorism does not appear to pose a large risk to life. Even in the unusual context of 2001 and the 9/11 attacks, the risk of dying from terrorism in the United States was just one in 101,000 (Mueller and Stewart 2010). That contrasts with the dramatically higher risks in that year of homicide death (one in 22,000), dying in a traffic accident (one in 8,000), and cancer-related fatalities (one in 540). In this same year, bathtub drownings (one in 79,000) posed a far greater risk to American lives than Osama bin Laden and al-Qaeda did. Since 9/11, al-Qaeda attacks outside war zones have killed few Americans (Mueller 2006).[2]

Complementary and equally surprising evidence has come from some counterterrorism officials. According to Michael Sheehan, assistant secretary of defense for special operations, "Al-Qaida wasn't as good as we thought they were on 9/11. . . . Everyone looked to the skies every day after 9/11 and said, 'When is that next attack?' And it didn't come, partly because al-Qaida wasn't that capable. They didn't have other units here in the U.S. . . . Really, they didn't have the capability to conduct a second attack" (Tilghman 2012).

In the face of this evidence concerning the absolute and relative risks posed by international terrorism, counterterrorism policies and practices have emerged as a transformation of American constitutional law and practice. They create an important new set of conflicts between rights protections and national security imperatives, placing limits on long-established domestic and international human rights protections. In doing so, they have dramatically expanded the coercive capacities of U.S. government agencies. They raise the possibility of further and potentially unpredictable uses by American presidents in the future.

Why Public Opinion?

This book examines the political sources and consequences of the war on terror through the lens of public opinion. We look at the attitudes and beliefs of ordinary Americans. We want to better understand when and why Americans have gone along with or actively embraced these policies, and where they may draw the line on what the federal government is allowed to do in the name of fighting terrorism.

Some critical observers of American politics, not to mention a number of our fellow social scientists, may be skeptical that much can be learned about the post-9/11 era and the new war on terror through a focus on mass opinion. If, for instance, readers doubt that there is anything of weight or real substance in the public's attitudes, they may be skeptical about the rationale and ultimate payoff behind our efforts. We hope throughout the rest of the book to provide material for skeptics to rethink a categorical dismissal of policy opinions among the public. For now, however, we want to briefly outline why we expect, indeed why we are compelled to believe, that mass public opinion deserves careful scrutiny if we are to gauge the full significance and relevant dynamics of the post-9/11 war on terror.

Elsewhere we have written at some length on the evidence that public policies are often affected by public opinion (compare Manza and Cook 2002; Brooks and Manza 2007; Manza and Brooks 2012). Our evaluation of that evidence, our own and others' (for example, Stimson, Mackuen, and Erikson 1995; Burstein 1998, 2003; Gilens 1999; Wlezien and Soroka 2010), leads us to the conclusion that public attitudes are frequently, but by no means always, an important determinant of government policy. Sometimes the influence of public opinion is direct—as when elected officials act preemptively in response to public preferences—or indirect, as when voters' attitudes on important issues influence election outcomes. Our conclusions do not mean that other factors—such as political institutions, elite and mass mobilizations, media discourses, and the legacies of past policies—do not also influence policymaking processes. Certainly the relationship between opinion and policy is a probabilistic one; opinion does not determine policy, but much more often than never the public gets policies closer to what majorities prefer, and few policies are sustained over long periods in the face of strong and mobilized public opposition. Persistently unpopular policies are perhaps like a door that is off the hinges; all it takes is a bit of a push and it will fall right over.[3]

To this point, then, our general expectation is that where public opinion is visible to democratically elected politicians, they will tend to respond, even if unevenly and sometimes only indirectly. Almost immediately, we can see the fruitfulness of this position, for it compels us to raise key questions and face central puzzles. If, indeed, Americans did not want new constraints on rights and liberties to be set in place after 9/11, why did counterterrorism policies persist and even expand over time? Alternatively, perhaps the public actually prefers these policies?

Still, the idea that public opinion and policy can be connected one way or another remains controversial. A quick review of what other scholars have said about public opinion will show a pair of objections commonly made against such conclusions.

First, some analysts believe that public opinion is simply too whimsical or easily manipulated by political elites to be worthy of much study. Given their privileged access to the mass media, political elites are capable of shaping the way people think about important policy questions. Mass opinion thus has no "independent" effect on policy outcomes.

In the case of the war on terror, or national security issues more generally, it has sometimes been argued that most Americans simply do not have sufficiently detailed knowledge of the policy issues in question (in this case, the kinds of counterterrorism measures under consideration) to reason about and form stable opinions that are measurable through surveys and alternative methods of data collection. One response to such arguments is that critics of public opinion conflate individual-level instability—that is, actual individuals may be confused, ignorant, or easily manipulated—with aggregate public opinion. But it is aggregate public opinion that frequently matters for politicians and policymakers, as it is generally in the aggregate that policy preferences are read by policymakers.

But aggregate opinion is meaningful to study for other reasons. In the aggregate, individual-level randomness tends to average out. The miracle of aggregation, as it is sometimes called, arises from the fact that sometimes people will mistakenly respond to a survey question one way or the other, but unless errors go disproportionately in one direction, they will tend to average out. Examining aggregate mass opinion is thus informative even when randomness is rife among a majority of individuals.

We also think that the case for a more analytically optimistic view of the mass public when it comes to even complicated foreign policy and counterterrorism questions is a good one. An important review of opinion research by John Aldrich and his colleagues (2006) delivers a thematic result for skeptics: the best evidence suggests foreign policy attitudes are no less real or reflective of prior beliefs and reasoning than domestic policy attitudes. Americans tend to have plenty of initial convictions as regards matters such as the appropriate use of military force,

globalization, and international agreements and treaties, and these issues also have considerable salience for the public. This doesn't mean, of
course, that these beliefs and dispositions are unalterable or insulated
from further thought and interaction with environmental stimuli. But it
does suggest an initial and nontrivial baseline and set of initial inclina-
tions among voters. In concrete settings, it is precisely these dispositions
that are the raw material, interacting with politicians' communications
and other environmental stimuli, out of which public opinion emerges.

From this perspective, it should not be particularly surprising that
counterterrorism measures may be salient and draw from deeply held
beliefs and emotional responses among ordinary Americans. In retrospect, it would be rather shocking if this were not the case. In addition to
the 9/11 attacks and accompanying media coverage (Nacos, Block-Elkon,
and Shapiro 2011), relevant stimuli relating to counterterrorism policies
since then include the following: "orange" threat levels; pat-downs and
full-body scans at U.S. airports; and the specter of foreign-trained, homegrown, and even underwear-loaded bomb suspects at times dominating
the mass media and public discussions.

A second argument against public opinion offers a distinct but no less
skeptical conclusion. Many social scientists, particularly in our own dis-
cipline of sociology, are doubtful that public policy, especially foreign
policy, is informed by public opinion at all, regardless of whether public
opinion exists. The argument here is that the role of powerful actors operating behind the scenes, as it were, is key to understanding political
outcomes. These actors may be powerful because of the money they con-
tribute to the political system, the network ties that bind them together
with elected officials, or their direct influence with government officials
and political party leaders. These beyond-closed-doors arguments could
seem especially powerful in the case of national security policies, which
are frequently shrouded in secrecy and where policy decisions are only
revealed after the fact, for example, through the work of investigative
journalists.

We do not doubt the importance of such actors in shaping policy in
general, and national security policies in particular. But this does not
mean that mass opinion is irrelevant to policy or even to policymakers.
The potential impact of public opinion on government decisions about
such questions as military intervention or foreign policies affecting
American citizens is apparent in memoirs and studies of presidents and
their inner-circle advisors. Presidents and other political elites devote
considerable effort to trying to understand public opinion through in-
house polling, and to manipulate it. We might ask, accordingly, why
politicians and other organized actors ever try to understand or influence public opinion if it is meaningless, or whether other factors are all
that matter?

In this regard, the work of Aldrich and his colleagues (2006) is again telling. They amass evidence that linkages between mass public opinion and the government's national security policies are often substantial (see also Foyle 1999; Sobel 2001). For example, according to the famous rally-around-the-flag thesis, voters can be expected respond predictably and favorably to U.S. presidents when wars or military conflict break out. But with the passage of time and an increase in casualties, government policies come under scrutiny from an impatient and readily dissatisfied public who may seek to recall and punish a sitting president or the incumbent's party at the next election (see also Mueller 1970, 2006). It would be difficult to rule out the relevance of these process in the post-9/11 era, and indeed evidence precisely to this effect exists (Schubert, Stewart, and Curran 2002; Campbell 2006). Far from being irrelevant to understanding the dynamics and consequences of the war on terror, what Americans think and believe looks to be critical.

Coming to Terms with the Dark Side of Public Opinion

If there is a compelling case for taking public opinion seriously, why would there ever be any reflexive skepticism on the part of some scholars and nonscholars? Here we can only offer a conjecture, albeit one that we probe in more detail in the chapters that follow. It goes like this. *The attitudes and beliefs of Americans have a dark side, a willingness to suppress otherwise strong support for civil rights and liberties in the name of national crisis and perceived threats.* Vigorous supporters of rights and liberties may not like it, but this "dark side" of public opinion has, we argue in chapter 1, deep roots in American political culture. The dark side is far from being a permanent condition, but it can be activated under the right conditions, and its impacts are magnified when threats come from unpopular social groups that elicit suspicion or resentment.

History suggests that it is in times of crisis or political contention that the activation of this less-than-liberal side of the American public is most likely to surface. Indeed, this is precisely what has often animated many of the more analytically challenging and normatively provocative episodes of public opinion research in the past (Sullivan, Piereson, and Marcus 1982; Stouffer 1992; Kinder and Sanders 1996). The case of the war on terror and post-9/11 counterterrorism policies may represent a similar, new case. Part of the task of this book is to explore this scenario and the light it sheds on the post-9/11 era.

Why Rights? Why Counterterrorism?

Before the 2001 attacks, a remarkable array of social theorizing suggested the seemingly inexorable march of human rights ideas around the globe.

In the United States, the civil rights and subsequent protest movements of the 1960s were said to have ignited a "rights revolution," presided over by new cadres of progressive experts and activist judges and increasingly entrenched in both political institutions and public opinion (Epp 1998; Skrentny 2002; Ignatieff 2007). An earlier body of scholarship had powerfully documented Americans' increasingly liberal attitudes toward First Amendment liberties and ethnic and racial diversity (Wilson 1994; Marcus et al. 1995; Schuman et al. 1997). On the global scene, international governmental and nongovernmental organizations were seen as sponsoring "world society" norms and international treaties based on individual liberties, rationality, and scientific expertise (Boli and Thomas 1997; Meyer et al. 1997; Frank, Hironaka, and Schofer 2000). Everywhere scholars looked, it seemed that democracy was expanding, dictators were being called to task for human rights violations, and war crimes tribunals were pursuing investigations and making cases against warlords and rogue nation-states.

The overall impression conveyed by these developments is one of steady movement toward ever greater recognition of human and civil rights. What of the war on terror? As regards public responses, the initial conclusion of some opinion researchers was that there was no evidence of any real decline in rights support among the American public. But for a slight dip in the immediate aftermath of the 9/11 attacks, Americans continued to endorse positions that would have pleased most of the Founding Fathers. According to the most comprehensive study, "Americans have not shown a penchant for tolerating restrictions on their freedom and civil liberties. . . . Over time, citizens became more protective of civil liberties than concerned about their security" (Davis 2007, 219).

But as we get further and further away from 9/11, such conclusions leave us with a puzzle. What if high levels of rights support in principle did not preclude favorable views of counterterrorism policies? Could this also be a feature of the post-9/11 era? For the most part, questions such as this go beyond the scope of much of the earlier rights-centered scholarship in the public opinion field. There is little doubt among scholars that Americans tended to view ideas of rights and liberties with favor in the 1990s, and, after an initial dip in the immediate aftermath of 9/11, would continue to do so. But with a decade's worth of hindsight, the assessments of initial scholarship and the long-standing trajectory of public opinion research do not seem to provide enough of a vantage point for getting at the realities of the contemporary era.

Scholars are now beginning to explore in more detail this new reality. We describe these efforts in more detail in chapter 2, but it is useful to highlight three key possibilities that provide a point of departure for this book. One powerful and dissenting interpretation emphasizes the susceptibility of Americans to threat manipulation (Merolla and Zechmeister 2009). When primed by politicians or the media to think about terrorism threats, individuals cope by shifting their preferences regarding what they want out of political leaders and public policy. In contrast to claims about their existential nature, terrorist threats need not be real to have powerful effects. Indeed, political leaders may actively manipulate threats to their advantage. Evidence demonstrates the recurrent use of terrorist threats in presidential communications in the media buttress post-9/11 policies.

A second view suggests an even more lasting foundation, not just with how Americans cope in a threat-laden environment, but in what the public already believes. The thrust of this second line of thinking emphasizes the central role of ethnocentrism in shaping attitudes toward the war on terror (Kam and Kinder 2007; Kinder and Kam 2009). Here, lasting attachments and identifications associated with social groups are central, and ethnicity is preeminent. In the post-9/11 era, the sense of "us versus them" is said to dispose the American public, particularly whites, to endorsing punitive and bellicose policies. Survey evidence reveals that after 2001, a measure of ethnocentrism predicts the public's preferences on a variety of policy-attitude items, including the Afghanistan and Iraq wars, spending on defense and the war on terrorism, and border control. Pushing the ethnocentrism thesis further is the possibility that other, even more encompassing definitions of outsiders underlie support for coercive, counterterrorism policies (Sides and Gross 2011).

A third and final set of ideas emerges from historically oriented scholars who have called attention to a different sort of us-versus rhetoric relating to national identity as a driver of public support for strong counterterrorism policies (Hutcheson et al. 2004; McCartney 2004; Lieven 2005). Nationalism and national identity status, separate from ethnocentrism, may provide a motivation for citizens to embrace post-9/11 policies. In this case, people with a stronger identity with America would be more likely to be positive about the country's direction in fighting terrorism. This also raises a set of questions about whether perceptions of the national origins of policy targets are a factor in the formation of attitudes.

Public Opinion and Path Dependence

Like any important policy innovation, counterterrorism policy—and public attitudes toward it—may become subject to path-dependent processes that tend to lock in those developments. Path dependency arises when particular kinds of rules or arrangements develop their own subsequent momentum. Path dependency is common in many arenas of social life. The degree of equal opportunity legislation and the use of majoritarian versus proportional representation rules in democracies are two dramatic examples, ones that also illustrate the remarkable variety of such processes.

An example that highlights the historical particularities of path dependency can be seen in the case of the QWERTY keyboard. Established in the context of the nineteenth century to reduce the occurrence of keys jamming, QWERTY is far less optimal in later historical contexts, where mechanical keys have been replaced by electronic technology. But, once established, QWERTY has proven impossible to dislodge despite numerous attempts to do so. A subtle feature of path dependency, as the case of the QWERTY keyboard suggests, is that it can persist in spite of inefficient or even perverse impacts (David 1985).

In the study of public policy, path dependence provides analytical leverage for understanding how developments at one time may come to shape what is possible at other times. Paul Pierson (1993, 2000) has advanced the claim that path dependence is likely because key constituencies form around a newly adopted policy and fight to maintain it in more or less its original form over time. Furthermore, important policy developments typically alter the context within which political contests take place, advantaging certain kinds of strategies and proposals and disadvantaging others, particularly those that argue for a model that departs from the now-established policy regime.

Another key source of path dependence in politics is that once adopted, policies may become popular with citizens and voters, so that they become entrenched or even simply taken-for-granted features of social and political life. In the area of U.S. social policy, we would point to Social Security and Medicare as examples of social policies that have become sufficiently entrenched in the public mind that efforts to substantially modify or even tinker with them tend to meet with sharp public backlash. Why do policies become popular after they are adopted? Sometimes it is because, as for Social Security or Medicare, large numbers of citizens benefit from the program and gain an interest-enhanced legitimacy. But other explanations are also possible, as, for example, when a policy or program mobilizes beliefs and convictions to which individuals already subscribe. Could coercive counterterrorism measures have activated authoritarian values or a pattern of antipathy toward key target groups on the part of citizens? If so, politicians may have new grounds for expansion. Even those with reservations may be reluctant to tamper with popular policies, fearing electoral reprisals if they do so.

Just how deeply entrenched and path dependent post-9/11 counterterrorism laws and policies ultimately prove to be remains to be seen. In the rest of this book, we first gauge the magnitude of and the mechanisms undergirding public support for the new counterterrorism policies and measures. But, at the outset, we note that if our hunches about the impact of public opinion on policy are correct, and if a process of path dependence has now garnered popular support for new counter-terrorism measures, their persistence becomes more likely.

The Plan of This Book

As we look at scholarship on counterterrorism and public attitudes, we see a rich field with a diverse array of theoretical perspectives that increasingly outstrip the available empirical evidence with which to resolve fundamental questions and controversies. In this study, we draw on three nationally representative surveys we conducted in 2007, 2009, and 2010. Each includes a range of survey experiments we have developed to explore various aspects of public support for counterterrorism. In our examination of these experiments, we probe the underlying beliefs and considerations that shed light on when and why Americans extend support to counterterrorism policies. The findings and results that emerge from our surveys may be surprising to some, pointing as they do to a mix of established as well as more novel biases that operate in the contemporary era. We also want to see just how malleable, or locked in, mass opinion ultimately is. That is a challenge that matters for democratic theory and practice, and our experiments provide perspective.

Our exploration of a darker side of U.S. opinion starts from, and calls for, situating it within the broader, historical context. The long history of domestic countersubversion, including campaigns against Native Americans, immigrants, socialists, communists, and civil rights activists, is a key part of the American political heritage. We discuss this history in chapter 1, noting how the rights revolution of the 1960s and 1970s appeared to render the long history of intrusive surveillance and repression of perceived enemies, foreign and domestic, as a thing of the past. But, if initially unexpected, the post-9/11 turn suggests a remarkable retreat back to an older era in the balance between rights and liberties versus national security claims and imperatives.

Complementing the historical background outlined in chapter 1, American public opinion in the post–World War II era also appeared to have shifted toward strong support for civil liberties and greater freedom from government surveillance or rights abridgment. In chapter 2, we consider such assessments of opinion liberalization, alongside the alternative scenario that people are instead vulnerable to bracketing rights support in the face of new perceptions of threat. We also consider theoretical approaches emphasizing stronger predispositional bases, stemming either from patterns of group identification or from prior beliefs about the group targets of policy. We summarize how and why competing theories differ in regard to causal mechanisms behind public responses and policy reasoning, and we indicate how our research questions provide leverage.

Chapter 3 introduces the first big empirical question: how, if at all, have public attitudes and responses to counterterrorism policies changed? The 2007 to 2010 period covered by our surveys is fortuitous. This is a critical era, spanning a widely discussed shift in political party control over the U.S. presidency and a deepening Democratic majority in Congress. If an explanation based on partisan reasoning is anywhere close to the mark, we should see clear evidence of over-time and between-group patterns of polarization based on partisanship. But as we will see, this is not what the data show. Instead, there are very few trends. That tells us that the 9/11 policy legacy is anchored in forces beyond partisan reasoning.

Beginning in chapter 4, we turn to an analysis of our survey experiments to explore the structure and complexity of Americans' attitudes more closely. We begin by asking whether threats and the national targets of counterterrorism policies matter to the formation of attitudes. Are these simply two sides of the same factor, or different forces in their own right? Results of our experiments provide dramatic evidence that the national identity target groups matters. Evidence indicates that this is also a quite different force than terrorism threat. That lends momentum to our initial hunches, and, more subtly, the results also shed light on the degree and source of malleability in U.S. counterterrorism attitudes.

Chapter 5 builds on the findings. We want to bring ethnocentrism into proper consideration to broaden our investigation of identity targets. We offer a contrasting and accompanying set of experiments into patterns of sentiment toward established versus more novel types of outsider groups. It is groups such as "Muslims," "foreigners," and "people of Middle Eastern background" that elicit particularly negative attitudes. Our experiments tell us how these distinctions influence policy reasoning. Especially important is whether the key cleavage on counterterrorism involves the national identity origin of target groups, or instead their identities with respect to an underlying dimension of transnational ethnicity.

In chapter 6, we consider a now-classic perspective on this process of adaptation to environmental change: the theory of cognitive dissonance. In contrast to traditional theories of reward-based learning, the cognitive dissonance thesis anticipates that individuals adapt their beliefs and attitudes more quickly in the absence of rewards, and specifically when they are confronted with undesirable tasks or conditions. But the established causal candidate of interest-related factors might also explain feedback pressures when it comes to the impacts of counterterrorism policy on opinion. We evaluate the evidence and in doing so unearth a new feature of policy feedback: our tests suggest that policy change acts primarily to enhance or leave intact, but not to reduce, support for counterterrorism practices.

Our concluding chapter brings these results together. They point to the importance of symbolic cues that go well beyond historical events and realities; particularly notable are the national and ethnic identities of the group targets of counterterrorism policies. They also suggest additional implications for the future of counterterrorism policies in America. Our results and interpretations suggest that public support for elements of the war on terror are substantial; under the right conditions, this support can also be propelled upward by communications about disliked groups and simple reminders of past terrorism plots. But our results also point to possible scenarios under which public reasoning might move in new directions toward reconsideration and greater mobilization of rights support may be possible.

Chapter 1

From Rights Revolution to War on Terror

"All you need to know is that there was a 'before 9/11' and an 'after 9/11.'
After 9/11, the gloves come off."

Cofer Black, director of the CIA's Counterterrorist Center,
testifying before Congress, September 26, 2002

How will future historians view the counterterrorism policies of the post-9/11 era? Situating the post 9/11 era in historical perspective is a valuable way to begin addressing the question. As we argue in this chapter, such a step provides perspective on the similarities and differences between contemporary counterterrorism and earlier episodes of government repression or rights contraction.

We draw from the work of influential political historians to unpack American political culture as characterized by enduring tensions between the goals of democracy, civil liberties, and the rule of law, on the one hand, and a deep suspicion of internal or foreign enemies, on the other. Although technologies of surveillance and legal foundations for the incarceration of alleged subversives have evolved, the underlying conflicts between rights-based liberalism and countersubversion directed at internal and foreign targets have persisted over nearly the entire course of American history. In some key periods, the countersubversive current has exploded into the political mainstream, generating mass mobilizations, media scares, and new laws and government surveillance of suspected enemies. The political upheavals brought on by 9/11 and the resulting adoption of domestic and international counterterrorism policies did not, in short, occur in a historical vacuum with no precedents or collective memories.

The historian Richard Hofstadter (1965) famously characterized the periodic rise of countersubversive movements as reflecting an underlying "paranoid style" in American politics. For Hofstadter, the paranoid style coexists uneasily alongside the liberal tradition. The political significance of fears of subversion is most clearly visible during those moments when governmental repression of allegedly subversive groups has been undertaken. These have included the long campaign against Native Americans and the "taming of the frontier," the anti-immigrant and anti-union crusades of the late nineteenth and early twentieth centuries, the Red Scare of 1919 to 1920, the roundup and forced internment of Japanese Americans during World War II, the Truman-McCarthy anti-Communist era of the late 1940s and early 1950s, and the surveillance and harassment of civil rights and protest groups during the Federal Bureau of Investigation's (FBI's) COINTELPRO (Counter Intelligence Program) designed to combat 1960s radicalism (for reviews and discussion of these campaigns, see Rogin 1987, chap. 2; Goldstein 2001).

The power of Hofstadter's paranoid-style metaphor arises from the fact that so many episodes of countersubversive mobilization appear to draw on similar themes and political frames. Among the most important of these are the alien character of the subversive group, the totalistic nature of the subversive challenge, the role of conspiracy hatched in secret, and finally the frequent targeting of hostility on unpopular religious subgroups, for example, anti-Catholicism in the anti-immigrant campaigns, anti-Semitism in the Red scares, and anti-Muslim sentiment in the current counterterrorism era (compare Davis 1971; Rogin 1987).[1]

It is, of course, important that if the counterterrorism policies of the post-9/11 era recall earlier periods of countersubversion in American history, they also, of course, are critically different. First, they were spurred by the second most lethal attack from a foreign source on American soil, trailing only Japan's bombing of Pearl Harbor at the start of World War II. In this sense, by comparison with earlier anti-Indian, anti-immigrant, or anti-Communist scares, the post-9/11 antiterrorist era had a truly violent starting point and an enemy that demonstrated a capacity to inflict real harm and repeatedly asserted an intention to cause further damage and loss of life.

Second, the target in post-9/11 mobilization was quite explicit about its intention to kill non-Muslims around the world in the form of global jihad. America, as the leading nation in the West and preeminent supporter of Israel, was a special target. The intention of previous alleged subversives to kill large numbers of Americans could only be inferred indirectly—for example, the Communist Party's support for a "revolutionary" overthrow of capitalism, which was reframed by anticommunists as advocating violence, even if little or no evidence of such violent acts could be found.

But before we conclude that the terrorist threat posed by al-Qaeda and unaffiliated homegrown groups by itself provides a sufficient explanation for the dramatic reversals of rights and liberties that have unfolded since 9/11 and the popular support they activated, it is worth keeping in mind the magnitude of the threat ten years after 9/11 and even in 2001.[2]

Turning to government responses, an intriguing contrast is provided by the bombing of a federal government building in Oklahoma City in 1995. This attack killed 121 people and was conducted by two members of a far-right militia, Timothy McVeigh and Terry Nichols. McVeigh and Nichols were part of a group that had long been preparing for violent actions against the U.S. government, and other violent militia groups were identified as well. Yet following the Oklahoma City bombing, an orderly criminal investigation unfolded, the suspects were arrested and tried in regular federal criminal court, and they were ultimately sentenced to death for their actions. No modification (much less a transformation) to rights and liberties protections was attempted, and no national dialogue over changing laws surrounding domestic surveillance ensued. Despite considerable loss of life and extensive public anger directed at McVeigh and Nichols, these public reactions and the responses by the federal government produced no larger institutional changes.

For many scholars and commentators, the tempered and seemingly proportional response to the Oklahoma City bombing confirmed growing recognition of the need to protect civil liberties and constitutional rights in the contemporary period since the 1960s. The abuses of the McCarthy era, the FBI under J. Edgar Hoover, and the Nixon administration's secret surveillance and wiretaps of suspected "enemies" produced major political backlashes that had culminated in legislative efforts seeking to ensure that the federal government could never spy on citizens without proper legal authorization. Alongside major pieces of civil rights legislation in the same period, a veritable rights revolution appeared to have become a permanent part of the legal landscape by the middle 1970s. The gradual strengthening of international legal covenants concerning human rights and due process—which the United States vigorously embraced during the Cold War—further contributed to this robust environment of rights protection.

The international legal environment is of central importance. A growing body of measures, beginning with the Geneva Convention Accords, both before and after World War II, created a set of rules for the humane treatment of prisoners of war, as well as a broader battery of international law concerning human rights. An international criminal court system for handling cases arising out of the violation of human rights was established and by the 1990s was functioning in The Hague, The Netherlands. The United States led the way in the immediate postwar world in encouraging the adoption of the Geneva Accords and had long abided by these provisions. These standards had seemingly triumphed, becoming widely practiced around the world. The rights revolution was not limited to domestic rights but extended, in principle, to encompass human rights enjoyed by all persons.

In this chapter, our goal is to situate the rise of post 9/11 counterterrorism laws and practices in the context of the history of countersubversion, but in particular in the displacement of the rights revolution that had seemingly provided strong protection against some of the very policies and programs that have characterized the U.S. government's response to the attacks. We examine specific laws and policies adopted in the post 9/11 era, as well as some of the secret practices pursued by covert action and intelligence agencies with the full backing and support of the Bush administration. We then turn, finally, to their surprising continuation after the election of Democratic majorities in Congress and of President Barack Obama in 2008. Obama had campaigned against several key Bush-era programs, yet once in office made only modest changes to those programs. In some cases, the Obama administration even extended their use, for example in sanctioning the execution of American citizens without trial, aggressively employing rarely used sedition laws against National Security Agency (NSA) whistleblowers, and permitting the confinement of a sergeant in the U.S. Army accused of leaking secret documents to the Internet-based Wikileaks.

A Brief History of American Countersubversion

The Constitution's Bill of Rights has provided an encompassing set of protections for individuals and groups against arbitrary state power. But these protections have also proven to be highly malleable in historical contexts where fear of enemies, internal or external, has been mobilized. Rights violations of the sort found in the post-9/11 era are not new in the United States.

Indeed, in the early days of the post-9/11 era, historically minded commentators drew analogies to such periods of rights retrenchment as the Red Scares of 1919 through 1920 and the 1950s, the World War II internment of Japanese Americans, and the FBI COINTELPRO's unlawful surveillance and harassment of civil rights and protest groups during the 1960s (Goldstein 2001; Chang 2002; Brinkley 2003). Affecting as they did the liberties and welfare of tens of thousands, these earlier episodes are suggestive of the historical ebb and flow of conflicts between individual rights and government overreach.

The first Red scare, and in many ways the origins of the paranoid style, can be traced to the eighteenth- and nineteenth-century campaigns against Native Americans. Native Americans stood in the way of the westward expansion of the United States. Their occasionally violent resistance to continual encroachment on Indian lands, combined with whites' often insatiable demands, led to repeated military interventions to root out and remove unwanted tribes from lands desired by whites. This process, halting and uneven over many decades, was presented to the American public as a necessary confrontation between a majority and the alien values and ways of a native people (see Rogin 1987, 45–51).

The second set of Red scares developed from the 1870s onward in response to the rising challenges posed of organized labor, especially in immigrant communities, and later with the growth of socialist and communist parties. The history of organized labor in America is remarkably violent in comparison with its much better organized European counterparts (compare Kimeldorf 1992; Voss 1994; Lichtenstein 2003). American workers and their unions were bitterly, and often violently, opposed by employers and their allies. The employment of Pinkertons and local police forces against striking workers led to many outcomes involving the loss of life—the Haymarket riot of 1886, the violent suppression of the Pullman strike in 1894—and the use of police, local militias, and the military to enforce legal injunctions against strikes were common before the 1930s, when the labor injunction was banned by the Norris-LaGuardia Act (Forbath 1992). Of particular note was the crushing of the Knights of Labor, the first union organization in the United States committed to organizing workers along both racial and skilled-nonskilled divides. Although notably successful in the early 1880s, during the mid-1880s employer associations banded together with local political elites to destroy Knights locals (Voss 1994).

The labor upsurge of the 1930s and the incorporation of unions into the New Deal political order generally ended the use of repressive public power against organized labor, at least outside the South. But the early 1940s witnessed a new episode of repression, against Japanese Americans on the West Coast in the aftermath of the attack on Pearl Harbor. Japanese American families, many of whom were second- or third-generation Americans, were forced to leave their homes and move to internment camps. This arbitrary roundup was based on ethnicity, not evidence of any acts (or even ideological commitment) to support the Japanese war effort. Its cruelty has been well documented: families were often forced to sell their homes at rock-bottom prices, businesses and farms were lost, and entire communities were wiped out.

The countersubversive logic can also be seen in a long series of campaigns and race wars involving African Americans. Every major political mobilization of blacks—beginning during Reconstruction and continuing through the twentieth-century civil rights campaigns, urban race riots (after World War I and again in the late 1960s), as well as in attacks on the Black Panthers and the Nation of Islam (under Elijah Muhammad and later Louis Farrakhan, but also in the vilification of ex-Nation of Islam leader Malcolm X)—has been framed by its opponents as a conspiracy against the American way of life. It is, of course, difficult to separate the role of racism and more general countersubversive motivations in these campaigns; and it is important that they tended to be far stronger in the South, where a long tradition of violent racial conflict and rumors can be found (Odum 1943; Foner 1999).

Later episodes of political repression, in particular the surveillance activities of the Nixon White House against its perceived enemies, are also worthy of note. Revelations about the Watergate break-in and the cover-up that followed exploded into the national consciousness in 1973 and 1974 and produced the most sustained backlash in civil liberties violations on record. We discuss these issues in more detail in the next section.

The Rights Revolutions, at Home and Abroad

The changing political contexts of civil liberties and civil rights in America are critical to understanding the rise and evolution of counterterrorism policy. The character of rights and rights-based political struggles have long defined key shifts in American political and legal institutions (Bowles and Gintis 1986; Foner 1999; Fisher 2005). Inalienable rights are mentioned in the Declaration of Independence. The first ten amendments to the U.S. Constitution are universally known as the Bill of Rights. Throughout most of the twentieth century, the gradual extension of rights to previously disenfranchised groups made it the core of progressive liberalism. It is hardly an exaggeration to say that where the U.S. Constitution—whether read literally or more contextually—has proven most open to progressive readings has been in the steady expansion of the scope and meaning of rights. Rights-based rhetoric and political challenges had, by the end of the twentieth century, become so common in discussing social or political reform that the phrase *rights talk* emerged as a shorthand description.

In the classic mid-century synthesis of T. H. Marshall (1950), three sets of rights—civil, political, and social—defined the evolution of modern citizenship in democratic polities. Marshall periodized the rise of rights-based citizenship from civil rights (beginning with freedom of contract, freedom of association, and the abolition of inherited privilege), through to political rights (with the rise of multiparty democracies, a free press, and the principle of universal suffrage), and finally to social rights (with the rise of the welfare state and a promise of a right to a basic standard of living "from cradle to grave," in the famous words of the 1942 Beveridge report proposing an expanded welfare state in the postwar United Kingdom). Marshall, and those who have followed in his footsteps, has seen these rights as inherently linked; for example, civil rights gain full meaning only when political rights have been extended to all citizens, ending the possibility of unjust governance and authority. Likewise, political equality is only possible when all citizens have been provided a minimally acceptable standard of living and have sufficient resources with which to participate in political life.

The evolutionary structure of Marshall's narrative is seductive, but it fits only loosely in many specific cases. The pathway to full citizenship in the United States, for example, was halting, uneven, and subject to reversals not anticipated in the Marshall model. The U.S. Constitution provided for an unprecedented level of political equality and political rights, as well as an important set of protections in the Bill of Rights. But these rights were often quite flimsy in practice. For example, the states generally limited the extent of the franchise to propertied white men until the 1840s, and women would not enjoy the benefits of full political rights until 1920, and blacks not until 1965 (Keyssar 2000). The predominant interpretation of constitutionally grounded rights in the nineteenth and early twentieth century was above all else the doctrine of freedom of contract and the rights of economic actors to be free of government regulation (for example, Horowitz 1992).

One of the most dramatic and consequential examples of this interpretation of constitutional rights in the late nineteenth and early twentieth centuries was the repeated injunctions that courts issued against unions and strikes (for example, Forbath 1992; Ernst 1995). When workers banded together to engage in collective action, courts routinely found them to have violated their employers' rights to contract with each of them individually. Another critical example was the invocation of states' rights, especially in the context of conflicts over Jim Crow laws. Where federal courts had to face questions of civil rights in the context of race, they generally provided the states with wide latitude in limiting equality under the law, even after the adoption of the Fourteenth Amendment in 1868 and its famed equal protection clause, as long as state laws did not explicitly use race as a criterion (Vallely 2004).

A recurring theme in the limiting of civil and political rights before World War II can be seen in the responses of federal courts to periodic countersubversive campaigns that erupted. In the case of freedom of expression, nineteenth-century courts generally adopted the view that governments had the authority to limit speech that could potentially facilitate a proscribed or bad outcome and that state governments (or the federal government in the time of warfare) would have a wide scope to make that determination. In the early twentieth century, however, this would begin to change. Key was the emergence of a civil liberties–civil rights legal community. Defending the rights of organized labor, most notably the Industrial Workers of the World, who faced numerous legal challenges throughout their heyday between 1911 and 1920, provided one key impetus, eventually leading to the creation of the American Civil Liberties Union (ACLU). The rise of the NAACP (National Association for the Advancement of Colored People) and its legal challenges to segregation would provide another.

Early freedom of speech cases sometimes involved organized labor, but the most influential early cases concerned the right to express opposition to World War I. The precursor to the ACLU was formed in 1917 to defend opponents of the American entry into World War I. Many such antiwar activists were imprisoned for their advocacy of opposition to the war, including the head of the Socialist Party, Eugene Debs, who received a ten-year sentence for opposing U.S. entry into the war. The ACLU would later vigorously defend aliens seized in the Palmer raids of 1919 to 1920, named after then U.S. Attorney General A. Mitchell Palmer, who sought to round up and deport supporters of Bolshevism and other radical views. In these contexts, when the paranoid style was dominant, rights protections tended to be readily bracketed in the rush to identify and punish aliens and dissenters.

The McCarthy period, when liberals and a timid ACLU often refused to support Communists accused of illegally advocating the overthrow of the Constitution, opened a key chapter in the legal fights over countersubversion. American courts generally allowed the firing of public sector employees and college professors for mere membership, or in some cases alleged membership, in the Communist Party. Ellen Schrecker (1986), for example, reports that some 400 professors would be fired for their political beliefs in the late 1940s and early 1950s. But the most shameful moment in the legal endorsement of countersubversive politics occurred in 1944, when the U.S. Supreme Court endorsed the mass internment of Japanese Americans in the infamous Korematsu v. U.S. ruling. After the bombing of Pearl Harbor, the federal government had ordered the internment of all Japanese Americans living on the West Coast. Some 110,000 Japanese, well over half of whom were American citizens, were forced to move to the camps, leaving behind homes, jobs, and communities. The Supreme Court approval of the mass internment suggested an extremely high level of deference to the president in times of war.

But this limited vision of the meaning of the rights granted under the Constitution would not hold forever. Although the development of a new conception of civil rights was halting and somewhat uneven, the legal and political challenges of the 1960s ushered in a much broader set of rights-based commitments across a number of domains. The stages of this process are well known. During the New Deal, an initially hostile Supreme Court gradually came to accept the power of the federal government to regulate the economy and promote social equality that necessitated "positive" governmental action (Starr 2007; Wolfe 2008). Other rights, most notably the right of workers to organize unions, developed in this period as well. A series of major Supreme Court rulings during the Warren Court years (1954 to 1968) provided a vast extension of rights under the Constitution. In particular, a remarkable string of major civil rights victories for African Americans, other minorities, and women would be issued by the Warren Court.

The most important of these decisions, Brown v. Board of Education (1954), overturned decades of Jim Crow segregation practices in public education. In combination with major civil rights legislation in the 1960s, the notion that everyone had a right to equal opportunity began to spread throughout American law and political institutions. As the civil rights movement and its liberal allies gained ground in the early 1960s, major pieces of civil rights legislation—most notably the Civil Rights Act of 1964 and the Voting Rights Act of 1965—were adopted by Congress and signed into law by President Lyndon Johnson.

The process of rights expansion did not stop there. As the sixties rolled on, the growing strength of new cultural and political forces in American life—notably the antiwar movement and the New Left, but also the gay rights movement and issues of free speech, privacy, and the right to protest government policy free from official harassment—increasingly came to the fore. These challenges pushed debates over civil liberties and the meaning of the right to political freedom further than ever before. The notion that the Constitution provided individuals with privacy rights, for example, emerged in the Supreme Court's famous ruling in Griswold v. Connecticut (1965), where the Court struck down a state ban on the selling of contraceptives. This right of privacy would be critical to one of the Court's most important rights-based decisions in Roe v. Wade, which held that women should have a right to choose to have an abortion in the first two trimesters of a pregnancy.

Other important and contested rulings surrounding individual rights concerned those of accused criminal offenders. The doctrine of habeas corpus—the requirement that no individual could be held in custody for an extended period without being formally charged—was clearly specified in the Constitution and, with the exception of wartime, a rigorously followed practice throughout American history. But other rights critical to maintaining an innocent until proven guilty model of criminal justice procedure were rarely implemented across the United States before the 1960s. Many states refused to provide indigent defendants with adequate legal representation before the Supreme Court's famous ruling in Gideon v. Wainwright (1963).

The emergence of limitations on aggressive police tactics also surfaced in this era. These included the requirement that police inform the accused of their right to counsel and their right not to incriminate themselves or answer questions. Somewhat more ambiguous have been limitations on legal searches and seizures of material. In that realm, federal courts have set only modest limits on police practices, deferring to local and state law in a long series of rulings over the years.

Aftermath of Vietnam, Watergate, and Rights-Based Limits on the National Security State

When it came to civil liberties and civil rights, the reform era did not end in the 1960s. The abuses of the Nixon administration, and revelations about FBI abuses under J. Edgar Hoover's COINTELPRO program—which was designed to spy on, and actively disrupt, domestic political organizations and movements, including the civil rights movement—would generate an unprecedented backlash. In August 1974, Nixon resigned the presidency under extreme pressure and threat of impeachment, as evidence of a high-level cover-up of the break-in at the Watergate hotel came to light, along with other evidence of administration-ordered spying on its domestic "enemies." The Democrats swept the 1974 elections, picking up some seventy-five seats in the House of Representatives, and momentum grew for laws banning the abuses revealed during the Watergate era.

With political momentum behind reformers, the floodgates opened and a wide variety of quasi-legal or outright illegal domestic surveillance and secret foreign operations came to light. The so-called Church Committee, a Senate investigatory body chaired by Senator Frank Church (D-Iowa), began investigating Central Intelligence Agency (CIA) and Federal Bureau of Investigation (FBI) activities in relation to both domestic spying and illegal foreign operations (by the CIA), including assassinations of foreign leaders (Johnson 1988; Smist 1990). The background to the establishment of the Committee was both a variety of investigative journalistic reports, most notably Seymour Hersh's *New York Times* accounts of illegal CIA activities in December 1974, and information that had been revealed during the Watergate and other hearings on domestic surveillance by the U.S. Army ("Huge C.I.A. Operation Reported in U.S. Against Antiwar Forces, Other Dissidents in Nixon Years," December 22, 1974; for hearings on U.S. Army domestic spying, see U.S. Congress 1974).

The Church Committee was a landmark in several respects. It included notables such as Walter Mondale and recently elected Senator Gary Hart on the Democratic side, and John Tower, Howard Baker, and Barry Goldwater on the minority Republican side. The committee delved into a full-scale investigation of a range of intelligence and military abuses. Many of its findings and documentation were classified and only some of these have yet been released to date, but the committee did publish a fourteen-volume "interim" report that covered illegal domestic surveillance (including unauthorized opening of mail and telephone wiretapping), the use of tax data and the Internal Revenue Service to harass dissidents, and illegal covert operations (such as CIA efforts to assassinate foreign leaders). The committee's final report and supplementary materials included evidence of the extensive FBI harassment of Martin Luther King, which was intended, in the words of one FBI official, to "neutralize" King: "No holds were barred. . . . We [have] used similar techniques against Soviet agents" (U.S. Congress 1976, 1).

The Church Committee's revelations led to a couple of key pieces of legislation designed to ensure that these abuses would not recur. Evidence of covert CIA efforts to assassinate individuals without due process, including heads of state deemed dangerous to U.S. interests, was now viewed by Congress as a gross and unambiguous violation of international law, and would be so understood by leaders of both major parties until the 9/11 era. An executive order issued by President Gerald Ford in 1976, and a second one issued by President Ronald Reagan in 1981, formally barred U.S. intelligence agencies from carrying out foreign assassinations. The second major legal change was the adoption of the Foreign Intelligence Surveillance Act (FISA) by Congress in 1978. The key provision of FISA was that all U.S. intelligence agencies were required to obtain permission to spy on anyone, including U.S. citizens, in a U.S. territory by going before a special federal court known as the Foreign Intelligence Surveillance Court, or FISA court. For any government agency to conduct covert foreign intelligence on U.S. soil, the agency was required to demonstrate that the intelligence being gathered both involved a foreign government and presented a clear threat to U.S. security. The Patriot Act would later amend this to include foreign terrorist organizations. The role of the FISA courts appeared clear: intelligence agencies could continue to gather intelligence on U.S. soil, but they would have to be authorized to do so by the court.

These restrictions on the national security state were of modest consequence until 9/11. All evidence suggests that more traditional law enforcement approaches were generally used to deal with domestic terror threats, although FISA courts did authorize dozens of wiretaps over the years. During the administrations of Ronald Reagan and George H.W. Bush, several highly questionable military operations were undertaken in pursuit of particular policy goals. Most notable was Reagan's invasion of the tiny Caribbean country of Grenada to overthrow the democratically elected Socialist government of Maurice Bishop in 1983, and the execution of Bishop himself. The Bush administration's invasion of Panama in 1989, aiming at the overthrow of the dictator Manuel Noriega, on the grounds that he was involved in drug smuggling, raised similar questions. But both interventions were over before international objections could be voiced.[3]

Under Bill Clinton (1993 to 2001), respect for human rights and the international rule of law probably peaked. But even the Clinton administration occasionally violated the rules in various contexts. This was apparent, for instance, in the use of American air power without congressional or United Nations (UN) endorsement against foreign military targets in several widely publicized incidents. But, in general, the Clinton administration operated within the parameters of the new model. One of the most striking examples can be seen in the Clinton administration's extensive debates over, and hesitancy to order, the execution of Osama bin Laden. Bin Laden and al-Qaeda emerged as a major international terrorist force with the 1998 bombings of the U.S. embassies in Nairobi, Kenya, and Dar es Salaam, Tanzania, and the 2000 attack on the USS *Cole* that caused the deaths of seventeen servicemen. In retrospect, the reluctance of the Clinton administration to authorize a kill order against bin Laden and its general restraint in the aftermath of the 1995 Oklahoma City bombing underscore the power of the rights revolution during these years.

The period from the 1970s through 2001 suggests that when compared with the full scope of post-9/11 war on terror programs, underlying commitments to both civil liberties and international law were quite robust. To be sure, some critics viewed the administrations of Ronald Reagan and George H.W. Bush as involving far more legal and human rights violations than this account implies. For example, the Reagan administration's support for right-wing anti-Communist regimes around the world, including many repressive governments, violated basic human rights policies. But again, in comparison with what would follow after 9/11, the U.S. government and its intelligence agencies balanced security versus rights trade-offs in ways that appear comparatively restrained and cautious.

The Internationalization of Human Rights

We have mentioned the role of international law as part of the larger rights revolution. We now expand on this topic as it bears in many ways on debates over post-9/11 counterterrorism policies. The advancing conception of human rights in the international legal community was a vitally important development at the global level. Among the well-known hallmarks was the creation of the United Nations after World War II and the adoption of ideas, legal frameworks, and eventually a set of legal institutions to enforce a concept of universal human rights. These developments can be seen in the UN's 1948 landmark adoption of the Universal Declaration of Human Rights.

Also important was the expansion and codification of a series of international agreements known as the Geneva Conventions regarding the treatment of enemy soldiers and civilians in wartime, which underwent significant revision and expansion in 1949 in light of the World War II experience.[4] The expanding role of the International Court of Justice in The Hague has been another important milestone in international law, and the role of the International Court has grown considerably in recent decades. In these courts, a series of dictators and rogue military leaders have been successfully tried and convicted for murder and other violations of international human rights (Hagan 2003).

In summary, then, the emergence and successful operation of international legal and human rights institutions provides a sharp contrast to the seamier legacies of rights vulnerability and violations within specific countries. As we discuss in chapter 2, it is precisely these international legal and governmental associations that animate scholarly models of a forward-looking "world society" (Meyer et al. 1997). And it is these international organizations with their associated treaties and laws, alongside relevant national protections such as the U.S. Bill of Rights, that provided the existing backdrop from which the war on terror began to dramatically depart.

The 9/11 Era

The attacks on the World Trade Center and the Pentagon by a group of al-Qaeda operatives sent into the United States were devastating. A total of 2,985 people would die on 9/11 from these attacks, and many thousands more, including rescue personnel and volunteers involved with the clean-up, would face serious health problems in the years to follow. Few who experienced that day, and the onslaught of media coverage that followed in its wake, will forget the searing images it provided, reinforced for days afterward by media coverage that was unsparing in its presentation of terror, disorder, and rumor.

It would later be revealed that the Bush administration and leading intelligence agencies had failed to interpret repeated signals about the impending attacks, including a famous August 6, 2001, briefing that warned the president about an impending threat in which hijacked airplanes could be used as potential terrorist weapons (National Commission 2004). The attacks, and the failure to respond to signals before 9/11, pushed a previously recalcitrant administration into overdrive to adopt a more aggressive set of new policies and military campaigns in a determination to respond on multiple fronts to the attacks. In addition to the two wars that would be launched in the name of fighting terrorism, in Afghanistan in 2001 and Iraq in 2003, the Bush administration—in some cases secretly and in some cases with congressional authorization—undertook the following measures:

- passage of the Patriot Act of 2001, later amended and expanded in 2006 and 2008, and renewed most recently in June 2011;

- authorization of the operational arm of the Central Intelligence Agency to seize, or "render," suspected members of al-Qaeda or associated organizations wherever in the world they might be found without seeking formal legal authorization from foreign jurisdictions and to bring them to one of a number of detention centers around the world for interrogation;

- where rendition proved difficult or impossible, authorized the killing of key members of al-Qaeda or other terrorist organizations, in many cases without obtaining formal legal authorization, and often through the use of missile, drone, or air attacks;

- authorized intelligence agencies to expand domestic surveillance, including wiretapping phones and reading email and other Internet communications without formal court authorizations, as authorized by the Patriot Act or in some cases with no legal authority at all;

- established the U.S. military base at Guantanamo Bay in Cuba as the primary holding location for suspected terrorists before they could be tried, but also established a number of "black sites" around the world in which suspects could be interrogated aggressively and outside the reach of U.S. law or treaties to which the United States was a party;

- authorized the use of enhanced interrogation techniques against suspected terrorists, including the use of waterboarding, in the hopes of gaining information about al-Qaeda or other terrorist plans and operations;

- established military courts as the primary legal forum to try suspected terrorists whom the administration decided could not be tried in open court for security reasons, with Congress authorizing these courts in 2006 with the passage of the Military Commissions Act (later modified by a Supreme Court ruling in Hamdan v. Bush), although still widely used by the Obama Justice Department; and

- adopted extensive new federal security requirements for airports, shipping ports, and federal buildings while encouraging state and local authorities to develop similar plans for public transportation and government buildings.

It is important to understand the reasoning and motivation behind the Bush administration's initial implementation of these laws and policy activities, especially because many of these programmatic developments appear to have largely become permanent since 9/11. In the aftermath of the attacks, a single powerful metaphor dominated much of the administration's thinking, exerting considerable influence within the media and broader public as well. The metaphor was the ticking time bomb, the idea that additional terrorist plots and attacks were imminent, and to foil them immediate and unconditional action was necessary.

Joel Surnow's popular TV series 24 captured and dramatically reinforced the metaphor. In each season of the show, counterterrorism operative Jack Bauer and his colleagues were confronted with the threat of one or more terrorist attacks on the United States, with the show set on a single day and a clock ticking off the minutes during each of the episodes. So effective was the show that one commentator was moved to suggest that "the most influential thinker in the development of American interrogation policy . . . is none other than the star of Fox Television's '24,' Jack Bauer" (Litwack 2008). In defending the use of torture, 24 was "quoted more often than the Constitution," and it was invoked by a wide range of commentators as exemplifying a larger set of tensions and conflicts between national security imperatives and civil and human rights considerations.[5]

Between 2001 and 2003, the legal foundation for the most controversial of these practices was provided to the Bush administration by John Yoo of the Justice Department's Office of Legal Counsel. A prominent young law professor at the University of California–Berkeley, Yoo authored the so-called torture memos, which argued that the Geneva Conventions did not apply to enemy combatants in the war on terror, and furthermore that the White House's executive authority permitted the use of torture to extract confessions in the name of preventing future terrorist acts. Yoo also provided authorization of the administration's warrantless wiretapping program, arguing that the FISA court did not need to be consulted in cases where a suspected foreign terrorist was involved in a communication with an American citizen.[6] Other advocates of the extreme antiterror measures within the administration, notably Vice President Dick Cheney, worked actively to ensure for a long period that dissenting and moderate voices within the administration would have limited policy influence for the first half-decade after 9/11.

The five most controversial legs of the emerging counterterrorism system have been the expansion of domestic surveillance, the indefinite detention of suspects, the rendition of subjects in foreign countries, the use of torture in interrogations, and a commitment to the use of military courts to try detainees who would be charged with a crime. We briefly discuss each of these next.

Domestic Surveillance

Seven months after 9/11, the NSA began to assemble a database of all telephone conversations, numbering in the hundreds of billions, in which one party was outside the United States. With the initial cooperation of telecommunications giant AT&T, beginning in 2003, the NSA also used data-mining technology to collect massive streams of Internet traffic. The same procedures were used to tap into Society for Worldwide Interbank Financial Telecommunication (SWIFT) databases in Belgium that route most of the world's major financial transactions (Lichtblau 2008, chap. 8).

Monitoring of telephone, Internet, and financial transactions were largely invisible. The way most Americans become aware of enhanced domestic surveillance is in visiting the airport. There, screening has increased significantly and continued to expand under the Obama administration, as suggested by the roll-out of full-body scanners at security checkpoints, which enable a technician to see what may be hiding in passengers' underwear or body cavities. Some 500,000 individuals— Americans as well as foreign nationals—have been placed on the CIA's watch list as a result of NSA intelligence gathering (Bamford 2008, 3) and are subjected to more intensive scrutiny any time they encounter law enforcement or security personnel, for example, at airports, or when stopped by a police officer, no matter how routine the matter at hand.

Enhanced Interrogation

Some of those suspected of being involved in terrorist activity in the period after 9/11 were taken to hidden locations where they could be subjected to "extreme interrogation" techniques in the hopes of gathering intelligence. Otherwise known as torture, many of the interrogation techniques used by CIA and special military units defied the international human rights protections codified in the Geneva Conventions. They also violated Eighth Amendment protections against cruel and unusual punishment.

The techniques used—especially in the period from 2002 to 2006— included sleep and sensory deprivation, isolation, repeated beatings as well as humiliation, forcible administration of drugs, and most famously waterboarding, a technique that simulates the sensation of drowning. Evidence of these top-secret interrogations was uncovered and revealed over an extended period, and the full story of the government's use of torture cannot yet be written. But the first unambiguous evidence of torture came with the release of photographs of inmate abuse at the Abu Ghraib prison in April 2004, reported by *New Yorker* reporter Seymour Hersh and broadcast in a special *60 Minutes* report. An official military review of treatment of inmates at Abu Ghraib rebuked the prison's commanding officers. Interviews with prison officials and military investigators, as well as evidence shown in the photos that were released (and more graphically in photos not released for public viewing), documented gross mistreatment of inmates. This included evidence that inmates had been raped and sodomized, physically and deliberately injured, urinated upon, and subjected to attacks by guard dogs. At least one inmate was killed, and many others suffered serious injuries.

The initial response of the U.S. military to the abuses at Abu Ghraib was primarily to place blame on specific, and mostly lower-level, military personnel and their immediate supervisors, implying that these were random, unauthorized occurrences (Hersh 2005). Whatever the particulars of the chain of command at Abu Ghraib, later evidence suggested that the systematic use of torture was relatively widespread. Abu Ghraib was only one of a number of sites where torture was employed. Some of these were black sites, foreign prisons operated by the CIA or the American military in which individuals accused of terrorist activities could be interrogated outside the reach of any legal authority. Secret prisons were located in countries such as Poland, Romania, and Lithuania, and other facilities have been identified in Africa and the Middle East. The existence of black sites was initially denied by the Bush administration, but in September 2006 President Bush acknowledged their existence. Suspects were also sometimes turned over to foreign governments known for their use of torture and other aggressive techniques of interrogation and punishment (Mayer 2008).[7]

Detention of Suspects Without Due Process

The long-term detention of suspects without trial has been one of the most contentious aspects in the handling of terrorist suspects since 9/11. The facts are well known. Of the thousands of suspected terrorists rounded up since 9/11, a handful were arrested in the United States or through conventional legal channels, but many were arrested during the wars in Afghanistan and Iraq or through their rendition from foreign countries. Initially housed in prison sites around the world, most of the long-term detainees would eventually be transferred to the prison facility at the U.S. military base at Guantanamo Bay, on the southeast corner of Cuba. Gitmo, as it has come to be known, has become a holding facility for suspects thought to be too dangerous to be released. Some 779 detainees had entered or passed through as of late 2008.[8] In late 2012, 172 detainees were housed there.[9]

The Bush administration and more recently the Obama administration have claimed that a significant number of these detainees cannot be tried in federal court or even in a military court, either because the evidence against them is not adequate for a legal proceeding, or because revealing the source of the evidence is said to threaten U.S. security interests. Some procedures for review, including the right of detainees to petition federal courts under habeas corpus doctrine, are in place but have rarely been successful. Because the war on terror, unlike other military contests involving nation-states, may never be declared as won or over, some of these detainees face the prospect of lifetime detention without ever having a trial.

Extraordinary Rendition

Democratic governments have developed legal procedures and bilateral treaties for arresting and transferring suspects in criminal cases in other countries (see Zimmer 2011). The law of extradition is, to be sure, often complicated, because it bears on one of the foundations of the nation-state system: the idea of national sovereignty. One of the principles of international law is that states have legal jurisdiction over all individuals residing in their territory. Many countries—including the United States—have set some restrictions on their willingness to extradite upon request. For example, some countries that have abolished the death penalty will not extradite a suspect to the United States if she or he might conceivably be subjected to capital punishment.

One of the most common reasons to refuse to extradite is that the suspect is accused of political crimes or is wanted for reasons pertaining to political activities. The United States has long been a staunch defender of the right to dissent and has generally refused to turn over political suspects. The first known instance of this was the refusal of New England Puritans to hand over alleged regicides who had signed petitions calling for the execution of King Charles I (Pyle 2001, chap. 1).[10]

Rendition of suspects has been used occasionally in the past. In the famous case of Adolf Eichmann, for example, Israeli agents seized the suspected Nazi in Argentina to bring him back to Israel to stand trial for his role in the Holocaust. But in this and other such instances, the goal was typically to bring suspects back to the home country to stand trial in a public courtroom. In the post-9/11 context, the U.S. government has frequently chosen to ignore both international and historical precedents. Government operatives have simply abducted suspected terrorists, with the intention of transporting them to an interrogation center or a black site. This process, known as extraordinary rendition, was frequently substituted for normal extradition as part of the war on terror. The use of rendition is controversial for many reasons, because it involves kidnapping—which is illegal everywhere—and frequently violates bilateral treaties or international laws regarding national sovereignty. The practice of extraordinary rendition, in which the suspect is taken not to stand trial but instead to be aggressively interrogated, adds yet another level of legal contention and complexity (for more detail, see Mayer 2008).

Military Commissions

In addition to its use of rendition and prolonged or indefinite detainment, the Bush administration established military courts (or military commissions) as the primary arena in which Gitmo detainees would be tried. Efforts to try detainees in federal courts using normal rules of legal procedure were viewed by the Bush administration as problematic on several grounds. First, there were serious questions about whether convictions would be possible. In many cases, the evidence against potential defendants was tainted by the manner in which it was acquired; many of the defendants could only indirectly be connected to actual terrorist acts; and witnesses who might be called to testify might be unwilling, not locatable, or unreliable. Second, it has been alleged that open public trials might reveal national security secrets, such as the identity of agents or informants in the field.

The use of military tribunals for criminal trials during wartime has a long history. Benedict Arnold was tried in 1780 before a military court assembled by George Washington. Military courts were used in a handful of cases in the North during the Civil War; during World War II, eight German saboteurs were tried using this procedure. The latter case was used as a precedent by the Bush administration, but it is one widely considered by legal experts to be a "rush to justice" (see Fisher 2005). Furthermore, the U.S. Supreme Court has long been wary of the expanded use of military courts; as far back as 1866, it ruled that military courts could not be used to try a pro-Confederate lawyer from Indiana (James 2009).

The use of military courts continued to be a source of constitutional conflict and intense debate after 9/11. President Bush's executive order authorizing the use of military courts was struck down in 2006 by the U.S. Supreme Court's Hamdan v. United States ruling in a stunning rebuke to the administration, that the president had exceeded his authority in ordering the use of military courts without an act of Congress, and that the proposed courts would violate the Geneva Conventions (see Mahler 2007). Shortly after the Hamdan decision, Congress passed the Military Commissions Act, which provided congressional authorization for the trials, and no further Supreme Court intervention has occurred.

U.S. military tribunals elicit constitutional controversy for a number of reasons. Among the most important are that defendants do not have access to all of the information used against them, and a military court can consider secret evidence without the chance of rebuttal. Rules of evidence are also much looser and defendants do not have a right to a jury trial. Instead, cases are heard by military officers, and only a two-thirds majority of those on the panel is required for conviction. Finally, defendants do not have full rights to choose counsel, are ordinarily assigned a military lawyer, have a limited right of appeal, and are not guaranteed an appeal. In the normal rules of American criminal jurisprudence, the maxim "better to let ten guilty people go free than to convict one innocent person" has long provided an orienting rubric for the entire system. In the case of military tribunals, by contrast, many observers would consider the deck stacked against the defendant (for a historically grounded perspective on military tribunals, see Fisher 2005).

Global Influence

In an era of globalization, just as the campaign for the universalization of human and political rights diffused widely, so too did some elements of the post-9/11 legal regime implemented by the Bush administration. The growing capacity for national governments to learn from, and copy, one another appears to have given U.S. policy developments a larger international dimension. In December 2001, for instance, the United Kingdom passed the Anti-Terrorism, Crime and Security Act, which includes provisions enabling the detention of "suspected international terrorists." New Zealand passed new counterterrorism laws in 2002 and 2003 that broaden the definition of terrorism and enable law enforcement to demand computer passwords and pin numbers upon receipt of a warrant.

In 2001, the Canadian Anti-Terrorism Act made provisions for new government surveillance capacities, secret trials, and preemptive detention, all of which rest uneasily with the Canadian Charter of Rights and Freedoms. In 2008, Sweden passed a wide-ranging new surveillance law also based on the Patriot Act; this authorized the National Defence Radio Establishment (FRA) to tap all cross-border Internet and telephone communication.[11] Diffusion of counterterrorism legislation has also been common in developing countries. By the start of 2004, fourteen nations in Africa, Asia, Latin America, and the Middle East had passed laws resembling the Patriot Act.

The Emerging Legal Regime

Taken together, the post-9/11 use of vastly expanded domestic surveillance, rendition, indefinite detention, torture, and military commissions constituted a sharp break from the recent past. In some cases, these contentious activities reached to precedents from the World War II era or even earlier, well before the modern conception of international human rights was fully established. Evidence for some degree of worldwide diffusion suggests a new potential to possibly reverse some globally important components of the rights revolution in years or decades to come.

All of the major policies now in place have been the source of controversy and debate to varying degrees. Consider first domestic surveillance. As the full range of the Bush administration's secret program of counterterrorist activities came to light, the small community of civil liberties lawyers and legal scholars expressed strong condemnation. Most—though not all—legal scholars viewed the new counterterrorism policies as representing a substantial redirection in the balance of liberty and security. Almost immediately, constitutional lawyers warned that the Patriot Act jeopardized Fourth Amendment liberties and privacy rights, setting up risky precedents (American Civil Liberties Union 2001; Evans 2001; Mell 2002). As additional counterterrorism laws and policies unfolded, legal experts cautioned against establishing further precedents with respect to the practices of detention and rendition (American Bar Association 2003; Strossen 2003; Wu 2004). Later constitutional scholarship would characterize the breadth of post-9/11 laws and policies as a new "preventative paradigm" (Cole and Lobel 2007; see also Lichtblau 2008).

Government agency and law enforcement targeting of Muslims, as well as of individuals with surnames that suggest Muslim identity or Arab ethnicity, has likewise been seen as problematic. Interviews and demographic data in U.S. Muslim communities suggest little sympathy for, much less participation in, terrorist organizations. But evidence of ethnic- or religious-based surveillance, as well as of a rise in hate crimes, is substantial (Cainkar 2004; Schanzer, Kurzman, and Moosa 2010). This includes the detention just after September 11 of more than 1,200 mostly Muslim individuals based on anonymous leads provided to the FBI, and the required fingerprinting and photographing of approximately 84,000 aliens from twenty-five majority Muslim and Arab countries through the National Security Entry-Exit Registration System. Neither practice led to any convictions for violent crimes (Schanzer, Kurzman, and Moosa 2010). From a social-scientific perspective, it is thus difficult to see these treatments of innocent individuals as anything but a perverse feature of war on terror practices.

Domestic surveillance is one of the most difficult of counterterrorism programs to gain information about, or assess with respect to effectiveness. John Mueller and Mark Stewart (2011) have estimated that the increased public expenditures on intelligence gathering for counterterrorism in the post-9/11 period have reached an extraordinary $700 billion. Yet in spite of these mammoth expenditures, the effectiveness of these programs has been called into question by numerous experts and observers (see Shane 2012). Among other issues are numerous cases of false accusations. Civil rights groups tracking these false accusations have noted that in many cases, the individuals in question have been active in political groups in one way or another. Among the cases of false identification and wrongful FBI harassment include antiwar activists in Pittsburgh, liberal Catholics in Nebraska, an anarchist and anticorporate activist in Texas, and animal rights advocates in Virginia (Moynihan and Shane 2011a).[12]

Next, consider the use of military courts. Comparisons between regular criminal courts and military courts are limited, but evidence with which to conclude that the latter are better suited to the handling of terrorism cases is even more scant. Military courts, in the eyes of the rest of the world, have a degree of illegitimacy that is virtually impossible to alter, and this is consequential. Some countries have, for example, refused to provide evidence if it is to be used solely in military courts (Moynihan and Shane 2011b). Even if the goal is taken to be long sentences, it is not clear that military commissions tribunals are effective. Through the end of 2010, terrorism suspects tried in civilian courts received, on average, sixteen-year sentences. In contrast, suspects convicted using the tribunal system in the Guantanamo Bay center had all been freed (Shane 2010a).

What about torture, the most controversial programs of the post-9/11 era? Although the use of torture was officially banned through presidential order in January 2009, it continues to have its advocates. Some have argued that enhanced interrogation procedures such as waterboarding are effective and at times the only way of stopping terrorist plots from unfolding further (Thiessen 2010). One specific contention was that the waterboarding of Khalid Sheikh Mohammad led to information about a 2006 plot to bring liquid explosives aboard ten planes headed to the United States and Canada. As asserted by former Vice President Dick Cheney and Bush administration legal advisor John Yoo, another claim has been that the use of torture ultimately led to the identification of Osama bin Laden's driver, which in turn led investigators to Osama bin Laden's hideout in Abbottobad, Pakistan.

But such claims have been called into question by evidence uncovered by investigative journalists and reports by law enforcement experts. There are four specific and distinct issues. First, information obtained using coercive techniques is frequently false; the subject may say whatever he or she thinks will cause the torture to stop. A common feature of information obtained using torture is thus the frequency of false confessions.[13] Indeed, more sober assessment of the information provided by Khalid Mohammad during his waterboarding is that he continually misled his investigators, including with respect to the identity of bin Laden's driver (David Cole, "Guantanamo: The New Challenge to Obama," *New York Review of Books*, June 11, 2011). A sense of how important such errors can be is vividly illustrated by information about a link between al-Qaeda and Saddam Hussein's alleged chemical weapons program in

Iraq that was obtained through the CIA's turning over a suspect, Ibn Sheikh al-Libi, for torture in Egypt. Although ultimately proven false, al-Libi's account was used in February 2003 by former Secretary of State Colin Powell in an influential speech at the UN advancing the case for war against Iraq.

Second, evidence indicates that information as good or better can be obtained with noncoercive, legal techniques of interrogation. For example, according to the then head of Scotland Yard's antiterrorism branch, information about the 2006 liquid explosives plot was "based entirely on Intelligence gathered in the U.K." (Mayer 2010). The use of noncoercive techniques provided the information that ultimately led to the killing of Abu Musab Al Zarqawi, the head of al-Qaeda in Iraq (Alexander and Bruning 2008). More generally, continued successes in disrupting terrorist cells around the world after the ending of enhanced interrogation in 2005 are closely in line with the conclusion that torture is unnecessary to information-gathering within this arena.[14]

Another set of negative consequences relates to the possibility that harsh policies lead to anger and resentment toward the United States among Arabs and Muslims, potentially making it harder to combat terrorism or possibly even providing motivation for young Muslims to join or sympathize with terrorist movements. The legacy of torture has left a deep stain on the image of the United States across the Muslim world. Its continuing and open embrace by prominent U.S. officials such as former Vice President Cheney is notable and has likely helped keep alive a debate that might otherwise be settled.

Finally, and perhaps more simply, the use of torture tends to be viewed as morally wrong in the modern world. Although torture was once regularly practiced in medieval societies, it is generally understood today to be a gross violation of the minimal standards of decency and respect for human life. One of the most compelling objections to its sanctioned use is that America's enemies will feel completely justified—and perhaps encouraged—in using it as well. One of the reasons that international agreements on the humane treatment of prisoners of war have been possible is that all countries recognize the maxim "that which can be done to others can be done to us." But for its remaining advocates, that possibility seems to have been forgotten.

The Obama Era

The 2008 election of Barack Obama and a Democratic Party–controlled House and Senate was viewed by many commentators as presaging a fundamental change in counterterrorism policy. The architects of the war on terror had been replaced with an administration that had been critical of many of these policies and that had pledged new directions. During his 2008 campaign, Obama ran as an early opponent of the Iraq war. Moreover, as a constitutional lawyer and former law professor, he had spoken out against a number of the new counterterrorism policies and practices. Obama repeatedly promised to close the Guantanamo Bay prison camp within one year of taking office, and he gave a number of speeches about the importance of not undermining American values in the war on terror. In a *Boston Globe* interview, for instance, Obama asserted both that "the detention of American citizens, without access to counsel, fair procedure, or pursuant to judicial authorization, as enemy combatants is unconstitutional" and that "the creation of military commissions, without congressional authorization, was unlawful (as the Supreme Court held) and a bad idea" (Savage 2007).

On coming to office, the new administration and the Democratic majority surprised many by leaving intact the large majority of the counterterrorism measures established by the Bush administration. Virtually all key laws and policies, including the Patriot Act, the military commissions system, and the 2008 FISA Amendments Act's retroactive authorization of electronic wiretapping, remain in place. In a blow to human rights advocates, the practices of rendition and detention of terrorism suspects were retained, the Obama administration reasserting the Bush administration's argument that inmates in facilities outside the United States have no legal right to challenge their imprisonment (Savage 2009). To date, the main change has been an executive order banning the use of torture. Given that approximately 170 prisoners remain in the Guantanamo facility, and approximately 3,000 suspects are still being held in the detention center at Bagram detention facility in Afghanistan (see, for example, American Civil Liberties Union 2010), Obama's original promise to close Gitmo and other foreign detention centers remains unfulfilled.[15]

In recent years, the emergence of new war on terror policies and practices are especially worthy of note. One of these has been, for the first time, an explicit presidential sanctioning of assassination. The public assertion of this authority involved the case of Anwar al-Awlaki, a U.S. citizen living in Yemen who had urged the killing of Americans through terrorism and who had assisted in the recruitment of underwear bomber Umar Farouk Abdulmutallab, the Nigerian national who had tried unsuccessfully to bring down a Northwest Airlines plane in December 2009 (Shane 2010b). Subsequently killed by a predator drone strike in September 2011, al-Awlaki appears to be the first U.S. citizen openly tracked for authorized assassination without trial.

Related to this is the rising and publicly acknowledged use of predator drone strikes in Afghanistan and Pakistan. Since January 2009, these strikes have killed at least 520 people. Of these deaths, approximately 110 appear to have been innocent civilians.[16]

For constitutional scholars and commentators, another key issue has been the willingness of the Obama administration to effectively ignore most of the legal and civil rights Gitmo detainees would have under international law. On March 7, 2011, President Obama issued an executive order creating a pathway for the permanent detention of some terror suspects (Peter Finn and Anne Kornblut, "Obama Creates Indefinite Detention System for Prisoners at Guantanamo Bay," *Washington Post*, March 8, 2011). Going beyond the earlier legal architecture of the Bush administration, the 2011 executive order applies to inmates who cannot be tried because of "evidentiary" problems and stipulates that they may be held for life in the absence of any legal conviction. Initially, the executive order is said to apply to forty-eight of the 169 current inmates, though nothing would preclude that number from growing should the Executive Branch decide to add names to the list.

In another area of concern to civil libertarians, the Obama administration has sought to prosecute government whistle-blowers who have leaked materials to the media or, in some cases, who simply discussed with reporters their concerns about top-secret war on terror operations. This directly contradicts Obama's earlier campaign claims about whistle-blowers as "often the best source of information about waste, fraud, and abuse in government" (Mayer 2011). The widely protested conditions of the incarceration of Private Bradley Manning, who was alleged to be one of the primary sources for Wikileaks's release of top-secret U.S. war on terror documents, have been an ongoing cause for concern and protest by leading constitutional scholars. Manning is being detained under harsh conditions awaiting trial, among other things being placed in solitary confinement twenty-three hours a day, being required to sleep naked except for a smock, and being inspected every five minutes around the clock.[17] The administration also pursued the prosecution of Thomas Drake, a former National Security Agency employee who was accused of removing secret files from his office. Drake's main offense appears to have been talking to a reporter at the *Baltimore Sun* about the potentially improper, and illegal, spying on American citizens (Mayer 2011). But this case was effectively dismissed when the trial judge ruled the government would have to reveal in open court what documents had been removed.

Policy Permanence?

Having thrown the full weight of the American military and U.S. intelligence capacity at stopping al-Qaeda and associated groups, these efforts had by all accounts succeeded in crippling organized terrorist cells around the world, which documents and files uncovered after the 2011 raid on Osama bin Laden's hideout evidenced. From an historical perspective, this is perhaps to be expected, as terrorist movements have rarely been able to sustain themselves over long periods (Goodwin forthcoming). To be sure, small-scale homegrown terrorists have popped up in the United States and elsewhere. But the organized international terrorist movement has largely receded in recent years.

Yet unlike war with a nation-state, which can have a clear endpoint, the war on terror raises the possibility of a more open-ended campaign. According to some legal commentators, as long as any individuals or groups declare an intent to harm Americans, the war on terror might be used as the basis for expanding "the national surveillance state" (Balkin 2008). Along these lines, the *New York Times* reported in the autumn of 2010 that the Obama administration was preparing new regulations that would extend existing Patriot Act rules to require telecommunications companies to adapt their software and hardware systems to allow for immediate compliance with any wiretap order. The administration has also sought to bring all social networking sites—such as Facebook—and "person to person" Internet communication systems, such as Skype, into compliance as well (Savage 2010b).

No clearer signs of the permanence of the war on terror in spite of its ostensible success can be seen in the aftermath of the death of Osama bin Laden. On May 1, 2011, a team of Navy Seals successfully stormed a compound in Abbotobad, Pakistan, where Osama bin Laden had been holed up for several years and under surveillance by the CIA for several months. Yet in spite of this symbolic end point in the long struggle against al-Qaeda, Republican and Democratic congressional leaders quickly agreed to a multiyear extension of the Patriot Act. The measure sailed through both houses of Congress, reaching President Obama's desk while the president was traveling in Europe. In what was reported to be "an unusual move," the White House explained that to avoid any delays the president "would 'direct the use' of an autopen machine to sign the bill into law" (Savage 2011).

Yet even the extension of existing policies with no change in their scope did not go far enough for some in Congress. For example, the House Armed Services Committee in early May 2011 passed a national defense budget authorization bill to formalize the powers of the president to lock up anyone, anywhere, deemed a threat to U.S. national security. A *New York Times* editorial (Editorial 2011) summarized the measure in the following terms:

> Osama bin Laden had been dead only a few days when House Republicans began their efforts to expand, rather than contract, the war on terror.

Not content with the president's wide-ranging powers to pursue the archcriminals of Sept. 11, 2001, Republicans want to authorize the military to pursue virtually anyone suspected of terrorism, anywhere on earth, from now to the end of time.

Meanwhile, some members of the Senate Intelligence committee, with access to data not publicly available, warned that the Obama administration was developing an interpretation of the act that went far further than even Congress intended. Ron Wyden (D-OR) remarked, "I want to deliver a warning this afternoon: When the American people find out how their government has secretly interpreted the Patriot Act, they will be stunned and they will be angry" (Savage 2011).

Looking at these developments nearly a dozen years after 9/11, a period in which not a single American had been killed in the United States as a result of an act of international terrorism, the new counterterrorism paradigm has reversed the movement of decades of civil liberties and rights protections. And it appears to now have both become institutionalized in public policy and emerged as a routine part of American political discourse.

Conclusion

The attacks of 9/11 and the sudden appearance of a visible foreign enemy seeking to subvert the American way of life—in the form of Osama bin Laden and al-Qaeda—provided a new and vivid link to past episodes of countersubversion in American political history. Al-Qaeda presents the classic profile of the subversive enemy: foreign in origin but with possible domestic supporters organized in covert cells, hidden yet seemingly everywhere, and providing a direct and open ideological challenge to American democracy and capitalism. To be sure, al-Qaeda presented a more literal threat to American society than previous enemies had, in that its demonstrated capacity to carry out a massive terrorist attack exceeded anything previous internal enemies had ever accomplished. But, at the same time, the magnitude of threat to the American public is surprisingly limited according to the best available social-scientific estimates, and it has receded dramatically since the original—and seemingly unique—attacks of 9/11.

The campaign against the threat of terrorism has been remarkable in its depth, breadth, and length. That the Bush administration's policy responses to the 9/11 attacks have continued and in some cases expanded under the Obama administration underscores the persistence of the war on terror. For instance, President Obama's executive order of March 7, 2011, now makes permanent detention for terrorism suspects who cannot be tried by the law of the land.

For social scientists, the war on terror thus offers a puzzle and ex-planatory challenge. The magnitude of this challenge is substantial in light of the growing body of scholarship and investigative journalism documenting their perverse empirical consequences and departures from established constitutional and legal traditions. The answer to the puzzle may reside in the behind-the-scenes influence of important play-ers in what is sometimes referred to as the military-industrial complex. It may also reside in elite partisan dynamics in Congress and the White House. But without the mass public's acceptance of these policy and legal changes, their continuation many years after 9/11 is difficult to en-vision. In the next chapter, we explore some of the opinion research that might help answer these questions.

Chapter 2

The Puzzle of Counterterrorism Policy Attitudes

How has the American public responded to new laws and policies of the post-9/11 era? In the previous chapter, we situated the rise of counterterrorism policies first under the administration of President Bush and in their later continuation following the election of a Democratic Congress and Democratic President Barack Obama. We also highlighted the long historical backdrop against which countersubversive movements and politics have periodically occurred. As we saw, these earlier episodes have both points of similarity and differences with the 9/11 era.

The question of how the mass public views counterterrorism policies connects to this history and raises questions that go to the heart of some of the most important and long-standing debates within the field of public opinion research. Scholars have puzzled over questions of rights and civil liberties support since the McCarthy era, and a variety of competing theories have been advanced. Studying public opinion on counterterrorism is important not only for understanding the trajectory of policy but also for its implications for scholarly research on mass opinion more generally.

There is no question that the events of 9/11 were of considerable significance for most Americans. But the precise direction and duration of these impacts is the subject of ongoing research and unresolved controversies. Widespread media reports and some very early survey results seemed, for instance, to suggest that Americans were responding to attacks by coming together in unprecedented ways. In the essay "Bowling Together," the political scientist Robert Putnam seized on evidence of a rebound in public trust in institutions, arguing that after the 9/11 attacks "we rediscovered our friends, our neighbors, our public institutions, and our shared fate" (2002, 20). But such predictions did not last long. Almost immediately, survey analysts found public trust in Congress, banks, and business declining to pre-2001 levels (Rasinski et al. 2002), and additional research reported no lasting trends in community involvement or feelings of civic attachment (Schmierbach, Boyle, and McLeod 2005).

Moving to post-9/11 war on terror policies themselves, the puzzle is why Americans would support policies and practices that depart from long-standing civil liberties and rights protections. Has the passage of time—that is, as we move ever further away from the events of 9/11— shifted Americans' attitudes toward less support for such practices as torture or the use of military commissions in place of regular criminal courts for terrorism suspects? Or have Americans come to accept these policies as more or less permanently necessary to ward off further terrorist attacks, even at the expense of constitutional protections and liberties?

These key questions connect with a richly diverse set of theoretical perspectives on American public opinion. Our goal in this chapter is to see how these perspectives can inform the research we present in the rest of the book. Our point of departure is scholarship on the liberalization of attitudes toward civil liberties (for example, Smith 1990; Sniderman et al. 1996). The opinion liberalism literature parallels broader arguments about the emergence of a set of global institutions and organizations that have been described as the "world society" (Meyer et al. 1997). Both bodies of literature offer powerful insights and both are notably optimistic about the strength of rights-based commitments. But, as we will see, this scholarship faces some significant difficulties when we turn to figuring out why the U.S. government would implement, and why Americans might welcome, policies that would seem to rein in established rights and liberties.

Things become more complicated as we allow for the possibility that "rights talk" and citizens' democratic values are in tension with the strategic deployment of terrorist threats on the part of political elites. In general, the communication of threats tends to enhance prejudice, solidify group boundaries, and mobilize authoritarian sentiments (Rousseau 2006). In the post-9/11 era, an important body of threat-priming scholarship has analyzed how politicians' messages about terrorism threats shape policy attitudes (Merolla and Zechmeister 2009). This well-grounded perspective is one that we will need to engage.

We then turn to a third set of possibilities, rooted in research on the cognitive-psychological processes through which individuals reason about policy and political questions. In the partisan heuristics tradition, citizens focus in on which political party is responsible for, or associated with, a policy (Bartels 2002; Bafumi and Shapiro 2009). These models hold that when policy details are complicated, or matter little to their perceived welfare, citizens figure out where to stand based on the available cues that policy sponsors or opponents provide. The approach also predicts that when influential political actors shift course, their supporters will follow. This leads to opinion trends and pressures toward change, including the possibility of polarization.

Another type of cognitive shortcut that may be relevant in relation to counterterrorism policies is biases that individuals have toward specific subgroups such as immigrants, welfare recipients, or even American citizens as a group. Whether policies are viewed favorably can depend on whom they are viewed as targeting (Sullivan, Piereson, and Marcus 1982). For instance, when government entitlement programs are seen as benefiting deserving groups or individuals, public support tends to be high (Steensland 2006; Oorschot 2008). Applied to the war on terror, target group theory anticipates that support for counterterrorism policies hinges on whom a coercive measure is seen as targeting. What is potentially at stake in the post-9/11 era is not, however, as well established as our knowledge about domestic groups such as African Americans. Instead, it is less studied groups defined by transnational ethnic identities, such as Muslims or people from the Middle East.

Also in line with target group theorizing is how politicians' discourse since the 9/11 attacks involved an us-versus-them rhetoric, in which national identity became a central point of division (Hutcheson et al. 2004; McCartney 2004; Lieven 2005). Could it be that national identity status, separate from ethnocentrism, matters to how the U.S. public reasons about counterterrorism? National identity and nationalism have not figured extensively in research on Americans' policy preferences, but in the case of counterterrorism policy national identity is a strong candidate. If national identity status operates in this manner, it would tell us about a potent way in which nations matter at the level of individuals. But before we get ahead of ourselves, it will prove useful to carefully assess the leading theoretical contenders that have defined scholarship on public responses to counterterrorism policies during the past decade.

Liberalization Trends

A major tradition of public opinion research has emphasized the importance of what we term *opinion liberalization*. The core idea is that, over time, citizens and elites have come to embrace civil liberties and human rights. In turn, this provides a foundation for the operation and expansion of democracy in the United States.

This is a bold thesis. The extent to which citizens' underlying commitments to rights and liberties are strong will tend to limit public willingness to support authoritarian policies. Politicians may have leeway to impose rights restrictions when there is a crisis, but over time, a democratic public will demand restoration of baseline rights, perhaps especially if information about rights restrictions or abuses begins to flow.

The scenario of a democratically inclined American public has elicited a good deal of scholarly controversy and debate. The field of public opinion research itself emerged in part out of deep suspicions that mass publics were easily led astray and could rarely be trusted with democratic stewardship (Lippmann [1922] 1997). In the twentieth century, prolonged wars and authoritarian governments likewise disposed scholars toward pessimistic views of the capacities of mass publics (for example, Adorno et al. 1950). But, rebounding from scholarship on authoritarianism after World War II and the McCarthy era, subsequent decades saw the emergence of a more robust view of Americans' attitudes on matters of democracy and tolerance.

In this rethinking, two influential literatures stand out. The first is interdisciplinary research on attitude trends relating to civil liberties and tolerance of diversity. Ironically, this tradition started with findings about high levels of mass intolerance and low support for constitutional liberties. In Samuel Stouffer's ([1955] 1992) work, based on a 1954 national survey, respondents only needed to hear that it was a controversial figure like an "admitted Communist" for large majorities to restrict the exercise of First Amendment liberties.

But Stouffer's contributions to scholarship did not stop there. Finding evidence that civil liberties attitudes among younger and more highly educated respondents appeared to be more liberal than those of their peers, Stouffer predicted that the passage of time would turn things around. Younger, more constitutionally minded cohorts would replace the older generation. Increased levels of education would likewise propel the U.S. public as a whole toward greater liberties support.

This scenario of opinion liberalization was taken up with new gusto in the 1970s. Careful replication and extension of Stouffer's measures of civil liberties attitudes found a dramatic and liberal trend in U.S. opinion (Davis 1975; Cutler and Kaufman 1975). In further line with Stouffer's original hypotheses was new evidence for the importance of education and generation as sources of pressure (Nunn, Crockett, and Williams 1978). Grounds for skepticism were, of course, reasonable, and an important criticism concerned the confounding impact of target group references in measures of opinion (Sullivan, Piereson, and Marcus 1982). The impact of target groups represented a lasting contribution, for evidence was clear that such "least liked" groups of the time as the Symbionese Liberation Army elicited very low rights support from the public.

Nonetheless, evidence for a liberalizing trend continued to accumulate, and a thematic result was the existence of civil liberties support across a wider array of stigmatized or threatening groups than Stouffer had considered (Wilson 1994). Another milestone was evidence of parallel, liberal trends in gender, racial, and sexual morality attitudes (Smith 1990; Page and Shapiro 1992; Schuman et al. 1997). Given the historical inequalities and cultural baggage associated with these domains, liberalizing trends represented a dramatic change in attitudes. The move toward greater tolerance spanning a variety of important rights domains and identities lent credence to the opinion liberalization scenario.

Growing attention by opinion researchers to social psychological mechanisms also provided a more robust analytical foundation for understanding opinion liberalization. There was growing evidence that education shaped rights and liberties support through both general ideological beliefs as well as cognitive sophistication (Bobo and Licari 1989; Sniderman, Brody, and Tetlock 1991; see also Marcus et al. 1995). Buttressed by multivariate analysis, this increasingly sophisticated research was able to begin unpacking the process of attitude formation. Contrary to the view of skeptics, it increasingly looked as if ordinary individuals were capable of actually reasoning about rights and liberties conflicts (Sniderman et al. 1996). From the perspective of the subfield's earlier views of antidemocratic and authoritarian tendencies, the opinion liberalization scenario had gained purchase. It had moved the scholarly goalposts in a boldly optimistic direction.

Global Parallels?

Opinion liberalization scholarship focused on the workings of democratic support with respect to the attitudes and beliefs of individuals. A complementary literature has offered evidence of increasing support for human rights and democracy at the macro level of national states and international organizations. In particular, the theory of *world society* developed by John Meyer and his colleagues (Meyer et al. 1997; Meyer 2000; Schofer and Hironaka 2005) has offered a systematic model of the spread of democratic norms and global human rights. According to this theory, the emergence of international organizations exerts rising influence over the behavior of nation-states, and, in turn, the fundamental ideas around which specific countries are organized. This is especially apparent in the postwar era, where the rapid spread of democracy, universal education, and the rights of sexual minorities is particularly suggestive (Frank, Camp, and Boutcher 2010; Meyer 2000, 2001).

How do these rights spread? Global society theorists have identified international nongovernmental organizations (INGOs) and nongovernmental organizations (NGOs) as especially important because they are more free of the established interests of businesses, states, and political parties (Boli and Thomas 1997, 1999). Sponsoring ideas of individual liberties, scientific authority, and the importance of institutions such as education, INGOs and the networks that connect them to national states are said to represent a genuinely global model of civil society. Challenger social movements, when they successfully sponsor new ideas of individualism or rights, often enter the INGO population (Frank and Mc-Eneaney 1999). International governmental organizations such as the United Nations also act as carriers of world society norms, particularly when they are less rooted in the experience and interests of a specific country or world region.

By virtue of its analytical focus, the world society paradigm acknowledges contingencies in the relationships between the ideas sponsored by international organizations versus the actual behavior of national states and their populations. But this phenomenon, called *decoupling*, is not entirely open ended either. A key expectation is that over time, decoupling should lessen as the policy influence of international organizations strengthens. Provocative evidence indicates, for instance, tighter coupling in the realm of environmental policymaking and treaty compliance (Schofer and Hironaka 2005). By the same token, nations are still located in unequal positions within the world system, and it is the more affluent—and democratic—countries that appear to be strongly connected to international organizations and world society norms (Beckfield 2003).

Together, these aspects of world society theory have considerable relevance in the U.S. context. As a core player in and one of the sponsors of world society, the United States should, in principle, be a country with particularly well-entrenched legal and human rights norms. Although the focus of world society is not public attitudes as such, this perspective identifies macro-level processes that should exert consistently powerful pressures toward rights support and democracy. It is possible, even probable, that world society mechanisms complement the demographic and psychological processes underlying the opinion liberalization hypothesis.

Applications to Public Opinion on the War on Terror

By the turn of the new millennium, it was fairly common for public opinion scholars to view Americans as generally supportive of civil liberties and diversity, and the U.S. public as residing in an environment in which legal experts and international organizations actively buttressed and sponsored democratic ideals. The expressions of a more paranoid politics of the past, when civil liberties and political rights were given shorter shrift, seemed to have receded. The characteristics of the new global environment, alongside a more flexible and cosmopolitan public, had propelled American society in a progressive direction.

How, then, would mass public opinion fare when confronted with a dramatic crisis and an accompanying set of policy challenges? Would opinion liberalization hold? The shock of the 9/11 attacks rapidly led to new empirical scholarship on public attitudes. Reviewing the initial poll data, Leonie Huddy, Nadia Khatib, and Theresa Capelos (2002, 420) found a high proportion of Americans (between 55 and 79 percent) expressing the belief that the fight against terrorism would require some freedoms to be relinquished. High levels of fear were also found in both population surveys (Huddy et al. 2003) and undergraduate student samples (Coryn, Beale, and Myers 2004), and negative views of Arabs and Muslims appeared to be common. Given that fear was associated with exposure to television news, the dominant focus by the media on terrorism and visual images of the 9/11 attacks was telling (Nacos 2007).

But as provocative as these early results were, the passage of time provided the grounds for reconsideration. Looking over a longer period than initial studies, a review of polling data by Samuel Best, Brian Krueger, and Jeffrey Ladewig (2006) found that support for privacy rights and civil liberties had returned to earlier levels of support. Repeated surveys (with a panel component) conducted by Hank Jenkins-Smith and Kerry Herron (2005) likewise found a significant decline in respondents' willingness to restrict speech in the name of preventing terrorism.

The political scientist Darren Davis's scholarship (2007) offered the most systematic analysis and interpretation based on opinion liberalization scholarship (see also Davis and Silver 2004). In the wake of the 9/11 attacks, Davis proposed that public fears and anxieties surrounding terrorism were fueled by both media coverage and cooperation across party lines. This led to support for policies such as ethnic profiling and the Patriot Act. National security threats, alongside a disposition to trust government in times of crisis, were thus seen as conditioning citizens' willingness to restrict liberties. But using data from innovative surveys he conducted by November 2001, and repeated in 2003 and 2004, Davis also argued that underlying public commitments to rights and liberties would quickly resurface, and indeed had.

Viewed as a whole, then, a significant body of initial scholarship on public responses to counterterrorism seemed to confirm core premises of the opinion liberalization scenario. But important questions remained. One critical issue was how, if principled civil liberties support had not declined, could scholars account for the existence of positive and possibly enduring attitudes toward the more coercive or rights-restricting of counterterrorism measures?

Davis's survey data illustrate the challenge at hand.[1] Items from other surveys repeated over time reveal a similar picture of frequently high levels of counterterrorism policy support. From 2006 to 2010, for instance, an ABC News/Washington Post Poll found that between 65 and 75 percent supported "investigate threats" when asked "What do you think is more important right now: for the federal government to investigate possible terrorist threats, even if that intrudes on personal privacy; or for the federal government not to intrude on personal privacy, even if that limits its ability to investigate possible terrorist threats?" (Polling Report 2012).

Such conflicting results suggest that much needs to be explained. The accomplishment of opinion liberalization scholarship was to demonstrate the continued reality of civil liberties support. But the unmet challenge is thus how to account for patterns of public support for key policies and measures of the post-9/11 era.

Threat Priming

If the opinion liberalization thesis focused on the strength and endurance of civil liberties principles, the threat-priming literature evoked themes closer to the classical countersubversion theme considered in chapter 1. Here, the central question is the extent to which citizens will change their policy preferences when they feel threatened. The social psychology of threat provides a rich foundation for anticipating such responses. Citizens under threat display greater distrust toward outsiders, tend to retreat to established ideas and prejudices, and even experience a rise in thoughts about death. After the 9/11 attacks, perceptions of a new and profound threat rippled through the American public. A key political impact was on public willingness to support coercive new policy measures.

The social-psychological literature on threat provides a powerful line of explanation for public support for counterterrorism policies. Initially, the threat-priming thesis seems to resemble the rhetoric offered by architects of war on terror policies themselves (Thiessen 2010). After all, the 2001 terrorist attacks killed thousands. Shouldn't even the firmest supporters of constitutional liberties be expected to take seriously government policies and measures that reduce the risk of attacks bringing loss of life? If indeed the "war on terror is working" (Jacoby 2007), isn't it reasonable to expect that citizens will support policies they see as enhancing their safety?

To be sure, the actuarial and investigative evidence we reviewed in chapter 1, war on terror policies have generated a broad array of perverse and counterproductive outcomes, including Type I errors where innocent individuals have been wrongly questioned, detained in jails or military brigs, or even killed. But all of this is perfectly consistent with the threat-priming thesis, which does not require the threats to be substantial or even real. All that must happen is that the public receives and processes threat-laden messages communicated by elites. Regardless of their veracity, such communications will tend to color the policy reasoning of individuals.

A powerful way to get at the effects of threat priming on policy-attitude formation in relation to counterterrorism policy is with experiments. In a series of laboratory studies conducted between 2004 and 2007, Jennifer Merolla and Elizabeth Zechmeister (2009) randomly exposed a subset of subjects to the threat of terrorism. They used audiovisual presentations in which U.S. government officials warned of further attacks by al-Qaeda. Compared with the control group, individuals exposed to these terrorism threats reasoned quite differently about government policies. For one thing, they exhibited greater preferences for unilateral foreign policy. Respondents who had been threat primed also wanted more spending on the war on terror and showed greater support for the use of torture and military action against terrorism suspects. Finally, the experiments provided evidence that priming threats led individuals to prefer "decisive" political leaders, and to give greater weight to these evaluations when deciding which candidate to support in an election.

The underlying psychological dynamics explain why threat perceptions have such powerful impacts on attitudes (see, for example, Pyszczynski, Solomon, and Greenberg 2003; Huddy et al. 2005; Rousseau 2006). When confronted with new threats, particularly those involving the larger community or nation, individuals seek to reduce anxiety by increasing their loyalty to existing groups and institutions. Familiar symbols and sources of attachment bring comfort and simultaneously a tendency to distrust outsiders and unfamiliar things. Together, this raises the likelihood that threat communication and threat responses will enter into a feedback loop. When established sources of authority like the president tell people about new threats to their country, it tends to confer high levels of trust on the message, in turn also screening out dissenting voices and sources of skepticism. As unearthed in Merolla and Zechmeister's experiments (2009), threat-primed preferences for strong leaders can buttress the feedback process.

There may also be connections between threat-priming processes and the degree to which individuals support authoritarian ideas and values. A laboratory study by Howard Lavine, Milton Lodge, and Kate Freitas (2005) provides evidence. When exposed to threats, individuals characterized by high levels of authoritarianism become newly disposed to seek out information already in line with their policy opinions. In contrast, less authoritarian individuals, when exposed to the same threats, appear more likely to tolerate balanced sources of information. In this way, the threat-priming processes may activate heterogeneous, cognitive responses on the part of voters, disposing those with authoritarian values to become more closed minded and less open to reconsidering policy views.

A different kind of connection between threat and authoritarianism has been uncovered in research by Marc Hetherington and Elisabeth

Suhay (2011). Analyzing survey data collected in 2006 and 2008, these authors find that the effects of authoritarianism and threat perceptions interact when it comes to support for war on terror policies. But, in contrast to established views of how authoritarian values operate (for example, Altemeyer 1996), it is respondents with lower levels of authoritarianism who appear to be most strongly influenced by threat priming. Threats appear to matter considerably to counterterrorism policy attitudes, but primarily because they enhance support among nonauthoritarian individuals. According to Hetherington and Suhay, the effect of deploying threats thus brings the attitudes of less authoritarian citizens closer into line with those of their more authoritarian counterparts. Authoritarians, already predisposed to support such policies, are less affected by threat priming.

The preceding applications of threat-centered scholarship extend the view that terrorism threats are perennially powerful. Threat-centered scholarship evokes a different set of conclusions than the opinion liberalization model. It suggests that a threat-saturated environment fundamentally changes the contexts in which citizens reason about civil liberties and security issues.

But if indeed the post-9/11 era has put "democracy at risk," as Merolla and Zechmeister (2009) put it, is there any way out? Certainly, earlier periods of paranoid politics and symbolic threat deployment ultimately ran their course and gave way to moderation. Otherwise, the taming of the frontier, the Progressive Era's focus on white slavery, and the Red scares of 1919 and 1920 and the 1950s would be with us still. So what might be the conditions under which threat priming would not affect policy attitudes? And if threats have been consistently exaggerated, why hasn't reality intruded more forcefully? And are heightened threat perceptions all there is, or could other mechanisms shape counterterrorism policy attitudes, perhaps also buttressing an underlying pattern of support?

These questions gain further traction when we consider an earlier literature on rally-round-the-flag processes. Initially advanced by John Mueller (1970) to understand the effects of war on public opinion, the rally model analyzes how presidential popularity rises in times of war but rapidly declines when casualties increase. There are thus sharp and predictable limits on the president's or incumbent party's capacity to influence public opinion and the policy agenda (Brody 1991; Mueller 1994; Schubert, Stewart, and Curran 2002). That may seem counterintuitive, but only if we fail to see that military conflicts and crises ultimately generate a real downside. Wars and national security threats matter. But they do so in a cyclical way that initially enhances, and then later detracts from, the power and communicative influence of political incumbents and governing parties.

According to the rally model then, we may expect the impact of threat priming on voters' reasoning to vary considerably over time, eventually declining in efficacy. Certainly the waning fortunes of President George W. Bush during his second term should have limited the communicative capacities of his administration. And during this time, John Mueller's (2005) analysis of the trajectory of the Iraq War's casualty rate indeed finds trends in presidential approval to closely follow the rally thesis. It is also worth emphasizing that electoral losses by the Republican Party in the 2006 elections, and subsequently in the 2008 presidential election, brought about a political transformation of U.S. government.

Together, these macro-political changes suggest the importance of re-considering the impacts of threat priming in recent years. What updated estimates would show is important. But so too is the possibility that there are other sources of influence over the formation of counterterror-ism policy attitudes. Voter receptiveness to post-9/11 policies may not be limited to the presence of threats and threat communication in the environment.

Heuristics and Biases

The literatures on threat priming suggest that we also need to consider other possible sources of counterterrorism policy attitudes. Part of what makes threats involving the entire nation so potent has to do with pat-terns of identification that circulate among citizens. In similar fashion, the rally-around-the-flag thesis points to the mediating role of trust and responsibility attributions. Periods of war or national security crisis can enhance public approval of government or political leaders, but only if their attributions remain positive. When negative outcomes and other costs begin to escalate, voters start distrusting and shoveling blame on political leaders. Public willingness to support an incumbent's agenda then plummets.

Patterns of identification and differential trust in major groups or or-ganizations take us into novel territory, one associated with the interdis-ciplinary tradition of heuristics and biases scholarship (Kahneman, Slovic, and Tversky 1982; see also Gilovich, Griffin, and Kahneman 2002; Kahneman 2011). Here, the focus is on the cognitive shortcuts and biases that shape how individuals respond to changes in the larger environ-ment. The key idea is that in the real world, individuals tend to view new stimuli through the lens provided by their prior, and often en-trenched, beliefs, emotional attachments, and perceptual dispositions. This can lead at times to rapid and unexpected shifts in attitudes, as, for example, in the cognitive dissonance scenario. In this case, individuals completing repetitive tasks with little rewards are expected to change their attitudes more, and in a more positive direction, than those given

larger payments for the same task. This expectation is based on laboratory studies finding that individuals seek to reduce stress (cognitive dissonance) caused by behavioral compliance with environmental demands
(see Festinger 1957; Aronson, Wilson, and Akert 2006; Cooper 2007). But
it is equally if not more common that prior beliefs and biases shape the
ways in which individuals respond and make decisions. Howard Lavine,
Milton Lodge, and Kate Freitas's (2005) earlier research exemplifies motivated reasoning, and it is a common occurrence.[2]

The heuristics and biases tradition has enjoyed rich application in
electoral politics and political psychology research (Sniderman, Brody,
and Tetlock 1991; Lupia et al. 2000; Chong and Druckman 2007). Initially,
its application is somewhat less developed for research on counterterrorism policy attitudes, but analytical points of relevance are promising and
easy to discern. We consider, in turn, two strands of research, one focused on attitudes toward the partisan sponsors of a policy, and the
other on the specific targets of a policy.

Partisan Heuristics: Whose Policies Do You Support?

Political parties are central to the operation and definition of democracy.
In V. O. Key's (1964) classic work, parties exist at three distinct levels,
giving structure to the political conflicts of an era. First is the party-as-an-
organization, as exemplified in national, state, and local organizations.
Then comes the party-in-government, indexed by the behavior of elected
office holders. Last are the voters themselves, the party-in-the-electorate.

It is the party-in-the electorate that introduces us to the power of partisan heuristics. How do U.S. parties matter to the cognition of voters?
We know that partisanship, once acquired, shows a significant degree of
continuity over the life course.[3] Like ethnicity or religion, once voters
become Democrats or Republicans, that identification can be quite durable in the United States. It provides a powerful shortcut that effectively circumvents the potential complexity of political judgment and
choice.

But what if reducing the complexity of political judgment is not the
only reason that heuristics and biases matter? What if what voters really
attend to is just whether an individual or policy is promoted by a political party they like? Then they may reach an evaluation by matching
things to their partisan leanings, and not just to save time or effort. Like
threat priming, partisan heuristics are easily mobilized by politicians'
communication, by media reports, and through social interaction with
peers (Green, Palmquist, and Schickler 2002; see also Zaller 1992). But
now the mechanism at hand involves the degree to which voters identify
as either Democrat or Republican. When information or some prior basis
for making attributions about which politicians are associated with a

specific law or policy is available, partisan voters will tend to reach a quick if potentially self-serving verdict.

Some of the strongest evidence to date comes from the realm of economic policy reasoning. Analyzing panel data from the National Election Studies, Larry Bartels (2002) finds that voter evaluations of President George H. W. Bush were shaped not only by their own, earlier evaluations but also by their current patterns of party identification. Further evidence suggests that even voters' perceptions of how the economy was doing depended on party identification. Taking into account their prior economic perceptions, Republican identifiers were still considerably more likely than Democrats to view the economy in favorable terms in the early 1990s during a Republican presidency, and that was true of Democrats during the Clinton years as well. In line with the partisan heuristics thesis, voters' economic perceptions were focused through the lens of partisanship. The same, objective economic conditions were viewed asymmetrically by Democrats and Republicans. Partisanship had an independent impact on the formation of voters' attitudes and evaluations.

A still broader statement about the centrality of partisanship to voters' decision-making has been developed by Delia Baldassarri and Andrew Gelman (2008). Looking at a wide array of domestic policy issues using National Election Studies data, these scholars find evidence of growing associations with party identification (see also Bafumi and Shapiro 2009). Related work on roll call voting in Congress finds party polarization to have originated earlier during the 1970s (McCarty, Poole, and Rosenthal 2006). Research on partisanship-related polarization among voters emerged later, and in response to elite polarization, during the 1980s and 1990s. Insofar as partisan polarization among voters continued through 2010, these results suggest that partisanship will tend to matter even more in the contemporary historical era than it did in the past. They powerfully hypothesize that the growing relevance of partisanship to policy reasoning may give politicians an exaggerated capacity to place blinders over the eyes of their faithful.

Turning to the war on terror, how might partisan heuristics have figured? The starting point is that the existence of a single, uniform public is unlikely. Instead, we might think about an underlying dimension of heterogeneity, depending on where voters see themselves in relation to the Democratic and Republican parties. As in the case of economic policy, voters' partisan identities will tend to matter to responses to counterterrorism policies, as long as the major parties took different stances, and, in turn, voters perceived these differences.

A fully worked-out analysis of partisan voters' responses to counterterrorism policies has not yet been developed, but its initial outlines seem straightforward. Although early responses by politicians to the 9/11 attacks were overwhelmingly consensual and bipartisan, the new and aggressive policy apparatus of the war on terror soon became a hall-mark of Republican President George W. Bush and Vice President Dick Cheney. Over time, partisan opposition to war on terror parties emerged, but primarily among either iconoclastic or very liberal Democratic politicians such as Russell Feingold and Dennis Kucinich. By the 2004 and 2006 elections, there was ample evidence that voters perceived and acted on the growing policy differences within the Democratic and Republican parties on national security issues and the war on terrorism (Campbell 2005; Aldrich et al. 2006; Brooks, Dodson, and Hotchkiss 2010).

A second source of evidence follows and extends Mueller's (2005) analysis of public opinion on the Iraq War. Analyzing a longitudinal sample of students during early stages of the Iraq War, Brian Gaines and his colleagues (2007) found that all their respondents had comparable, and fairly accurate, assessments of trends in war casualties. But where partisanship mattered and created considerable divergence was with interpretations given to these facts: the same number of casualties was viewed as smaller among Republicans than Democrats. Looking over time, Gaines and his colleagues also found that Republican identifiers' highly positive evaluations of President Bush were unchanging. By contrast, Democrats' and Independents' presidential evaluations more closely tracked the trajectory of their beliefs about casualties.

Where does this all lead us? If partisan heuristics have also been key to counterterrorism policy attitudes, we should see strong relationships between partisan identification and the dynamics of support for war on terror policies. Republican identification will enhance the depth of support, particularly when levels of conflict among political elites are high. Over time, such a relationship may have strengthened and become entrenched. Similarly, it seems likely that Democrats and Independents may have begun to rethink or otherwise lessen their support of counterterrorism policy. These circumstances might manifest in a pattern of higher polarization, or more simply with respect to a greater degree of stability in the policy attitudes of Republican identifiers. Either way, the dimension of time will be critical to gauging the relevance of partisanship as a candidate factor behind attitudes on post-9/11 policies.

Target Group Effects

Partisanship is not the only type of heuristic likely to be relevant to counterterrorism policy attitudes. Who the perceived targets of a policy are may affect how citizens react to such policies. Sentiments and patterns of identification, when focused on a policy, can have an impact on the policy attitudes of individuals. Target groups thus operate as an alternative type of cognitive heuristic. Just like partisanship, all that is required is for individuals to have a preconceived attitude toward a given group, and for these perceptions to be stimulated in conjunction with their evaluation of a specific policy. What makes target group biases of further interest is that they may involve mistaken attributions. Individuals may, for instance, view a policy as applying disproportionately yet incorrectly to a specific group.

We can see this type of target group bias in scholarship on policy attitudes toward welfare in the United States. Initially, when Americans think about welfare policies, they tend to focus disproportionally on African Americans as the targets and clients (Gilens 1999). African Americans were not a majority of the recipients of means-tested programs like the earlier Aid to Families with Dependent Children (AFDC). But even if factually exaggerated, racialized perceptions are nonetheless of real consequence, for they tend to generate negative attitudes toward cash assistance programs.

At the same time, other social welfare programs, such as Social Security, call to mind a quite different group of perceived recipients. Here, group perceptions of the elderly are not particularly erroneous and are a good deal more positive (Cook and Barrett 1988). As a result, public attitudes toward pensions and health provisions for the aged show a pattern of greater support in comparison with many cash benefit programs. In both this and the preceding research example, preexisting emotional biases and prior judgments toward target groups are consequential. Public responses to the welfare state depend in part on the underlying images of clients and policy targets associated with specific policies (Steensland 2006). Who is seen as receiving welfare shapes how individuals evaluate and respond to specific programs.

Psychological research shows the considerable strength of target group perceptions. Implicit association methodology (Greenwald, McGhee, and Schwartz 1998; Fazio and Olson 2003) analyzes how people retrieve and reason on the basis of groups stereotypes. In implicit association testing, individuals are compelled to rapidly categorize a pair of dichotomous groups—for example, female versus male, black versus white—using specific attributes. The speed at which test subjects link specific attributes to a particular group, rather than to the other, tells researchers how strongly linked in memory a group bias is. If, for instance, individuals take longer to associate the word *good* with a black versus a white subject, that tells us about the presence of underlying racial bias. Implicit association scholarship has also linked test measures to subsequent behavior (Nosek, Greenwald, and Banaji 2007), showing the power of unconscious group biases.

What about target group biases and the case of the war on terror? To date, the strongest case advanced is that of Donald Kinder and Cindy Kam (2009). Their theoretical focus is on ethnocentrism, which they define as a broad-based notion of prejudice organized around beliefs about ethnic groups' intelligence, degree of trustworthiness, and work ethic. Using 2000 to 2002 National Election Study data, they offer a detailed analysis of linkages with policy attitudes. Controlling for the potentially confounding influence of partisanship, threat perceptions, and also authoritarianism, Kinder and Kam find evidence that a measure of ethnocentrism is associated with attitudes toward defense spending, spending on the war on terror, and policies concerning the Afghanistan and Iraq wars. They also find evidence that the effects of ethnocentrism increased over time, mattering more to policy attitudes in 2002 than in 2000. The 9/11 attacks and the policy responses of the U.S. government appeared to have made ethnocentrism more relevant to voters' reasoning on counterterrorism policies.

Kinder and Kam's theoretical assumptions about ethnocentrism are a good deal broader, however, than the empirical measure they use in the analysis. Empirically, their measure is based on survey items that ask individuals to evaluate whites, blacks, Asian Americans, and Hispanic Americans with respect to group traits. Theoretically, however, their claim is not inherently restricted to either the specific preceding groups or to major domestic ethnic groups in the United States.

Why might this matter? A likely scenario is that salient target groups in the war on terror fall along a quite different axis of ethnic cleavage. One major set of candidates is Muslims and Arabs. Evidence indicates that the public views both groups in exceptionally negative ways in the post-9/11 era (Panagopoulos 2006). In this context, violence and hate crimes against these groups after the 9/11 attacks are telling (Schanzer, Kurzman, and Moosa 2010). So too are trends during this time involving negative depictions of Arabs and Muslims in the media (Nacos 2007).

It is here that the ethnocentrism thesis has propelled research in a promising a new direction. Arguing that stereotypes of Muslims are key, John Sides and Kimberly Gross (2011) analyze data from the 2004 National Election Studies and the 2006 to 2007 Cooperative Congressional Election Studies. They find evidence that negative stereotypes toward Muslims and Muslim Americans are associated with voter attitudes toward war on terror policies, controlling for partisanship, threat perceptions, and Kinder and Kam's (domestic group) measure of ethnocentrism. Although partisanship and threat perceptions have significant effects, Sides and Gross find little evidence of any connection between war on terror policies and Kinder and Kam's measure of ethnocentrism. This finding is suggestive for scholarship on target group effects.

Where does it leave scholarship on counterterrorism policy attitudes? In contrast to the better-developed tradition of threat-priming research, neither Kinder and Kam's nor Sides and Gross's studies were able to harness experiments to buttress and give firmer confidence to causal interpretations. That said, the theoretical idea that target group effects involving ethnic identity seem to provide a plausible starting point.

Consideration of target groups brings us to a final cleavage in the war on terror. This involves groups defined by their national identity. Does it matter, for instance, whether counterterrorism policies are seen as targeting Americans or foreign nationals? When national identity status involves individuals who are not American citizens, will we find negative attitudes to color how individuals see war on terror policies?

In both cases, we anticipate the answers will be in the affirmative. We suspect that Americans may make a distinction between, say, Muslims who are and are not U.S. citizens. Yet this hypothesis is not specifically entertained in the existing target group literature, which has concentrated on domestic targets such as African Americans, who are in all likelihood assumed to be citizens. Theoretically, we think it is promising and important to go beyond an exclusive focus on domestically defined target groups. As noted earlier, one potential yet tractable drawback of ethnocentrism theory is a tendency to focus empirically on minority groups that are nonetheless composed exclusively of American citizens. In essence, this holds constant the separate and cross-cutting cleavage that distinguishes Americans from foreign nationals and may thereby conflate two kinds of group biases.

In general, we know that the political salience of target group animosity varies considerably over time. During World War II, for instance, animosities toward Japanese Americans emerged as a palpable force with respect to U.S. internment policies (Goux, Egan, and Citrin 2008), creating a willingness on the part of the public to tolerate those rights-violating policies. In the quite different context of the 1970s and 1980s, novel political-psychological research found that violence associated with the Symbionese Liberation Army and the Ku Klux Klan tested the willingness of Americans to support civil liberties for each group (Sullivan, Piereson, and Marcus 1982; Marcus et al. 1995). In the contemporary era, globalization and international conflicts suggest the importance of national identity as part of the public's repertoire of negative target group perceptions.

The issue of national identity and its political salience has been an important staple of scholarship on U.S. political culture and American exceptionalism (Lipset 1996; Smith 1997; see also Higham 2002). Much of the content of politicians' and intellectuals' discourse about national identity is stylized, seeking as much to create as to describe the essential American creed. Indeed, polemicists such as Samuel Huntington (2004) have simultaneously pointed to, and argued for, an idea of American identity that emphasizes national uniqueness, though without collapsing into the type of ethnic, racial, or religious distinctions discussed earlier.

What grounds are there for anticipating that national identity distinctions have emerged to actively shape counterterrorism policy attitudes? The key is probably not that the 9/11 attacks and government responses created a brand new set of ideas the public then adopted. Instead, the post-9/11 era was a context in which national identity distinctions came to be activated and thus made newly relevant to the public. The 9/11 hijackers were all foreigners; al-Qaeda is a foreign organization with an alien ideology.

As Anatol Lieven (2005) argues, many of the most memorable symbols invoked by President Bush and other politicians referenced precisely this underlying cleavage. *Americans* and *America* were powerful keywords in President Bush's post-9/11 speeches and were accompanied by an underlying idea of national mission that demanded immediate use of military force, and an accompanying moral certainty that left little room for debate or dissent (McCartney 2004). According to Lieven, the overall message from the Bush administration was that of a "wounded and vengeful" nation. This contrasted with a more upbeat and optimistic side of American nationalism during much of the twentieth century, one that often emphasized liberty or economic development.

It may have thus enhanced the long-term political viability of counterterrorism policy for the architects of the war on terror to frame it as an international conflict against a foreign enemy. This pits America and its people against a foreign aggressor—not just al-Qaeda, the Taliban, or even Saddam Hussein. It was also the "axis of evil" and "violent extremism" around the globe that was said to demand an immediate redirection of U.S. policy (Frum and Perle 2004; Yoo 2006).

Media scholars have extended the empirical reach of this line of argument. In the wake of the 9/11 attacks, John Hutcheson and his colleagues (2004) presented evidence of a powerful dissemination of national identity ideas. Analyzing *Time* and *Newsweek* articles published after the 2001 attacks, these scholars found a sharp rise in mentions of national identity–related themes. In 97 percent of these instances, President Bush was the key source. During this time there was also a growing divergence in the degree to which nationalist rhetoric was used by different groups of elites and experts. Hutcheson and colleagues found that print journalists relied primarily on the national identity rhetoric of the Bush administration. But that wasn't inevitable. Instead, it reflected the disproportionate influence of the Bush administration and its supporters on the media.

By design, a number of the most notorious counterterrorism policies target foreign nationals. This has been particularly true of the practices of rendition, detention, and torture. Moreover, as David Cole discussed in a *Boston Review* article, the U.S. government maintained from the start a double standard as regards implementation, giving noncitizens harsher treatment (December 2002/January 2003). When, for instance, U.S. citizen John Walker Lindh was captured in Afghanistan as a Taliban soldier, he was transferred not to Guantanamo Bay or another secret detention center but instead to Virginia, where he was later indicted in civilian criminal court. Likewise, applications of the Patriot Act appear at times to focus extensively on the immigration status of suspects, where here as well prosecutors have tended to focus on violations pertaining to foreign nationals. These subtleties are not immediately visible to the public, but the broader framing of counterterrorism policy as aimed at foreigners is likely to enhance its popular appeal.

Of course, the real proof is in analyses this perspective enables. In this context, a point we emphasize is that to get convincing results, it is critically important to be able to distinguish national identity status from the potentially confounding impacts of both threat priming and ethnocentrism-related target groups. This is a thematic challenge, one that applies equally to the task of disentangling, in turn, threat priming from ethnocentrism. Building closely from methodological innovations and political psychology scholarship, we will harness the power of survey experiments. We begin that task in the next chapter.

Chapter 3

A Critical Era?

I N THE midst of the 2007–2008 presidential election campaign, accumulating reports of the Bush administration's war on terror and policies fueled significant legal and constitutional controversies. Combined with the declining popularity of wars in Iraq and Afghanistan, a rethinking and reformulation of counterterrorism policies very much seemed to be in the air. Initially at least, the 2008 election appeared to usher in a transformation, voting out of power a Republican Party that had provided the leadership and policy architecture behind the war on terror. The Democratic Party extended their control of both the House and the Senate. Barack Obama, the first African American to hold the office, became forty-fourth president of the United States.

As a lawyer who had "taught the Constitution" while a lecturer at the University of Chicago Law School, Obama articulated numerous doubts on the campaign trail about the rationale and conduct of both the Iraq War and the larger war on terror. He promised to shut down the detention center at Guantanamo Bay, Cuba, and questioned the scope and legality of the National Security Agency's domestic surveillance programs. In 2006, he had voted against the Military Commissions Act, a minority position that signaled skepticism toward a central piece of the Bush administration's war on terror. He had also been an early and vigorous opponent of the Iraq War and had not wavered in his stated goal of bringing that conflict to a rapid end.

During his first week in office, Obama moved decisively on a couple of fronts, using executive authority to carry out key campaign promises. Executive Order 13491 sought to bring government treatment of captives into accord with U.S. and international law, explicitly banning the use of waterboarding and other torture techniques. Executive Order 13492 called for the closing of the Guantanamo Bay facility, alongside the restoration of habeas corpus and a commitment to comply with Geneva Convention principles regarding the treatment of prisoners. Obama's attorney general, Eric Holder, was tasked with reassessing the use of military courts for terrorism suspects and beginning planning for the transfer of detainees out of the Guantanamo Bay facility. Plans to try key al-Qaeda leaders in open federal courts were made, including a proposal (later abandoned) to try Khalid Sheikh Mohammad in the federal district court in lower Manhattan, not far from the site of the World Trade Center.

For both critics and proponents of war on terror policies, these early actions seemed to confirm where the new president stood and where his administration was inevitably going. Also of note with the new president came a seeming redirection in rhetoric concerning terrorism, alongside a cautious embrace of the Muslim world that symbolically signaled a new direction in American foreign policy. To be sure, as discussed in chapter 1, all such predictions about the direction of the new administration would turn out to be premature. Virtually all war on terror policy reversals came during the new president's first week on the job. But it would be some time before the full extent of the new president's extensions and even enlargements of many counterterrorism policies would be clear.

Taken as a whole, the rise of Barack Obama to the presidency provides us with a powerful context in which to begin our investigations. It allows us to gauge whether the American public started to move away from the Bush-era counterterrorism policies once they were no longer being vigorously defended by the White House. We can thus see just how much public support for these programs would survive in the absence of presidential leadership and promotion from the commanding heights of the federal government. It also permits examination of the impact of partisan factors, or partisan heuristics (as we called them in chapter 2), the idea that rather than all voters' opinions moving in tandem over time, voters' underlying identification as Democrats versus Republicans moderates the impact of changes in the partisan political environment.

Environmental pressures on the formation of mass opinion preceding and following the 2008 elections afford us a second unique opportunity. After a relatively long period following the 9/11 attacks, a widely covered series of new terrorist plots and attempted bombings unfolded in the United States in late 2009 and 2010. These events, like the changes to the political environment, may have propelled public attitudes toward counterterrorism in new directions.

In this chapter, we begin to draw from our unique set of three national surveys fielded in 2007, 2009, and 2010. Using these surveys, we assess the impact of political and historical events on public attitudes toward war on terror policies and practices. First, however, we briefly consider what repeated polls and surveys tell us about public attitudes before 2007. We then turn to our original evidence about the critical period after

2007, when Obama came into office and when official policy discourse about counterterrorism shifted dramatically. Overall, what we find is surprising in the face of these numerous shifts and transformations, for public attitudes toward counterterrorism policies show far greater stability than change between 2007 and 2010.

Public Attitudes Toward Terrorism and Counterterrorism, 1995 to 2008

Even before the 9/11 attacks, historical events and some poll data provide us with a partial yet informative initial portrait of how the American public might think about policy responses to terrorism. Indeed, two critical events in the first half of the 1990s began to make domestic terrorism more of a threat, and one worthy of attention from pollsters. A failed attempt to bomb the World Trade Center in 1993 by several members of a radical mosque in New Jersey generated intense interest, making headlines for a brief time until the perpetrators were caught.

An attack of greater consequence for loss of life occurred in 1995. Two members of a right-wing militia group, Timothy McVeigh and Terry Nichols, carried out a bombing of the federal building in Oklahoma City on April 19 of that year as a protest against the federal government's use of violent tactics against armed right-wing groups. The Oklahoma City bombing killed 168 people, and the outpouring of national outrage and media focus was enough to begin to generate sustained interest among pollsters in the threat of domestic terrorism.

Following the Oklahoma City bombing, the Gallup Organization began asking Americans the following question: "How worried are you that you or someone in your family will become a victim of a terrorist attack similar to the bombing in Oklahoma City—very worried, somewhat worried, or not worried at all?" This question was asked between 1995 and 1999. After 9/11, Gallup tweaked the item so that it is not strictly speaking comparable with the earlier item. The post-9/11 item asked, "How worried are you that you or someone in your family will become a victim of terrorism—very worried, somewhat worried, not too worried, or not worried at all?"

For two years after the Oklahoma City bombing, approximately 40 percent of Americans were either very or somewhat worried about being the victim of a terrorist attack. Subsequently, however, concern dropped, bottoming out in the low 20 percent range in 1999 and again in April 2001. Not surprisingly in the immediate aftermath of the 9/11 attacks, concern about being the target of a terrorist attack jumped to over 60 percent (with a full third of Americans saying they were "very worried"). Over the next five years, concern remained at or near 50 percent and was still in the high 40 percent range as late as 2008.

Even more telling perhaps are results concerning attitudes toward society-wide threats. From 2001 to 2007, a Fox News/Opinion Dynamics item asked respondents, "How likely do you think it is that another terrorist attack causing large numbers of American lives to be lost will happen in the near future: very likely, somewhat likely, not very likely, or not likely at all?" Between 74 and 83 percent of respondents chose either "very likely" or "somewhat likely."

An item seeking to capture trade-offs between civil liberties versus fighting terrorism was introduced in the CNN/USA Today poll after 2001. It asked,

> Which comes closest to your view? The government should take all steps necessary to prevent additional acts of terrorism in the United States, OR the government should take steps to prevent additional acts of terrorism, but not if those steps would violate your basic civil liberties.

When the question was first posed in January 2002, Americans were nearly evenly divided in their willingness to give up civil liberties to fight terrorism, but by the spring of 2002 a clear preference in favor of civil liberties emerged, one that has been more or less constant, with some trendless fluctuations, since the middle of 2002. Results of this sort informed the idea of a return to normalcy among the American public (for example, Best, Krueger, and Ladewig 2006; Davis 2007).

But as discussed in the previous chapter, a quite different picture begins to emerge when the focus is shifted more centrally onto measures of counterterrorism policy attitudes. In one repeated item fielded by Fox News/Opinion Dynamics, respondents have been asked, "Do you think the military prison at Guantanamo Bay should be closed, or not?" At the start of this series in 2005, 59 percent choose the "should not" option, and in the most recent survey in late 2009, the corresponding figure was 60 percent.

Between 2006 and 2010, ABC News/Washington Post surveys asked respondents, "What do you think is more important right now: for the federal government to investigate possible terrorist threats, even if that intrudes on personal privacy; or for the federal government not to intrude on personal privacy, even if that limits its ability to investigate possible terrorist threats?" At the start of this series, 65 percent choose the "investigate threats" option, and in 2010 the corresponding figure was 68 percent.

Together, the preceding repeated poll items convey what is a powerful and perhaps surprising message about the American public in the post-9/11 era: measures of attitudes toward counterterrorism policy suggest a good deal of support. Looking at these and other repeated items (Polling Report 2012), there are ample, if initial, grounds for asking whether new environmental pressures and events registered much impact on public preferences. To answer this question, it is useful to examine specific war on terrorism policies and practices, and we now turn to a fuller and more systematic consideration than has been previously developed in the scholarly literature.

Public Responses During a Critical Era, 2007 to 2010

The change in partisan control of government in 2006 and especially in 2008, when Obama captured the White House, gives us traction to consider the partisan heuristics scholarship discussed in the previous chapter, and more generally to consider how the very different framing environment ushered in by a Democratic president affected public opinion. This literature leads to expectations of a large divergence in the counterterrorism opinions of Democratic versus Republican identifiers. Viewed through the lens of voters' partisan biases, the election of a Democratic president who had been openly critical of key elements of the war on terror should matter, but in an asymmetric fashion. Self-identified Democrats can be expected to experience pressure to move away from earlier levels of policy support. Doing so brings attitudes more in line with new perceptions, at least with respect to specific issues of detentions, torture, and military commissions toward which Obama had expressed criticism in the course of the campaign. Republican identifiers, for their part, are unlikely to have been so moved. Their policy attitudes may have remained unchanged, or possibly even deepened in response to growing perceptions of party-based conflicts.

The period from 2009 to 2010, however, is likely to have exerted pressures in the opposite direction. Given a new environment saturated by highly publicized reports of terrorism plots, it is possible that citizens either became more fearful of a terrorist attack or increased their support for counterterrorism measures. Of course, if the operation of partisanship heuristics remained or even grew in relevance, it is instead possible that self-identified Republicans were more responsive to these environmental changes than others. Ultimately, then, what we find will move us forward in understanding the trajectory and some initial dynamics of how the American public views the war on terror.

Data: The 2007 to 2010 Surveys of American Policy Attitudes

To look systematically at Americans' attitudes toward counterterrorism policies and practices, we need survey data. In this chapter and throughout this book, we draw on three national surveys we conducted, the Surveys of American Policy Attitudes (SAPA).[1] Several features make these data suited to the tasks at hand.

First the SAPA data provide us with the necessary over-time coverage.

Fielded first in 2007, then in 2009, and again in 2010, the SAPA surveys powerfully bracket the campaign and outcome of the 2008 presidential election. In turn, the 2009 and 2010 surveys span a period that witnessed the emergence of a series of new terrorist attacks and foiled plots.

A second feature of the SAPA surveys is their fielding of a suitable range of policy-attitude items, alongside experiments with which to systematically unpack mass policy reasoning. We postpone a more detailed discussion of the experimental design of SAPA until chapter 4. But right now, the substantive breadth of SAPA's policy-attitude items is important. As discussed in the following section, these items span a broad range of laws and activities associated with the war on terror.

A third and final feature is that these data are nationally representative. A good deal of scholarship on counterterrorism attitudes has derived from laboratory samples. These offer important results harnessing controlled experimental designs, yet these primarily college-student samples can also have limitations in terms of their validity outside of the laboratory. The SAPA data enable us to generalize across the entire U.S. population.

Measures of Counterterrorism Policy Attitudes

The scope and complexity of post-9/11 counterterrorism policies is important. The SAPA data provide us with measures across multiple policy domains, from specific pieces of law and policy legislation to de facto activities associated with the war on terror.

In all, the surveys contain ten items with which to measure counterterrorism policy attitudes. These items have each been designed around a set of experiments, in which alternative question wordings introduce one or more treatments of interest. For now, our focus is on the version of each question that has been repeated across multiple SAPA surveys. This allows us to see just how, and for whom, opinions have shifted over time. Question wordings for these repeated items are listed in table 3.1.

A number of SAPA policy-attitude items draw from past instrumentation used in national surveys. The detentions item derives from an item fielded by Darren Davis and Brian Silver (2004), and the ethnic profiling and airport security items are based on a format employed by the Gallup Organization (Saad 2006). The Patriot Act, National Security Agency (NSA) surveillance, and rights violation items are also based on Gallup survey items (Polling Report 2007, 2009). The torture, waterboarding, assassination, and Military Commissions Act items are of our own design.

All policy-attitude items make use of a branching methodology. In this two-part approach, respondents first answer a question that has binary (agree-disagree, support-oppose) response options. A follow-up

Table 3.1   Wording of Surveys of American Policy Attitudes Policy-Attitude Baseline Items

National Security Agency surveillance
"Do you think that the federal government should monitor telephone conversations between American citizens in the United States and suspected terrorists living in other countries?"

Military Commissions Act
"As you may know, Congress passed the Military Commissions Act in 2006, creating a separate set of courts and prisons in which individuals classified by the government as "enemy combatants" can be held indefinitely. Supporters of the Military Commissions Act say it gives the government the power to protect our country from terrorist attacks. Critics of the Military Commissions Act say it denies individuals their legal rights. What do you think?"

Patriot Act
"As you may know, shortly after the terrorist attacks on September 11, 2001, a law called the Patriot Act was passed which makes it easier for the federal government to access phone and email records. What do you think? Do you support or oppose the Patriot Act?"

Assassination
"In recent years, the U.S. government has sometimes targeted individuals suspected of being al-Qaeda or Taliban leaders for assassination. Do you [approve/disapprove] of targeting for assassination individuals suspected of being al-Qaeda or Taliban leaders?"

Rights violation
"As you may know, in 2009, the FBI [Federal Bureau of Investigation] arrested a number of terrorism suspects, including several American citizens, who were plotting attacks in Illinois, New York, and North Carolina [The government should take all steps necessary to prevent additional acts of terrorism in the United States even if it means foreign nationals' individual rights and liberties might be violated/Even if it means foreign nationals' individual rights and liberties might be violated, the government should take all steps necessary to prevent additional acts of terrorism in the United States.]."

Detentions
"Next, please tell me if you would favor or oppose each of the following as a means of preventing terrorist attacks in the United States. How about—Detaining someone who is not a U.S. citizen indefinitely if that person is suspected of belonging to a radical Muslim organization?"

Airport security
"How about—Requiring Muslims, including those who are U.S. citizens, to undergo special, more intensive security checks before boarding airplanes in the United States?"

Ethnic profiling
"How about—Allowing law enforcement to bring in for questioning people of certain ethnic backgrounds if these groups are thought to be more likely to engage in terrorist activities?"

Table 3.1   (continued)

Waterboarding
"In recent years, the government sometimes used a technique known as
waterboarding on terrorist suspects in an effort to gain information about
threats to the United States. Do you [approve or disapprove] of the use of
waterboarding on terrorist suspects?"

Torture
"Do you agree or disagree that government authorities should have the right to
torture a suspect who is American if they think it will help prevent a terrorist
attack from taking place in the United States?"

Source: Authors' compilation.

question probes opinion strength. This branching design yields response
categories ranging from strongly agree to strongly disagree, or strongly
support to strongly oppose. Because it breaks the cognitive task of responding to questions into easier-to-digest parts, the branching format
reduces the chance that survey respondents will guess or misunderstand
things. That has been found to significantly improve the quality of attitude measurement.[2]

How Americans Viewed Counterterrorism Policies, 2007 to 2010

Let's first look at where Americans end up by the end of the SAPA surveys. For eight of the counterterrorism items, 2010 is the final survey and
data point, and 2009 is the last survey in which the remaining two of the
items were fielded. Figure 3.1 presents our analysis of these data, and
symbols indicate the mean level of support for a specific counterterrorism policy or practice. SAPA counterterrorism items have a range of 0
through 1, higher scores indicating greater support.[3]

Of the ten policies and practices at hand, it is NSA surveillance of
American citizens and suspected terrorists that elicits the highest level of
support. With a score of 0.76, the NSA surveillance item's score is well
above levels of support for the next three counterterrorism items, all of
which cluster together: airport security (0.67), the Patriot Act (0.66), and
the Military Commissions Act (0.65). Next is assassination, where the
targeting of "individuals suspected of being al-Qaeda or Taliban leaders" receives a score of 0.60.

These first five counterterrorism items show what amounts to a fair
amount of support. All scores are well above the 0.50 scale midpoint.
The right panel of figure 3.1 presents data for the remaining five items.
The rights violation item leads the way, 0.57 indicating that respondents'
average opinion is shaded toward agreement with the position of taking

Figure 3.1   Counterterrorism Policy Opinions

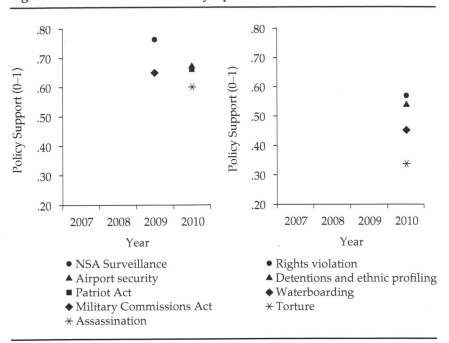

- NSA Surveillance
- Airport security
- Patriot Act
- Military Commissions Act
- Assassination

- Rights violation
- Detentions and ethnic profiling
- Waterboarding
- Torture

Source: Authors' calculations based on SAPA (Brooks and Manza, various years).
Note: NSA = National Security Agency; SAPA = Surveys of American Policy Attitudes.

"all steps necessary to prevent additional acts of terrorism." Not far behind are opinions on detention, the mean for which is 0.54.

In the 2010 SAPA survey, the detention and ethnic profiling items have the same item score of 0.54. The waterboarding item is next with a score of 0.45. With an even lower score of 0.34, the practice of torture easily elicits the highest level of public opposition. Given that waterboarding is best understood as a subset of torture, the contrast between opinions on these two counterterrorism practices merits a note in passing because it anticipates the cognitively induced framing effects we probe more systematically in chapters 4 through 6.

So far, a key result that stands out is how relatively positive attitudes toward many counterterrorism policies were, nearly a decade after the 2001 terrorist attacks. The SAPA items by design make no effort to sugarcoat or otherwise lower the bar when it comes to measuring support for contentious counterterrorist activities. Nonetheless, seven of our ten items show positive and quite strong support in many cases. As dismaying as it may be to civil libertarians, this is quite consistent with past polling on post-9/11 policies that we discussed in the previous section.

With this in mind, we are now in a position to emphasize two further findings. Opinions across the range of counterterrorism issues are heterogeneous. The diversity of war on terror policies registers for the public. Although some practices, such as the use of torture, are clearly unpopular, others, such as government surveillance and even targeted assassination, elicit much higher levels of support.

Had we found a more homogenous portrait of policy opinions, we might have been tempted to see the U.S. public as reflexively and wholeheartedly behind counterterrorism efforts. Perhaps this would indicate an encompassing impulse toward authoritarianism. In contrast, however, the variation in policy opinions revealed by the 2010 SAPA data suggests something else. Americans as a whole appear quite capable of a significant degree of policy reasoning, incorporating differences across counterterrorism measures into their attitudinal responses.

That said, there is a pattern to these differences in policy opinion. When the activity at hand involves a specific government agency or piece of legislation, public attitudes are a good deal more supportive, as in the cases of NSA surveillance, the Patriot Act, and the Military Commissions Act. The assassination and rights violation items also make reference to, respectively, the U.S. government and the Federal Bureau of Investigation, and these items also suggest relatively positive attitudes.

Of the four remaining items, the two for waterboarding and torture show notably low levels of support. On average, opinions on detentions and ethnic profiling are a good deal less positive than those on the government law and agency-related items. A clear anomaly is the airport security item. The lack of specific reference to government agencies or authorities does not prevent quite positive attitudes on the part of Americans toward "more intensive security checks" (targeted at Muslims).

What should we make of these further results? One take-away point is simple and important. The idea of government and law can itself be quite persuasive. This has been an important theme in public opinion and political psychology research (Sniderman, Brody, and Tatlock 1991, chap. 11; Tyler 2006), though it is also potentially offset by steady declines in trust in government since the 1960s (Hetherington 1998; Smith 2012). Certainly not all government institutions elicit positive responses on the part of the public.

But what our current results suggest is that for counterterrorist activities, adoption of formal legislation and the involvement of government agencies in their administration has seemingly enhanced support. By contrast, covert coercive activities are not, by themselves, seen in such a favorable light. This implication calls for greater scrutiny. We do just that in chapter 6 when we look at the contribution of policy adoption as a force capable of itself influencing the formation of counterterrorism policy attitudes.

Figure 3.2   Only One Over-Time Trend Is Significant[a]

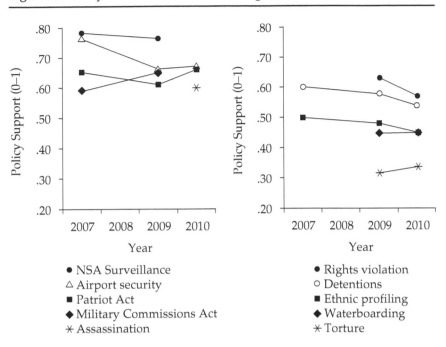

Source: Authors' calculations based on SAPA (Brooks and Manza, various years).
Note: NSA = National Security Agency; SAPA = Surveys of American Policy Attitudes.
[a] Significant trend (airport security) indicated by triangles.

How Did the U.S. Public Respond Over Time?

We want to know not just where the American public ended up but also where they started before 2008. Looking at the years covered by the SAPA data tells us whether, as we might expect, critical events and environmental changes registered, propelling counterterrorism policy opinions in new directions. Was there a significant shift in counterterrorism policy opinion? Did the 2008 election coincide with a decline in policy support? And did a subsequent increase in terrorist plots and attempted attacks rekindle greater public preferences for war on terror policies?

The over-time SAPA data in figure 3.2 extend our portrait. As before, item means in a survey year are plotted. Five of the items were fielded in all three surveys, and four items were fielded in just two of the three. The final item—targeted assassination—was available in only the 2010 survey.

The SAPA data deliver a resounding set of answers. In only one case—airport security—is there statistical evidence that aggregate opinions changed, where attitudes moved in the direction of lower support, over time, between 2007 and 2009. A casual observer, looking at the SAPA data in figure 3.2, might initially see the four other instances of down-

Table 3.2 Tests for Over-Time Trends[a]

	Linear Change	~ Linear Change
2007-2009-2010 items		
Patriot Act	$F(1) < .01; p > F > .99$	$F(2) = 1.48; p > F = .23$
Detentions	$F(1) = 2.07; p > F = .15$	$F(2) = 1.18; > F = .31$
Airport security	**$F(1) = 11.81; p > F < .01$**	**$F(2) = 7.17; p > F < .01$**
Ethnic profiling	$F(1) = 1.42; p > F = .23$	$F(2) = .82; p > F = .44$
2007–2009 items		
Military Commissions Act	$t(1) = -1.62; p > F > .11$	$t(1) = 1.62; p > F > .11$
NSA surveillance	$t(1) = .52; p > F > .60$	$t(1) = .52; p > F > .60$
2009–2010 items		
Rights violation	$t(1) = 1.78; p > F > .08$	$t(1) = 1.78; p > F > .08$
Torture	$t(1) = -.59; p > F > .56$	$t(1) = -.59; p > F > .56$
Waterboarding	$t(1) = .00; p > F = 1.00$	$t(1) = .00; p > F = 1.00$

Source: Authors' calculations based on SAPA (Brooks and Manza, various years).
Note: NSA = National Security Agency; SAPA = Surveys of American Policy Attitudes.
[a]Bolded entry indicates significance at the .05 level.

ward-sloping item means as indicative of opinion trends. But that judgment would be incorrect, because over-time changes in these items means are well within the margin of sampling error. Likewise, in three cases, upward-sloping lines indicate nothing more than random fluctuation.

Before considering what these dramatic results mean, we spell out the statistical reasoning a bit more. In table 3.2, we present results for two different tests for over-time change in counterterrorism policy opinions. As shown in the top third of this table, when we have three survey years worth of data we can see whether there is evidence for either linear or nonlinear trends in opinion. We can also see from the first column that in only one case—airport security—is the test's p-value low enough to reject the null hypothesis of no change. In the second column, we consider the more complicated scenario of nonlinear change. As before, only the case of airport security returns evidence of a significant time trend in attitudes.

The remaining test results in table 3.2 are for the five items available in only a pair of surveys (that is, 2007 and 2009, or 2009 and 2010). In all cases, the statistical results lead to the same conclusion. There is simply no evidence to reject the hypothesis that counterterrorism policy opinions were stable during the time periods in question.

What, then, are we to make of these results? Starting with the changing environment of late 2009 and 2010, we find no evidence for any impacts of historical events on counterterrorist policy opinions. Dramatic events like the attempted bombing of a Northwest Airlines flight on Christmas Day in 2009, alongside the failed Times Square car bombing attempt in May 2010, received considerable national news coverage. But even so, they did not appear to prime the public to rethink terrorism and demand greater government policy action. Counterterrorism policy opinions during this time period were unchanged.

Of course, it is possible that shifts in threat and related perceptions occurred earlier in 2009. That seems somewhat less likely, given that the largest (and most) of the new terrorist attempts occurred during or after the 2009 SAPA data collection. But as a hypothetical, that should still lead us to see evidence of trends toward rising counterterrorism policy support between 2007 and 2009. And recall that the only evidence of change during this time is for the case of declining support for airport security measures.

This brings us to the importance of the 2007 to 2009 results themselves. The election of Barack Obama in 2008 appears to have done virtually nothing to reorient public attitudes toward war on terror policies. If that had happened, we should see trends toward declining support for counterterrorism policies from 2007 to 2009. The single possible exception is the case of airport security opinions. But this trend is modest in magnitude and by itself insufficient to substantiate any expectations of large campaign effects or parallel influence on mass opinion stemming from a partisan change in government control.

It is, in principle, possible, even probable, that counterterrorism opinions changed before the 2007 SAPA survey, contributing in some way to the later emergence of challenger and antiwar presidential candidate Barack Obama. But even so, that would still leave intact the notable stability of the counterterrorism attitudes we have measured between 2007 and 2009. It is this relatively short stretch of time that provided the electorate as a whole with ample opportunity to observe partisan differences in policies, including those related to counterterrorism.

Partisan Heuristics and Group-Specific Trends

We now turn from looking at the public as a whole to a finer-grained set of portraits, which is particularly informative with respect to partisan differences in opinion. In general, we should expect Democrats and Republicans to view policy issues from different vantage points. The war on terror is a fertile ground for partisan heuristics. Additionally, what if rising patterns of party-based conflicts over counterterrorism have, over time, increasingly pushed the partisan faithful in different directions? A divergent set of trends involving Democrats and Republicans would then cancel out at the level of the entire electorate.

Let's see what the SAPA data have to say. As before, we can consider scenarios of linear as well as nonlinear change when items are available in more than two surveys. The first column in table 3.3 presents results with which to consider scenarios of partisan divergence.

Of the entire set of twenty-six statistical tests, only two provide any evidence for a partisan group-specific trend in opinion. One of these is for Democratic identifiers with respect to a linear trend in airport security opinion. We already know that there was a population-wide opinion

Table 3.3 Additional Tests for Group-Specific Trends[a]

	Democrat/ Republican	Liberal/ Conservative	College-Educated/ Non-College-Educated	White/ Nonwhite	Christian/ Non-Christian
Linear change					
Patriot Act	$p = .14/.55$	$p = \mathbf{.04}/.72$	$p = .23/.33$	$p = .68/.32$	$p = .65/.15$
Detentions	$p = .36/.11$	$p = .81/.46$	$p = .82/.37$	$p = .33/.11$	$p = .14/.62$
Airport security	$p = \mathbf{.03}/.38$	$p = \mathbf{.04}/.60$	$p = \mathbf{.00}/.18$	$p = \mathbf{.00}/.36$	$p = \mathbf{.01}/.11$
Ethnic profiling	$p = \mathbf{.02}/.56$	$p = .32/.22$	$p = .72/.59$	$p = .33/.60$	$p = .71/.07$
Military Commissions Act	$p = .89/.53$	$p = .82/.84$	$p = .50/.58$	$p = .20/.50$	$p = .45/.05$
NSA surveillance	$p = .80/.83$	$p = .66/.08$	$p = .59/.13$	$p = .62/.80$	$p = .80/.52$
Rights violation	$p = .43/.70$	$p = .63/.58$	$p = .69/\mathbf{.01}$	$p = .27/.41$	$p = \mathbf{.03}/.57$
Torture	$p = .56/.45$	$p = .99/\mathbf{.00}$	$p = .69/.28$	$p = .79/.22$	$p = .62/\mathbf{.00}$
Waterboarding	$p = .70/.68$	$p = .52/.99$	$p = .72/.67$	$p = .79/.57$	$p = .81/.89$
~Linear change					
Patriot Act	$p = .10/.30$	$p = .08/.58$	$p = .22/.62$	$p = .28/.32$	$p = .43/.09$
Detentions	$p = .46/.28$	$p = .82/.29$	$p = .82/.24$	$p = .53/.27$	$p = .12/.36$
Airport security	$p = .08/.05$	$p = .05/.58$	$p = \mathbf{.01}/.31$	$p = \mathbf{.00}/.44$	$p = \mathbf{.01}/.21$
Ethnic profiling	$p = .06/.59$	$p = .59/.15$	$p = .85/.42$	$p = .61/.74$	$p = .80/.20$

Source: Authors' calculations based on SAPA (Brooks and Manza, various years).

Note: NSA = National Security Agency; SAPA = Surveys of American Policy Attitudes.

[a]Entries are probabilities associated with F-tests for items available in three years (Patriot Act, detentions, airport security, ethnic profiling) or t-tests for items available in only two years (Military Commissions Act, NSA surveillance, rights violation, torture, and waterboarding).

trend on this issue. For Democratic identifiers, movement toward declining support over time is similar, from a score of 0.74 in 2007 to 0.64 in 2009 and 0.61 in 2010. The second group-specific trend is also for Democratic identifiers on the issue of ethnic profiling, even though the sample as a whole showed no evidence of trends on this issue. But focusing just on Democratic identifiers, we can see that group opinions shifted significantly during the 2007 to 2010 period covered by the SAPA surveys.[4]

But the much more dramatic finding concerns the absence of anything like a comprehensive movement toward partisan polarization. Republican identifiers' counterterrorism policy opinions did not change during a period when many former Bush administration officials and war on terror architects have been steadfast in their positions. For their part, the opinions of Democratic identifiers remained at a constant distance from those of their Republican counterparts on seven of the nine policy issues under consideration. We find that surprising, because during this period it was specific Democratic Party politicians, particularly as exemplified in the emergence and election of Barack Obama, who moved toward more skeptical postures on a number of counterterrorism policies.

Still, however, the over-time story is not yet complete. Other relevant groups are important to consider with respect to time. The remainder of table 3.3 presents those results. Looking first at ideology tells us whether and for what issues self-identified liberals and conservatives may have experienced group-specific trends. As shown in the table, three trends are significant. Two are for liberals with regard to the Patriot Act and airport security. The third is for self-identified conservatives on the issue of torture. We consider these trends in greater detail in the following section.

Six additional subgroups round out the trend analyses. In addition to respondents who are or are not college-educated, we consider, in turn, whites versus nonwhites and Christians versus non-Christians. In parallel fashion to the earlier results, the large majority of the tests deliver evidence of a good deal of stability in counterterrorism policy opinions. Of the nine instances in which there is evidence for group-specific opinion change, six relate to the airport security issue and are quite similar to the population-wide trend on same issue.

Three instances of group-specific trends are left to consider. The first two are for non-college-educated respondents and Christians on the issue of rights violation. In both, between 2009 and 2010 policy support declined significantly. By contrast, the third—for non-Christians—involves an increase in support for torture between 2009 and 2010.

A Closer Look at Group-Specific Trends

Three domains of policy opinion merit additional scrutiny. They merit it because we have found evidence of group-specific trends in opinion. Al-

Figure 3.3   A Closer Look at Airport Security Opinions[a]

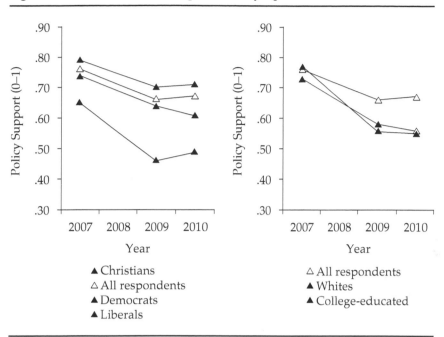

▲ Christians
△ All respondents
▲ Democrats
▲ Liberals

△ All respondents
▲ Whites
▲ College-educated

Source: Authors' calculations based on Surveys of American Policy Attitudes (Brooks and Manza, various years).
[a] Significant trends indicated by open triangles.

though these trends do not change the larger picture of evidence, they are still worth considering. We look first at the case of airport security opinions. As displayed in figure 3.3, the opinion trend affecting all respondents is illustrated using open triangle symbols. In summary, overall support for airport profiling measures experienced a significant if modest decline between 2007 and 2009, and little change between 2009 and 2010. This population-wide trend provides a baseline for gauging the group-specific trends in figure 3.3.

The group-specific trends our tests unearthed are comparable to the population-wide trend and are indicated using solid black triangles in figure 3.3. Democrats and liberals, college-educated and white respondents, and also Christians experienced a significant drop in support for airport security measures between 2007 and 2009. There is no instance in which a group moved in a divergent direction. What this is telling us is that the main story about opinion change on airport security is the one told by initial estimates for the public as a whole.

When we turn to the Patriot Act, we find there is just one group for which there is evidence of a time trend: self-identified liberals. As displayed by the dark triangles in figure 3.4, we can see how liberals

Figure 3.4   A Closer Look at Patriot Act Opinions[a]

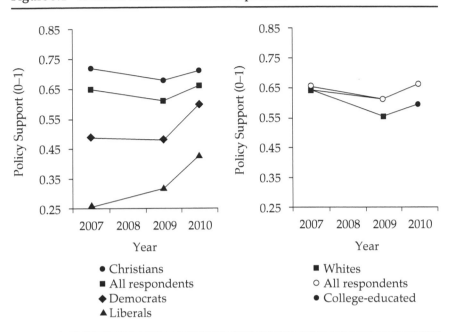

- ● Christians
- ■ All respondents
- ◆ Democrats
- ▲ Liberals

- ■ Whites
- ○ All respondents
- ● College-educated

Source: Authors' calculations based on Surveys of American Policy Attitudes (Brooks and Manza, various years).
[a] Significant trend (Patriot Act) indicated by triangles.

changed. An initially unfavorable view of the Patriot Act began to thaw by 2009, and this trend continued through 2010, as enforcement of the act lay in the hands of the Obama administration.

A final pair of group-specific trends is evident on the issue of torture. As displayed in figure 3.5, self-identified conservatives' and non-Christians' opinions shifted significantly between 2009 and 2010. The attitudes of all other groups, and of the public as a whole, were stable and unchanging during this time.

The shifts in attitudes toward torture among conservatives and non-Christian respondents are both toward greater support for counterterrorism policies. Non-Christians started out with much lower initial levels of support in 2009 but changed their opinions as much as self-identified conservatives did.

The deepening of support for torture among conservatives most closely approximates the kind of group responsiveness suggestive of polarization in counterterrorism opinions. This case is also remarkably singular. There are other instances of group-specific trends—such as non-Christians (torture) and self-identified liberals (Patriot Act)—but in these cases segments of the population with relatively distinct attitudes have

Figure 3.5   A Closer Look at Torture Opinions[a]

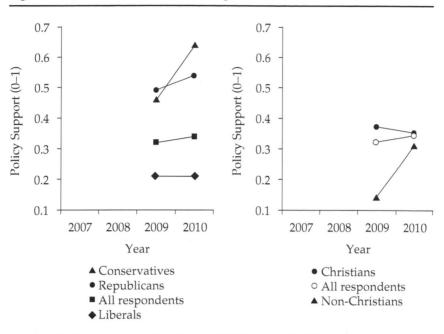

- ▲ Conservatives
- ● Republicans
- ■ All respondents
- ◆ Liberals

- ● Christians
- ○ All respondents
- ▲ Non-Christians

Source: Authors' calculations based on Surveys of American Policy Attitudes (Brooks and Manza, various years).
[a]Significant trend (torture) indicated by triangles.

moved over time to positions more similar to those of the public as a whole.

None of this is good news for theoretical expectations of group-specific responsiveness to environmental events. Again, this does not mean that groups defined by ideology or identities share identical views of counterterrorism policies. But it is to say that these groups have tended to share a similar degree of stability in their overall opinions on war on terror issues that, almost a decade after 9/11, is largely independent of the external environment.

What Have We Learned?

The results of our analyses of opinion trends in this chapter begin to cast doubt on one important hypothesis. A distinguished literature provides compelling grounds for anticipating that voters frequently view policy issues in an unabashedly and perhaps unreflectively partisan fashion, taking their cues from politicians and party leaders. In general, however, we find no evidence that an historic change in partisan control of U.S. government was preceded by, or led to, a corresponding shift in public attitudes toward counterterrorism policies. In this way, we can rule out the explanatory scenario in which voters' attitudes toward the war on terror were closely linked to the positions or persuasive arguments communicated by the administration of President George W. Bush. A weaker expectation is that partisan voters responded asymmetrically to political changes, leading to a growing pattern of polarization that is difficult to observe when considering the electorate as a whole. But here too the lack of evidence is noticeable.

With this in mind, it is useful to consider an historical case that offers intriguing parallels, one to which we return in chapter 6. This is President Bill Clinton's 1996 reform of the Aid to Families with Dependent Children (AFDC) program. A strong expectation among many political strategists and scholars was that voters would give the Democratic Party credit for moving against an unpopular and widely resented program. Because the AFDC program was viewed as exemplifying everything white voters disliked about welfare, its reform was also seen as potentially bolstering support for other redistributive social policies. By downsizing AFDC, the issue of race could be taken out of the picture. Or so some Democratic strategists hoped.

The expected impacts of welfare reform on public attitudes, however, did not happen. Instead, as demonstrated by Joe Soss and Sanford Schram (2007), the public's attitudes toward the poor and toward specific welfare programs did not change much. That is, the electorate as a whole had failed to rethink its earlier views of social policy. Even if only white voters, political independents, or Democrats had responded, public attitudes as a whole should have been carried along by opinion change among a large group within the electorate. Clearly, then, U.S. welfare attitudes in the 1990s were not readily dislodged or remade by simple historical events or a prominent instance of partisan-sponsored policy change. Other, more powerful mechanisms shaped the attitudes of voters. So what was going on?

A second important clue emerges from scholarship on welfare reform and U.S. public opinion. Focusing on race-related biases as key, Joshua Dyck and Laura Hussey (2008) found that AFDC retrenchment failed to dislodge the strong impacts of racial attitudes on policy opinions. These impacts persisted even though the policy changes in question were also accompanied by declining stereotypes of welfare recipients in the media (2008, p.596). These results suggest that it was the public's existing racial attitudes that made them inattentive to historical change and unwilling to rethink their initial views of both welfare programs and the poor.

We think these results for the case of public opinion on welfare have a payoff for our focus on counterterrorism policy attitudes. In both cases, what we are dealing with are similar and rather striking instances of public opinion appearing nonresponsive to seemingly dramatic changes in the environment. In the case of welfare attitudes, it is an historic reform of the AFDC program. In the case of counterterrorism attitudes, it is the election of a new president and the emergence of a series of terrorist plots and foiled attacks that received extensive media coverage.

For this chapter's analyses, then, three initial themes stand out. First, our SAPA surveys provide ample evidence that Americans carve distinctions when they evaluate distinct counterterrorism policies and measures. We see this as evidence that the public can and does reason about the differences in these programs rather than merely responds, for instance, monolithically in a single voice.

Second, we find counterterrorism policy opinions to have been remarkably stable in the period before and after the historic 2008 presidential election. This tells us a good deal. It is quite clear that partisan shifts in government, even an electoral displacement of leaders that introduced the war on terror, did not by itself lead to any substantial rethinking of counterterrorism policies. And, paralleling this phenomenon, the emergence of a series of new terrorist plots did not move the public as a whole toward higher levels of policy support.

But evidence nonetheless indicates that shifts in counterterrorism policy attitudes have tended to involve movement toward lower rather than higher levels of support. This can be seen in the case of opinions on airport security. Moreover, if we extend the as-yet nonsignificant movement of items beyond 2010, it seems possible that a number of these, with the accumulation of data, might eventually show similarly declining trends.

But what of the as-yet unspecified factors holding policy opinions in place? Given the SAPA data showing counterterrorism policy opinions remaining largely untouched by a series of important events, the key must lie beyond recent historical events and the operation of partisan heuristics. It is to those factors that we turn in the next three chapters.

Appendix: Surveys of American Policy Attitudes (SAPA)

The Surveys of American Policy Attitudes were developed in cooperation with Dr. John Kennedy and the Center for Survey Research (CSR) at Indiana University. Data were collected using computer-assisted telephone interviewing methods (CATI), and numbers were randomly generated using the Genesys list-assisted method. This method allows for unpublished numbers and new listings to be sampled. After selecting a random sample of telephone numbers, numbers were matched to a database of business and nonworking numbers, and all matches were subsequently purged from the sample. The sample was nationwide, and at each residential number a respondent from all household members age eighteen or older was selected.

The data collection staff included eleven supervisors and forty-nine interviewers. All interviewers received at least 20 hours of training in interviewing techniques before production began. Interviewers were instructed to read questions and response categories at a pace slower than conversation and to use neutral probes and feedback phrases. Audio and visual monitoring was regularly conducted by the telephone survey supervisors using the CSR facilities. Monitoring was conducted randomly, with each interviewer being monitored at least once during each three-hour shift.

All cases with confirmed valid telephone numbers were called up to fifteen times, unless the respondent refused or there was insufficient time before the end of the study. Cases with unknown validity (persistent no answers or answering devices) were called a minimum of eight times, with calls made during the morning, afternoon, evening, and weekend. Interviewers attempted to convert each "refusal" at least twice. When possible, a conversion attempt was made at the first instance of refusal and a second attempt was usually made after a few days.

For the 2009 survey, questions were pre-tested on April 7, and production began on May 15, finishing on August 4, 2009. The average interview length was 29.8 minutes. For the 2010 survey, questions were pre-tested on July 27 and 28, and production began on August 6, finishing on November 29, 2010. The average interview length was 25.7 minutes.

Final Disposition Summary

The following table classifies every case according to its final disposition. These dispositions are based on the guidelines for Final Disposition Codes for Random Digit Dialing (RDD) Surveys established by the American Association for Public Opinion Research (AAPOR) Standard Definitions for Final Dispositions of Case Codes, 2004. Using AAPOR's RR3 (Response Rate 3 formula), the response rate was .1527 (15.3 percent) in 2009 and .1133 (11.3 percent) in 2010.

These response rates are closely in line with declines in participation found in telephone surveys. Research on the impact of these trends on data quality suggests that declining response rates are not by themselves tantamount to response bias, or that probability sampling should necessarily be abandoned in favor of such alternatives as quota sampling (Groves 2006). A relevant result of experiments into effects on data quality (Keeter et al. 2006) is that low rates are likely a source of bias only insofar as the probability of survey participation is correlated with one or more measured variable of interest. However, in SAPA, the majority of nonresponses (unknown eligibility or not interviewed) were a product of conditions such as no answers on the line and an initial refusal to participate before the start of the survey itself (or any item) was described.

Table 3A.1 Response Rates

	2009	2010
Interview		
Completed interviews	1542	1216
Partial completions	17	9
Total interviews	1559	1225
Refusal	4436	4450
Break-off (refused after starting interview)	146	131
Respondent never available	969	1122
Telephone answering device (message confirms housing unit)	141	525
Respondent away for the duration of the survey	20	4
Physically or mentally unable/incompetent or deceased	38	36
Language	169	143
Miscellaneous	7	0
Total eligible, non-interviews	5925	6411
Unknown eligibility, non-interview		
Always busy	121	102
No answer	1820	1467
Telephone answering device (unknown if housing unit)	1788	2147
Call barrier	2	6
Technical phone problems (line/circuit problems)	855	1996
Respondent not found	111	0
Total unknown eligibility, non-interviews	4697	5718
Not eligible		
Fax/data line	1014	757
Nonworking/disconnected number	3495	4363
Temporary nonworking/disconnected number	54	186
Number change	70	50
Cell phone	13	13
Call forwarded	22	42
Business, government office, other organization	615	932
Institution	27	11
Group quarters	7	18
Seasonal home	31	12
Not eligible—no adult household members	11	132
Total not eligible	62	6517
Total sample	17602	19871

Source: Authors' calculations based on Surveys of American Policy Attitudes (Brooks and Manza, various years).

Chapter 4

Threat Priming and National Identity Targets

L AWS AND public policies dole out punishment and distribute rewards. When people see government as punishing groups they dislike or do not trust, they may feel good about government action. If a policy rewards a group that citizens see in a positive light, that policy will also tend to be viewed favorably. But when laws and policies reward disliked groups, they can become deeply unpopular.

This is target group theory. Looking at limits to tolerance and civil liberties support, classic public opinion scholarship focused on domestic groups that gained the dubious status of least liked among survey respondents (Sullivan, Piereson, and Marcus 1982). Analyzing support for voting rights, we found that Americans were less likely to extend the franchise to violent ex-felons or those convicted of a sex offense than a generic ex-felon (Manza, Brooks, and Uggen 2004).

A widely discussed example concerns welfare. A survey experiment provided evidence that white Americans were twice as likely to support providing welfare benefits to a hypothetical white mother over a black mother with otherwise identical characteristics (Gilens 1999). Support for a range of social policies drops when the group receiving the benefit is identified as black or Hispanic (Kinder and Sanders 1996).

Target group theory is well established in the study of public opinion and political psychology. Our application of these ideas in this chapter is an extension. We hypothesize that national identity is a key source of target group differences when it comes to the domain of attitudes toward counterterrorism policies. Our concern in this chapter focuses on a particularly novel kind of national target: the difference between Americans and non-Americans, or alternatively between U.S. citizens and foreign nationals.

Complementing target group theory is the idea of threat priming: the process whereby information about terrorism plots or attacks is communicated to individuals. We know from past work that such communications are likely to be consequential for individuals' reasoning about counterterrorism. What we do in this chapter is update and extend scholarship by considering how threat priming works in relationship to national identity, and more specifically in the context of counterterrorism policies. We are able to develop this analysis using a set of novel experiments contained in the 2010 Surveys of American Policy Attitudes (SAPA) data.

Most broadly, our results provide some new support for the relevance of target group theorizing. For understanding public support for counterterrorism policies, it can matter who people think these policies are targeting. But certain complexities are important as well. We find that attitudes toward the contentious practice of torture are unaffected by the national identity of a target. We contrast that result with the far greater degree of malleability in attitudes toward airport security and rights violations in the name of combatting terrorism. We also unpack a degree of complexity stemming from evidence that how much threat communication and target group perceptions matter can depend on factors such as level of education.

Threat Priming, Target Groups, Experiments

In investigating these questions, we face two related challenges at the outset. The general challenge is to make sure that it is really the national identity of a target that shapes counterterrorism attitudes, as opposed to something else. When survey respondents hear key phrases like "American citizens" or "foreign nationals," we hope that they are thinking about the national identities of policy targets. But if they are thinking about something else, our evidence is flawed and inconclusive at best.

So we begin with a simple question: What exactly are survey respondents thinking about when answering questions about American citizens or foreign nationals? This brings up a second challenge: the relevance of the threat-priming thesis. According to this theory, it is remarkably easy to get people primed to think about terrorism threats. Threat priming is relevant if key phrases like "foreign nationals" also carry with them an implicit threat. When people hear this kind of language, do they feel threatened? Until we determine a way of distinguishing the intrinsic target group component from any overlap with other potential threats, we will not have fully gotten at the mechanism behind policy reasoning.

The challenge of distinguishing target group impacts from threat processes applies, in turn, when we consider threat priming as a candidate mechanism behind counterterrorism policy attitudes. An interesting possibility is that threat stimuli might themselves cause individuals to think about specific groups that they associate with threats. If that includes foreign nationals, we are right back at the heart of the problem. For both foci in this chapter, developing an analysis that can distinguish terrorism threats from the national identity of target groups is thus essential.

The Payoff of Experiments

In figuring out why individuals reason about policy questions is the way they do, a key problem is accounting for unmeasured factors, and thus ruling out plausible alternative interpretations of results. Consider, for instance, what happens if we observe that individuals who identify themselves as conservatives dislike paid family leave or resist tax increases on the wealthy. We might be tempted to conclude that conservative political orientations dispose individuals to oppose egalitarian social policies.

But that conclusion could, in principle, invite a host of skeptical rejoinders. Could it instead be that these individuals' beliefs about social policies are what dispose them to identify as conservatives in the first place? Alternatively, perhaps the reason lies with unmeasured personality characteristics. Maybe those who are temperamentally resistant to change tend to both identify as conservatives and oppose egalitarian arrangements?

These are fundamental problems faced in varying degree by all observational, that is, nonexperimental, data analysis. Getting a handle on what really matters is where experimental designs can be useful. It is particularly the case when a mechanism of interest may overlap with other, real-world processes, a critical challenge in the case of counterterrorism policy attitudes. With experimental designs, we can randomize the assignment of individuals to conditions in which a particular factor of interest is manipulated. With these procedures, we sweep away the unmeasured processes that at times frustrate causal inference in conventional observational data analysis. We end up with a more confident handle on subsequent results.

In our earlier example, consider if we had primed a random half of our sample to think about ideology before answering a question about family policy. If the individuals exposed to this prime then showed lower support for paid family leave, it would constitute experimental evidence that ideology matters in the formation of attitudes toward social policies. We would be much more confident in pinning a causal interpretation on the results.

The methodological benefits of experiments are particularly relevant in the study of attitudes and policy reasoning. Here, processes of interest and sources of error frequently move together. Indeed, the well-known tendency of individuals to rationalize existing biases creates precisely the kind of interconnections that may need to be untangled (Vaisey 2009; see also Lord, Ross, and Lepper 1979). For these reasons, experiments in the laboratory and population survey have proven invaluable to public opinion research (Sniderman and Grob 1996; Chong and Druckman 2007). Experimental analyses of counterterrorism policy attitudes have been a central hallmark of much scholarship on our topic of interest (Lavine, Lodge, and Freitas 2005; Davis 2007; Merolla and Zechmeister 2009).

Airport Security, Rights Violation, and Torture Experiments

The experiments from SAPA we discuss in this chapter and the rest of the book all focus on counterterrorism policy attitudes. They use as a control an initial version of each policy-attitude item, which provides a baseline for comparisons with other versions of the same item. In the alternative versions, we introduce experimental treatments that prime individuals to think about either a new terrorism threat or, instead, a new target group defined by national identity. There is, of course, the scenario discussed earlier, in which threats and target groups overlap in the minds of actors. One further set of experiments probes this possibility in detail.

Our first experiment relates to airport security. The issue we take up here is whether threat priming generates, as expected, higher levels of support for intrusive new counterterrorism measures. This provides us with a way of extending Merolla and Zechmeister's (2009) experiments on the topic. We want to see whether, indeed, threat priming still matters. But we have an additional query as well: does it matter if the threats are real ones, or do hypothetical threats also compel people to readjust their attitudes toward counterterrorism policies?

We list in table 4.1 the three versions of the airport security item that make up our experiment, fielded in the 2010 SAPA data collection. The control group item asks respondents whether they favor or oppose the following: "Requiring individuals who traveled to countries in the Middle East, including those who are U.S. citizens, to undergo special, more intensive security checks before boarding airplanes in the United States?" In the first, experimental condition, the same item is prefaced by reference to an actual terrorist attack that took place a year earlier: "As you may know, in 2009, government authorities arrested a terrorism suspect after he tried to set off a bomb on a plane bound for Detroit." If, as expected, priming respondents to think about terrorism threats influences their attitudes toward counterterrorism policies, support for airport security measures should be higher in the second (experimental) condition than in the first (control group).[1]

But our work with the airport security experiment is not yet done. In a second experimental condition, the control group item is prefaced by

Table 4.1   SAPA Item Wordings and Experiments

Airport security
  How about—"Requiring individuals who traveled to countries in the Middle East, including those who are U.S. citizens, to undergo special, more intensive security checks before boarding airplanes in the United States?"
  Experimental condition 1: Control group item prefaced by, "As you may know, in 2009, government authorities arrested a terrorism suspect after he tried to set off a bomb on a plane bound for Detroit."
  Experimental condition 2: Control group item prefaced by, "What if the government was responding to a terrorist act that had just taken place?"

Rights violation [+ experiments]
  "[The government should take all steps necessary to prevent additional acts of terrorism in the United States even if it means foreign nationals' individual rights and liberties might be violated/Even if it means foreign nationals' individual rights and liberties might be violated, the government should take all steps necessary to prevent additional acts of terrorism in the United States.]"[a]
  Experimental condition 1: *foreign nationals'* changed to *Americans'*
  Experimental condition 2: Control group item prefaced by, "As you may know, in 2009, the FBI arrested a number of terrorism suspects, including several American citizens, who were plotting attacks in Illinois, New York, and North Carolina."
  Experimental condition 3: Control group item prefaced by, "As you may know, in 2009, the FBI arrested a number of terrorism suspects, including several American citizens, who were plotting attacks in Illinois, New York, and North Carolina." And *foreign nationals'* changed to *Americans'*

Torture 2009 [+ experiment]
  "Do you agree or disagree that government authorities should have the right to torture a suspect if they think it will help prevent a terrorist attack from taking place in the United States?"
  Experimental condition 1: *suspect* changed to *suspect who is American*

Torture 2010 [+ experiments]
  "Do you agree or disagree that government authorities should have the right to torture a suspect who is an American citizen if they think it will help prevent a terrorist attack from taking place in the United States?"
  Experimental condition 1: *American citizen* changed to *American citizen of Middle Eastern background*
  Experimental condition 2: Control group item prefaced by, "As you may know, in 2009, the FBI arrested a number of terrorism suspects, including several American citizens, who were plotting attacks in Illinois, New York, and North Carolina."

Source: Authors' compilation.
Note: SAPA = Surveys of American Policy Attitudes; FBI = Federal Bureau of Investigation.
[a]Order of presentation of phrases in brackets is randomized.

asking, "What if the government was responding to a terrorist act that had just taken place?" This experiment gives new leverage. Now we can see whether the priming of a hypothetical terrorist attack matters as much or less than a real one.

Next is the rights violation experiment, which is also from the 2010 SAPA data collection. In contrast to the airport security experiment, the rights violation experiment has three treatment-effects conditions. This is because we have a full 2 x 2 design with two underlying factors. The first is for national identity status, foreign nationals versus Americans, and the second is for the presence versus absence of threat priming. This design enables us to systematically parse out and detect any cognitive overlap between the target group and threat stimuli.

In the rights violation experiment's control group, respondents are asked, "The government should take all steps necessary to prevent additional acts of terrorism in the U.S. even if it means foreign nationals' individual rights and liberties might be violated."[2] The first experimental condition holds constant the target group reference to foreign nationals but now prefaces the item by stating the following: "As you may know, in 2009, the FBI [Federal Bureau of Investigation] arrested a number of terrorism suspects, including several American citizens, who were plotting attacks in Illinois, New York, and North Carolina." This introduces the threat-priming stimulus. As before, we make reference to actual, historical instances of terrorist plots. By design, however, the terrorist plots at hand are different ones than the 2009 attempted airplane bombing used for its relevance to the airport security experiment.

As summarized in table 4.1, the two remaining conditions for the rights violation experiment change the target group reference from foreign nationals to Americans. Both items thus ask, "The government should take all steps necessary to prevent additional acts of terrorism in the United States even if it means Americans' individual rights and liberties might be violated." Whereas the first of these conditions contains no threat priming, the second condition uses the same prior reference to FBI arrests of terrorism suspects in 2009.

The final two experiments considered in this chapter concern attitudes about the use of torture. In the 2009 SAPA data collection, respondents were asked, "Do you agree or disagree that government authorities should have the right to torture a suspect if they think it will help prevent a terrorist attack from taking place in the United States?" That is the control group version. For the experiment, the suspect is redefined as an American: "Do you agree or disagree that government authorities should have the right to torture a suspect who is American if they think it will help prevent a terrorist attack from taking place in the United States?"

The 2010 torture experiment uses a modified question, where the control group question already makes reference to an American citizen as the policy target: "Do you agree or disagree that government authorities should have the right to torture a suspect who is an American citizen if they think it will help prevent a terrorist attack from taking place in the United States?" In the first experimental condition, a qualification is added to American citizen, changing the wording to American citizen of Middle Eastern background. In the second experimental condition, the control group item is prefaced by a threat-priming stimulus: "As you may know, in 2009, the FBI arrested a number of terrorism suspects, including several American citizens, who were plotting attacks in Illinois, New York, and North Carolina."

The 2010 torture experiment does not, then, employ the kind of 2 x 2 design used in the rights violation experiment. But this turns out to matter little. Indeed, to anticipate the thrust of our results, the issue of torture is such that neither threat priming nor national identity has any effect on policy-attitude formation. This is a notable result in its own right. As we will see, attitudes toward other counterterrorism policies and practices are typically malleable when new conditions and considerations are brought to bear.

Independent Variables and Interaction Tests

Ultimately, our analyses cannot stop with the experimental results. What we also need to do is combine the experiments with a regression analysis that explores possibly confounding factors. What we then have is a set-up in which both experimental conditions and nonexperimental variables are covariates in a regression model. There are two reasons for this procedure.

The first is that it provides a way of comparing the magnitude of both experimental and nonexperimental factors. Suppose national identity status matters in one of our experiments into counterterrorism policy-attitude formation. Suppose also that a nonexperimental factor like education also shapes policy attitudes. Incorporating both factors into a combined statistical model allows us to directly compare their effects. This can tell us a lot more than just that the effects in question are statistically significant.

The second reason is that it is entirely plausible to wonder whether the true effects of the experimental treatments differ across layers of the population. For instance, what if national identity status has quite different effects among white respondents than among minorities? That would mean the experimental treatment effect interacts with race. If so, the experimental results would be incomplete, and even misleading, by themselves. We would need to reestimate to take into account the interaction in question.

This line of thinking has powerful implications for the kinds of tests we must conduct. When initial grounds for considering an interaction between one of our experimental treatments and a nonexperimental co-variate are compelling, we should look into it. Failure to do so would produce a faulty interpretation. Just as important, if we indeed find evidence for interactions of this sort, it will shed further light on how mechanisms like national identity status shape counterterrorism policy reasoning.

We think six variables are reasonable candidates for interaction tests. Three we have already discussed in passing: threat perceptions, authoritarianism, and partisanship. Each aligns with existing theories that we reviewed in chapter 2. Three sociodemographic variables—education, religion, and race—are introduced here for the first time; all reflect factors that previous scholarship has highlighted as important.

We start with threat perceptions, which is a different process from threat priming. Threat perceptions are static in our analyses and thus not manipulated like the threat-priming treatments in our experiments.[3] Instead, threat perceptions are survey respondents' self-reports, as measured by the following question: "All in all, how concerned are you that the United States might suffer another terrorist attack in the next twelve months?"[4] This is an established measure in the literature (for example, Davis 2007), and testing for interactions tells us whether individuals with high levels of existing threat perceptions are more, or less, inclined to process a specific experimental treatment. In the airport security experiment, for instance, it is conceivable that threat priming has the greatest effects among individuals who already feel high levels of threat in the environment. If so, we would find evidence of an interaction between threat perceptions and threat priming. By contrast, it may be that those with low perceptions of threat are most affected by a threat prime, being "reminded" of threats they had forgotten about.

Our next candidate for interaction is authoritarianism. In line with classical ideas about authoritarian values presented by Theodor Adorno, Else Frenkel-Brunswik, Daniel Levinson, and Nevitt Sanford (1950), some notable recent work has pointed to the possibility that threat-related stimuli have different effects on individuals depending on the degree to which they subscribe to authoritarian values (Lavine, Lodge, and Freitas 2005; Hetherington and Suhay 2011). Authoritarianism emphasizes conformity, a preference for order, and obedience to authority. We want to make certain that we take into account its main effect, and any interaction effect, in gauging the influence of threat perceptions on attitudes.

Our measure of authoritarianism, drawing from recent work on the subject (Kam and Kinder 2007), is a scale of three items that probe respondents' preferred traits in children: "Which one is more important for a child to have: Independence or respect for elders? Obedience or self-reliance? Good manners or curiosity?"[5] These items and the resultant scale they generate have desirable properties in measuring authoritarianism, for they do not simultaneously invoke the policies with respect to which they are expected to shape opinion. We follow past practice in summing items into a scale after first standardizing the items. Higher scores on the scale indicate a greater tendency toward authoritarianism, and we test for interactions with our experimental treatments.

We next consider partisanship. The partisan heuristics thesis anticipates that voters may respond quite differently to political stimuli depending on their underlying patterns of party identification (Bartels 2002). Following convention, we measure partisanship using the traditional seven-point scale, where <7> indicates strong Republican and <1> indicates strong Democrat. In testing for the possibility of interactions with experimental treatment effects, we also test for interactions using an alternative measure, whereby Republican identifiers and Democratic identifiers are treated as binary variables. Both measures of partisanship yield the same interaction test results.

Turning now to the three sociodemographic variables, education has long been viewed as a key variable in the literatures on democratic tolerance and opinion liberalization (Bobo and Licari 1989; Sniderman, Brody, and Tetlock 1991). Because greater exposure to education tends to bolster support for rights and liberties, it is possible that individuals will respond differently to experimental stimuli involving trade-offs between rights-liberties versus security-order. In the analyses presented here, education is a continuous variable, measured in years.

The final two candidates for interaction are variables for religion and race. In past scholarship, religion and race have figured as long-standing influences on policy preferences in the United States (for example, Kinder and Sanders 1996; Steensland et al. 2000). In testing for interactions, we treat both religion and race as binary variables, coded, respectively, <1> evangelical Protestant and <1> white and <0> otherwise. Additional schemes enabling further group contrasts are possible, but they do not change the results of the interaction tests presented.

Other Independent Variables

To obtain satisfactory main effect estimates for the preceding independent variables, we also include in the models independent variables as controls, in addition to the six with which we conduct the interaction tests. We would not want, after all, to unwittingly exaggerate the true effects of such variables as threat perceptions or race. This also applies to interaction effects, so we include our entire roster of independent variables prior to conducting tests for interaction.

Age and economic performance evaluations are continuous variables.

Figure 4.1   The Power of Threat Priming

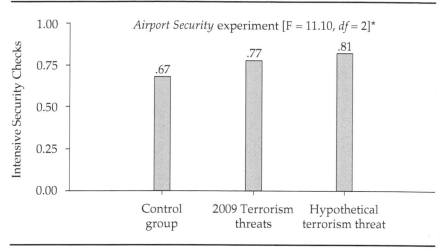

Source: Authors' estimates based on Surveys of American Policy Attitudes (Brooks and Manza, various years).
*Indicates significance at $p < .05$.

Age is coded in years. The economic evaluations item's scores are <1> gotten better, <2> stayed the same, and <3> gotten worse in response to the question, "Thinking about the economy in the country as a whole, would you say that over the past year, the nation's economy has gotten better, stayed about the same, or gotten worse?"

Female, retired, and labor force participant are all binary variables, coded <1> for the status in question, <0> otherwise. A final variable, church attendance, is continuous. Scores range from <1> never to <7> every day in response to the question, "Regardless of your religious views, how often do you attend religious services? Would you say every day, more than once a week, once a week, two or three times a month, once a month, a few times a year or less, or never?"

Analyses and Results

We begin with figure 4.1's airport security experiment and its focus on threat priming. The control group item in the experiment lacks the threat-priming stimuli. In the second condition, priming respondents with reference to the 2009 attempted airplane bombing raises support for airport security measures. That is very much in line with expectations, and it means that the threat-priming thesis has remained of considerable relevance in recent years. But somewhat more surprising is the substantial impact of our second experimental condition. Priming respondents with a deliberately hypothetical terrorism threat also matters. Indeed, it has

Table 4.2 Do Experimental Treatments Have the Same Effects?[a]

	× Threat Perception	× Authoritarianism	× Partisanship	× Education	× Religion	× Race
Airport security	$F(2) = .65$ $p = .52$	$F(2) = .49$ $p = .61$	$F(2) =1.47$ $p = .23$	$F(1) = 6.86$ $p = .01$	$F(2) = .16$ $p = .86$	$F(2) = 1.10$ $p = .33$
$\beta_{2009\,threats}$ (SE)	.01 (.04)	<.01 (.01)	-.02 (.01)	<.02 (.01)	-.03 (.06)	.02 (.07)
$\beta_{hypothetical}$ (SE)	-.03 (.03)	-.01 (.01)	-.01 (.01)	**.03 (.01)**	-.03 (.06)	-.08 (.07)
Rights violation	$F(3) = .32$ $p = .82$	$F(3) = .45$ $p = .72$	$F(3) = .81$ $p = .49$	$F(1) = 5.66$ $p = .00$	$F(3) = .45$ $p = .72$	$F(3) = 1.65$ $p = .18$
$\beta_{Amer.+threat}$ (SE)	-.03 (.04)	.01 (.01)	-.02 (.02)	-.01 (.01)	-.01 (.07)	-.13 (.09)
$\beta_{for.+threat}$ (SE)	<.03 (.04)	-.01 (.01)	-.02 (.02)	**.03 (.01)**	.04 (.07)	.05 (.09)
$\beta_{Amer.+threat}$ (SE)	-.01 (.04)	<.01 (.01)	-.02 (.02)	**.02 (.01)**	-.07 (.07)	-.07 (.08)
Torture, 2009	$F(1) = .21$ $p = .65$	—	$F(1) = .24$ $p = .62$	$F(1) = .12$ $p = .73$	$F(1) = .14$ $p = .71$	$F(1) = .40$ $p = .53$
$\beta_{American}$ (SE)	.02 (.04)	—	-.01 (.01)	<-.01 (.01)	.03 (.07)	-.08 (.12)
Torture, 2010	$F(2) = .53$ $p = .59$	$F(2) = 1.53$ $p = .22$	$F(2) = .21$ $p = .81$	$F(2) = 2.49$ $p = .08$	$F(2) = .10$ $p = .90$	$F(2) = .65$ $p = .52$
$\beta_{ME\,back.}$ (SE)	.03 (.04)	<.02 (.01)	.01 (.01)	<-.02 (.01)	.03 (.07)	.09 (.08)
$\beta_{2009\,threats}$ (SE)	-.01 (.04)	<.02 (.01)	<.01 (.01)	<-.02 (.01)	<-.01 (.07)	.05 (.08)

Source: Authors' estimates based on Surveys of American Policy Attitudes (Brooks and Manza, various years).
Note: Amer. = American; for. = foreign national; ME back. = Middle Eastern background.
[a]Bold coefficient indicates significance at $p < .05$.

Figure 4.2   Education Effects in the Airport Security Experiment[a]

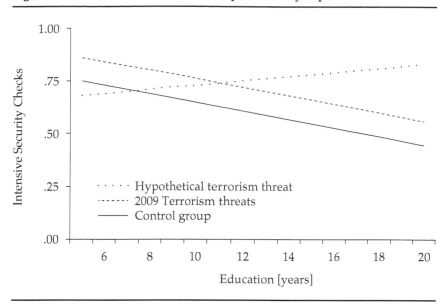

Source: Authors' estimates based on Surveys of American Policy Attitudes (Brooks and Manza, various years).
[a] Predicted effects of education in the hypothetical threat condition are not significant.

essentially the same impact on airport security policy attitudes as the priming of a real threat.

From the airport security experiment's F-test, we can see that overall group differences are significant. And with scores of 0.77 and 0.81, the two experimental groups appear to have notably comparable effects on policy attitudes. Post hoc statistical tests confirm this: the two treatments are indistinguishable.[6]

Provocative as they are, the results from the airport security experiment are still preliminary. Recall that we must look into the possibility that experimental treatment effects differ across layers of the sample or population. We do so in table 4.2, where we present F-tests and accompanying *p*-values for testing the significance of interaction candidates; coefficients and standard errors for these tests appear in successive rows.

Significant test results are in bold. In the airport security experiment, there is evidence for an interaction. We can see that the interaction involves education and one of the experimental treatments, pertaining to the hypothetical threat-priming condition.[7] This is the only significant interaction unearthed for airport security, but it is an important one and must be taken into account when interpreting results.[8]

We can begin to appreciate how the interaction changes things using the new results in figure 4.2. This figure shows how education affects

Table 4.3   Comparative Magnitude of Factors Behind Airport Security

	Effect	| Effect |
Education, control/threat-priming conditions	−.30	.30
Hypothetical threat priming (education = 20)	.28	.28
Threat perceptions	.18	.18
Hypothetical threat priming (education = 14.52)	.14	.14
Authoritarianism	.13	.13
Threat priming	.11	.11
Hypothetical threat priming (education = 5)	−.10	.10
Partisanship	.06	.06
Education, hypothetical threat-priming condition	.00	.00

Source: Authors' estimates based on Surveys of American Policy Attitudes (Brooks and Manza, various years).

airport security policy attitudes. Because of the interaction, however, the effects of education depend on which condition we are considering in the experiment. As shown by the downward-sloping lines for the predicted effects of education in both control group and real terrorism threat conditions, education appears to exert a constraining effect on support for the airport security measure. Higher levels of schooling are predicted as slightly lowering support for the counterterrorism measure in question, and this effect is identical across the two conditions in question.

Where things diverge is on the impact of education in the final condition, where we have primed respondents with the hypothetical terrorism threat. In this condition, education has quite different effects on policy attitudes. In fact, its effects are surprisingly nil, contrasting with results for the control group and real terrorist threat condition.

So far, we have looked at how the effects of education differ across conditions in our experiment. Now, we turn to looking directly at the effects on policy attitudes of the two types of threat priming. We also want to make comparisons with other predicted effects in our model. These results are summarized in table 4.3. Here we present range-standardized estimates of the magnitude of effects. Range standardization is a useful technique for comparing effects when independent variables have heterogeneous levels of measurement. We can, for instance, compare the predicted effects of binary versus continuous variables, as in the current application. What we are doing, in particular, is calculating effects across the full range of each variable: for binary variables, the range is a movement from 0 to 1. For continuous variables, the range is the difference between the highest versus lowest observed score.

To determine the predicted effects of threat priming, we must also take into account interaction effects, when significant. Because there is interaction between the hypothetical threat condition and education, the effects of the threat—relative to the baseline condition—are conditional on a respondent's education level. Of course, the education effect in turn depends on whether respondents have been exposed to the hypothetical threat versus alternative conditions in the experiment.

We start by looking at calculations for the impact of threat priming among respondents at the highest level of education, which is twenty years. This estimate is presented in the second row of table 4.3. At 0.28, the estimate indicates that relative to the control group, exposing highly educated individuals to a hypothetical threat massively boosts support for airport security. This is indeed a sizeable effect, the second largest of all estimates in table 4.3, but, to be sure, for respondents at the highest level of education. We emphasize that point because given the presence of an interaction with education, all estimates of the hypothetical threat treatment must be calculated for specific values of education.

At the other end of the spectrum, the parallel effect of threat priming among respondents at the lowest level of education, five years, is both small and negatively signed, –0.10. Before we take the absolute value to compare magnitudes, the –0.10 estimate indicates that the effect of hypothetical threat priming is to slightly lower support for airport security. This means that at the lowest level of education, threat priming has both smaller and different impacts on attitudes about airport security.

What about the effect among respondents with the average level of education, 14.52 years? This calculation rounds out our interpretation, and we now have an estimate of 0.14. The magnitude of this effect is typical of those presented in table 4.3. It indicates that stimulating the typical person to consider a hypothetical terrorism threat raises support for the airport security procedure by a likewise average amount.[9]

Let us now turn to the other experimental contrast, between priming the terrorism threat through the mention of real events versus the control group condition. This yields an estimate of 0.11. This predicted effect is, of course, constant across individuals because there are no interactions involving this treatment effect. To provide some comparative perspective, we compare this 0.11 estimate with the earlier 0.14 effect of hypothetical threat priming among individuals at the mean level of schooling. The hypothetical threat-priming effect is, according to this comparison, slightly larger in magnitude. But we should still keep in mind that that hypothetical threat-priming effect depends on level of education, and this effect is smaller among less-educated respondents and larger for those at high levels of education. To summarize, then, priming respondents with information about real threats raises support for airport security measures by a constant and nontrivial amount, 0.11, and this effect is smaller in magnitude than the parallel effect of hypothetical threat priming among the highest-education respondents (0.28) and larger than the hypothetical threat priming among the lowest-education respondents (–0.10).

Turning to the remaining estimates, partisanship is of generally minor relevance to airport security policy attitudes. With an estimate of 0.13, authoritarianism clearly matters to policy attitudes. Predictably, those endorsing more authoritarian values tend to give higher support to the coercive security measures at hand.

The 0.18 estimate for static threat perceptions is well worth noting. Recall that the latter measure is based on what individuals self-report, different accordingly from our experimentally manipulated threat cues. But even in the face of experimental manipulations of real and hypothetical threats, these existing threat perceptions still matter substantially for counterterrorism policy attitudes. What this means is that coming into the 2010 SAPA survey, individuals with higher levels of terrorism concern were also significantly more disposed to favor the airport security measures at hand. And as with other covariates that do not interact with the treatments, threat perceptions have a constant effect on policy attitudes for all individuals.

The remaining estimates are for education. Here, the interaction across the hypothetical threat condition versus the other conditions yields two estimates. In the control group and real threat-priming conditions, education has a substantial, even overwhelming, –0.30 effect. The negative sign of this effect means that higher levels of schooling lead to much lower support for airport security measures among respondents not exposed to the hypothetical threat treatment. But in contrast, education has no impact whatsoever in the hypothetical threat-priming condition. How education matters to counterterrorism policy reasoning can thus depend on what kind of threats are communicated. Together, then, these results underscore the substantial relevance of education to the first of our counterterrorism policy domains.

National Identity Targets

The rights violation experiment allows us to begin to see whether policy targets might matter in shaping attitudes. In this experiment, we are looking into the issue of taking all steps necessary to prevent additional acts of terrorism. A key experimental contrast is between taking all steps necessary to prevent additional acts of terrorism when it is foreign nationals versus Americans whose rights and liberties are on the line. But in this experiment, we also shake things up according to whether survey respondents are assigned to threat-priming or to no-threat conditions. What we have is a 2 x 2 factorial design, in which one factor varies target group characteristics, and the other the presence versus absence of threat. This design is useful in that it ensures that we can systematically test for, and distinguish between, the effects of threat priming versus those of policy targeting.

Most broadly, the F-tests in figure 4.3 show that both experimental

Figure 4.3   National Identity and the Rights Violation Experiment

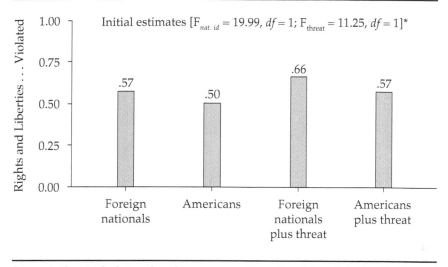

Source: Authors' calculations based on Surveys of American Policy Attitudes (Brooks and Manza, various years).
Note: nat. id = national identity.
*Indicates significance at $p < .05$.

factors matter. Manipulating terrorism threats shapes counterterrorism policy attitudes, and the same is true with respect to the more novel factor of national identity status. The 2 x 2 design of the experiment enables us to directly test for an interaction between the two experimental factors, and we find no evidence to this effect.[10] We conclude that there is no cognitive overlap between the threat priming and target group stimuli. That is an important finding in its own right. It tells us that we can treat threat priming and target group cueing as separate inputs in the attitude formation process.

The results displayed in figure 4.3 suggest that the impacts of threat priming and target group manipulation are comparable. In the no-threat condition, changing the policy target from *foreign nationals* to *Americans* lowers support for rights violations by 0.07. Doing so in the threat-priming condition lowers support by 0.09. Holding constant *foreign nationals* as the policy target, threat priming raises policy support by 0.09; holding constant *Americans* yields a parallel estimate of 0.07.

But these results are also incomplete, and we must thus regard their interpretation is initial. Although we have ruled out an interaction between the experimental factors, we have not yet taken into account any interactions involving nonexperimental factors. And looking back to the results of table 4.3, we see that there are indeed precisely interactions of this sort. It is again education, and only education, that yields evidence of significant interaction. We can also see that the interaction between

Figure 4.4   Education in the Rights Violation Experiment[a]

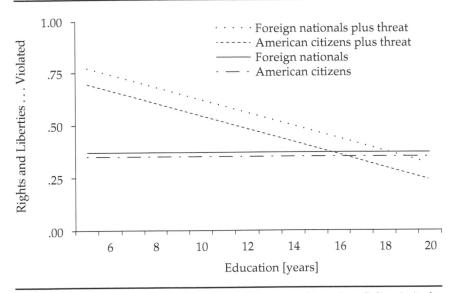

Source: Authors' estimates based on analysis of Surveys of American Policy Attitudes (Brooks and Manza, various years).
[a] Predicted effects of education in the no-threat conditions are not significant.

experimental treatment and education takes a specific form. Here, it is the two experimental conditions involving the absence of threat priming that interact with respondents' education level. The third interaction, involving education and the presence of threat priming in the American versus foreign national contrast, does not achieve statistical significance (see again table 4.2); it is safely dropped from the model.

We can now determine what the interactions are telling us that was not apparent from the initial, main effects–only results in figure 4.3. Let's start with the predicted effects of education on attitudes toward rights violation. Because of the interaction, we look at the effects of education across all four groups in the experiment. These results are presented in figure 4.4.

In the two no-threat conditions, education does not exert appreciable influence on policy attitudes. We can see this by observing how the relevant estimates for education run parallel to the chart's x-axis. When we vary respondents' level of education in the two no-threat conditions, we see little differences in their expected counterterrorism attitudes.

Staying with the figure 4.4 estimates, we can see that lines connecting estimates in the two threat conditions clearly slope downward. That is, at higher levels of education, individuals who have been exposed to an explicit threat respond quite differently in their policy reasoning than

Table 4.4   Comparative Magnitude of Factors Behind Rights Violation

	Effect	|Effect|
Threat priming (foreign condition)	.56	.56
Threat priming (American condition)	.48	.48
Education, threat conditions	−.45	.45
Partisanship	.24	.24
Threat perception	.24	.24
Authoritarianism	.13	.13
American versus foreign (threat-priming condition)	−.08	.08
Education, foreign/~threat condition	.00	.00
Education, American/~threat condition	.00	.00
American versus foreign (~threat-priming condition)	.00	.00

Source: Authors' estimates based on Surveys of American Policy Attitudes (Brooks and Manza, various years).

those at lower levels of education. In contrast to their less-educated counterparts, then, more highly educated respondents adjust to threat priming
by lowering their support for the counterterrorism goal in question. This
is an interesting result and very similar to the airport security experiment's results in the control group and (real) threat-priming conditions.

In table 4.4, we turn to comparisons involving the magnitude of key
effects. As before, we use range-standardized estimates to facilitate these
comparisons. And we again present effect calculations first without taking the absolute value (see column 1 of table 4.4), so we can see whether
a specific factor raises (or lowers) counterterrorism policy support.
Using as an example the −0.45 estimate for the effect of education in the
threat-priming conditions, the negative sign tells us that more education
disposes individuals to downgrade their support for rights-violating
practices. The size of this estimate is quite large, one of the most impressive in the rights violation experiment.

Staying with large-magnitude effects, the single biggest is for threat
priming. With estimates of 0.56 and 0.48, respectively, threat priming
matters enormously regardless of whether we are stimulating respondents to think about foreign nationals or instead Americans as the policy
targets.[11] Confronting people with a simple reminder about terrorism
plots in 2009 by itself substantially shores up their willingness to fight
terrorism, even at the cost of protecting rights and liberties.

With identical estimates of 0.24, partisanship and existing threat perceptions also matter a good deal to counterterrorism attitudes. In contrast, authoritarian predispositions have a relatively more modest impact. Still, the 0.13 estimate is not by any means trivial, particularly
because it takes into account so many potentially confounding processes.

What about the effects of national identity targets themselves? Starting with the no-threat conditions, we see in the table 4.4 estimates that

changing the target group from foreign nationals to Americans has no effect. We emphasize that this non-effect is constant across all levels of education, even though there is an interaction between the two no-threat treatments and education. Why is this the case? The key lies with the coefficient estimates from our preferred model of the rights violation experiment: the main effect estimates of the two treatments are identical in magnitude ($\beta = -0.56$, SE = 0.16), and the same is true of the two interactions between these treatments and education ($\beta = 0.03$, SE = 0.01). Mathematically, this means that when we calculate the difference in predicted effects to estimate the American versus foreign contrast, the resultant sum is 0 at all levels of education.

Next we consider the different picture obtained for the American versus foreign target group manipulations in the threat-priming conditions. Here, the -0.08 estimate tells us that redefining the policy targets as Americans lowers support for fighting terrorism at the cost of rights violations. National identity targets can thus have discernible effects on counterterrorism policy attitudes. But in this context we also emphasize that the magnitude of their influence is smaller than the effects of threat-priming processes.

The Case of Torture

The final experiments considered in this chapter concern torture. Looking over the relevant test results in table 4.2, no significant interactions with treatment effects occur in either the 2009 or 2010 experiments. This means that experimental group comparisons tell the entire story, and we present these results in figure 4.5.

The 2009 experiment manipulates the target of torture to be an *American*. As summarized by the nonsignificant *t*-statistic, policy attitudes do not vary across condition. The national identity of the policy target seems to matter little with respect to the practice of torture.

We fielded a new version of the torture experiment in the 2010 data collection. In this experiment, the target of torture is defined as an *American citizen* and is held constant across control group and treatment-effect conditions. What we are now testing is whether a target group redefinition affects attitudes, and, furthermore, whether instead priming respondents with terrorist threats also affects policy reasoning. But as seen in the F-test for comparing across all three groups, neither treatment has an impact on the formation of attitudes toward torture.

The torture experiments thus present us with some informatively divergent results. Neither threat priming nor target groups seem to matter much. One obvious point at hand is that counterterrorism policy attitudes are at their lowest when torture is under consideration. This is true of the SAPA data collection, and it is also established in the larger archives of polling on counterterrorism opinion on torture, as we noted in

Figure 4.5   Lessons from the Torture Experiments

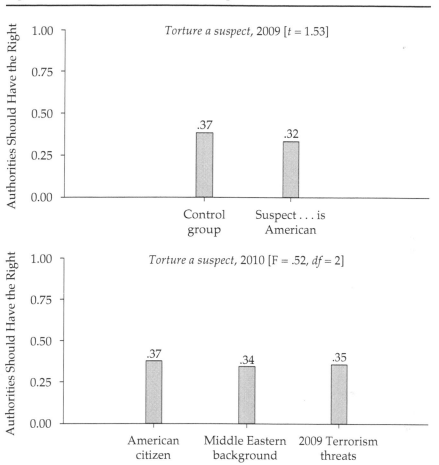

Source: Authors' estimates based on Surveys of American Policy Attitudes (Brooks and Manza, various years).

chapter 3. Not all war on terror practices have been popular, and our torture experiment tells us that on this issue Americans' attitudes are far less malleable than elsewhere.

Conclusion

Our results in this chapter put us in a position to appreciate something fundamental about counterterrorism policy attitudes. These attitudes— with the exception of those about torture—are readily dislodged and re- adjusted in the face of new cues and references. This is, of course, one of the unique benefits of experiments into policy attitudes. We can learn not just something about current configurations of policy attitudes, but also what alternative considerations may have the power to shake things up.

In this way, we can see that the empirical portrait of chapter 3, informative as it was, did not tell us enough. What we reported in that chapter was that the counterterrorism policy opinions had nearly all been very stable between 2007 and 2010. Using experiments, what this chapter's results show is that with just a pointed cue or two, individuals are rapidly prompted to reason a bit, and sometimes a lot, differently about counterterrorism measures.

But there is something of a catch as well. When we step back and look across our experimental effects in this chapter, they point suggestively in a specific direction. When subtly prompted through experimental cues and priming, Americans' reasoning around counterterrorism moves them toward greater support. To be sure, our experimental estimates are relatively few in number and can hardly be considered a random sample of the conceivable population of counterterrorism treatments.

This limitation is, of course, shared by virtually all experimental survey research. We would not know before deploying our treatments that the ultimate effects would be statistically significant. It is, for instance, quite conceivable that nearly a decade after the 9/11 attacks, the priming of cues regarding actual or hypothetical terrorism threats leaves Americans unmoved when they think about specific counterterrorism-related policies and practices.

But this is not what we find. In the airport security experiment, communication of actual and hypothetical terrorism threats matters, propelling individuals toward enhanced support for a controversial counterterrorism practice. This tells us that when Americans are thinking about counterterrorism and related issues, they may have a less positive view of relevant policies than when they are cued to instead think about the prospect of new attacks or threats. Because such threats appear to be easy to communicate, and indeed have been a hallmark of media discourse in the post-9/11 era (Nacos, Block-Elkon, and Shapiro 2011), this result points to a significant asymmetry in how conflicts over the possibility or likelihood of terrorism are as yet likely to shape mass attitude formation.

Threat Priming

Our threat-priming results call for additional consideration. We find striking confirmation and extension of Merolla and Zechmeister's (2009) earlier, laboratory-based experiments into threat priming and counterterrorism policy attitudes. Getting people to think about the specter of terrorism tends to bolster anew their willingness to support coercive new measures. This is readily apparent in the airport security and rights violations experiments.

But the results also illuminate some novel aspects of threat priming.

First is the striking disjunction between impacts of experimentally induced threats and the non-effect of historical events. Recall that our statistical comparisons across the 2009 and 2010 SAPA surveys found no
evidence that aggregate policy opinions had responded in any way to a
series of real terrorist plots and attempted attacks in the United States.
How can we square this finding with the thrust of this chapter's experimental results?

Ultimately, the explanation rests with the fact that historical events
involving terrorism are different from experimental preferences to terrorism in surveys. Initially perhaps, we might assume that it would be
historical events rather than experimental survey cues that matter most
to the formation of people's attitudes. But that is not borne out by our
data, because real historical events registered far less than survey references to terrorism. This leads us to a refined interpretation, in which
the formation of attitudes toward war on terror policies appears to be
readily shaped by simple communications, some of which involve symbolic cues, exemplified by a hypothetical terrorism attack and the national identity of a policy target. In this context, the indistinguishable
effects of experimental references to actual versus hypothetical terrorism
raise further the theme of symbolic cueing. Indeed, this compels us to
consider possible points of relevance to John Mueller's scenario of a
"perpetual-motion machine" (2008), where strategic communications
about terrorism threats register rapidly among citizens, potentially creating new demands for policies and further buttressing leaders' willingness to justify and extend such policies.

Further suggestive is how the threat-priming process appears to have
little to do with any underlying fears of terrorism itself. Recall that the
SAPA data enable us to measure respondents' initial level of concern
with terrorism. If experimental threat priming worked by simply mobilizing existing fears, we should see an interaction between individuals
with high levels of initial concerns and experimental exposure to terrorism threats. But there is no evidence for this. What threat priming is
doing is not magnifying latent fears and concerns with terrorism. Instead, even when it involves deliberately hypothetical cues, it is creating
a nearly automatic response and demand for coercive policies.

There is, of course, a significant interaction involving the effects of hypothetical threat priming and education. This translates into higher-education
individuals being even more susceptible to this kind of threat priming
than their less-educated counterparts. It looks as if the power of threat
priming is not something limited to cognitively vulnerable individuals.

The Importance of Education

In the two experiments in which experimental treatments shape policy
attitudes, we have found substantial evidence for the importance of edu-

cation. In the airport security experiment, higher levels of education enhance the impacts of hypothetical threat priming. In the rights violation experiment, education lowers support for fighting terrorism without regard for rights. The presence of an interaction also matters for the target group estimates, where national identity status affects policy attitudes in the threat-priming conditions, but not in the conditions in which threats have not been manipulated.

Education has long occupied a central position in public opinion and political psychology scholarship. On the basis of the results reported here, we can now suggest an important and little-studied feature of education: it can moderate otherwise powerful treatment effects in the survey context. What the interaction effects involving education tell us is that when we consider the reasoning behind counterterrorism policy, the American public tends at times to respond quite differently to key symbols and stimuli depending on whether they have more or less education.

This interactive relationship involving education will receive further scrutiny in the next chapter as well. But for now we emphasize the absence of interactions involving some other initially strong candidates. It is plausible to view party identification as a filter on individuals' willingness to incorporate political stimuli into their policy attitudes. In the current experiments, for instance, we might expect Republicans to be more receptive to reformulating their attitudes in the face of threat priming or the targeting of Americans by counterterrorism measures. But this is not the case. Furthermore, the main effects of partisanship in the current estimates are also not large. So far, these results suggest partisanship heuristics to have somewhat limited relevance to war on terror policy reasoning. What about other major groups within the population that might respond in cognitively divergent ways when it comes to terrorism threats and stimuli of relevance to counterterrorism policies? Established cleavages such as race and religion shed little light. The impacts of experimental treatment effects are independent of these group characteristics.

This brings us, finally, to authoritarianism, an important focus in recent scholarship (Lavine, Lodge, and Freitas 2005; Hetherington and Suhay 2011). Some scholars have seen authoritarianism as a newly mobilized foundation for counterterrorism policy support. Others have turned this argument on its head, arguing that although authoritarians are disposed to support these policies, it is nonauthoritarians who, when exposed to new terrorism threats, tend to respond in ways that bring their policy attitudes in line with those authoritarians. Using our experiments to directly test for authoritarianism x threat-priming interactions, we find no evidence to this effect across the three counterterrorism policy domains considered in this chapter. Threats matter in our experiments, but in ways that appear independent of authoritarian predispositions. These predispositions, for their part, exert a nontrivial impact, but it is largely static and not malleable in the way that the dynamic factors manipulated in our experiments are.

Target Groups and National Identity

What about target groups defined by national identity? This question has been a major focus in this chapter. The results offer a measure of support, but with qualifications. The rights violation experiment provides compelling evidence that target group priming is a different process than threat priming. In doing so, this confirms that more factors are behind counterterrorism opinion malleability than just threat-related stimuli.

By the same token, the interaction between respondents' education level and the absence or presence of experimental threats spills over into how we interpret target group effects. In no-threat conditions, the experimental contrast between Americans versus foreign nationals had little impact on policy-attitude formation. Under these conditions, national identity targets simply did not matter.

Where the results tell a different story is with respect to the other two conditions of the rights violation experiment. In this case, the movement from foreign nationals to Americans significantly lowers support for combating terrorism at the cost of violating rights. The magnitude of this effect is much smaller than the massive effects of threat priming in the same experiment. But, that said, the result at hand tells us that whose rights are seen as being at risk is an ingredient in people's reasoning about counterterrorism measures. When counterterrorism policy support is high, it may in part be due to the public's thinking that foreign nationals are being targeted by the policy in question.

The 2009 torture experiment found national identity to be largely irrelevant to policy-attitude formation. Public support for the practice of torture is already fairly low with respect to the baseline item, and the prospect of exposing an American subject fails to reduce support further. The 2010 extension of this experiment held constant the target as an American citizen, and we found neither terrorism threats nor the novel status defined by Middle Eastern background to have any impact on policy reasoning.

What the torture experiments suggest is that for some counterterrorism issues, target group identities and even threat priming will have little impact in the current historical era. When it is described as such, the American public has apparently made up its mind and the policy attitudes of both opponents and proponents are not easily reconfigured through new cues and cognitive stimuli. But this looks to be the exception, because counterterrorism policy attitudes on other issues are clearly quite malleable. In the next chapter, we explore more systematically a group cleavage that is a second candidate for shaping attitudes toward counterterrorism policy: transnational ethnic distinctions.

Chapter 5

Who Is "Us"?

WHO ARE the principal insiders and outsiders in the contemporary era? Or to use an earlier formulation provided by Robert Reich (1990), "who is 'us'?" When Reich posed this question, his idea was that the interests of workers and consumers alike were undergoing a rapid transformation at the hands of globalization. No longer, for instance, could consumers simply assume that "made in America" meant profits derived from a product's purchase would flow directly back into American workers' pockets and bank accounts. Instead, the complexity of the global economy meant that a non-U.S. or foreign-owned firm might at times provide better wages and other economic benefits for Americans, and that "buying American" might well involve purchasing a product whose constituent parts were assembled elsewhere. Popular perceptions might be slow to catch up. But according to Reich, globalization was transforming the fundamentals of identity and interest.

Two decades later, rhetoric and concern about the impact of globalization have spread widely. International migration, the increasing flow of capital across borders and the subsequent outsourcing of jobs, alongside the internationalization of culture and social and political movements, highlight just how dramatic these changes have been. Among its many consequences, high rates of migration across borders raises anew classic questions about insider versus outsider groups, and tensions between conceptions of national identity have become increasingly contentious. Conflicts generated by a more global, integrated world have no obvious political resolution in sight. Globalization is at the heart of the age in which we live.

But at the same time that globalization seems to be reaching into all corners of economy and society, much public opinion research in the United States has remained steadfastly domestic in its orientation. Consider, for instance, the rich fields of research on attitudes toward disadvantaged groups. When studying perceptions of, and attitudes toward, such groups as women, African Americans, Hispanics, or gays and lesbians, the underlying issue of whether group members are "American" is usually held constant or simply ignored.

But do people view the status of groups differently if they are not U.S. citizens? More generally, what is the impact of a group boundary that spans more than a single nation? When survey respondents are prompted to think about virtually any group of importance, such as Christians, Hispanics, whites, or women, does the degree to which they think of members of the group as American citizens (or not) affect their views? These are critical questions in a global era. They define a novel agenda concerning how confounding transnational processes influence perceptions and attitudes about insider versus outsider groups.

These issues are especially important in the context of counterterrorism, because perpetrators and sources of the threat are often thought to be foreign nationals, even though a number of key incidents have involved American citizens. The relevance of the citizenship status of the presumed targets of counterterrorism policies to understanding public responses to the war on terror is thus potentially strong. Indeed, in the previous chapter we found initial evidence for the relevance of national identity to public attitudes toward war on terror policies. Now we want to take a few more steps to firm up the case at hand. We need to make sure that national categories involving, for instance, "U.S. citizens" are not actually a proxy for a different sort of transnational boundary, particularly one involving an ethnic category or group, such as Christians or Muslims. In doing so, we are approaching questions about insiders versus outsiders from a new and, we think, potentially fruitful vantage point.

We find, to anticipate the thrust of our results, support for our general expectations. National identity distinctions matter and are not simply a proxy for cross-cutting ethnic categories. Our new analyses of group affect dynamics deliver particularly strong findings about how affect toward popular and unpopular groups can be experimentally manipulated when national identity status is brought into the picture. Finally, a new experiment into military commissions extends our focus on counterterrorism. Here, we find that both national and transnational identity cues matter to policy-attitude formation.

Domestic Versus Transnational Approaches

Within past scholarship, an underlying distinction concerns the degree to which an analyst is investigating one or multiple nations. Often, a single-nation focus is implicit. Yet in all cases we seek to show how distinctions across national contexts tend to be of consequence for understanding how identities of groups matter to policy-attitude formation.

Domestic Group Boundaries

Insofar as groups are central to social life, subjective classification of individuals as group members (or nonmembers) is inescapable in the United States and other national contexts. Individuals everywhere are attributed statuses based, for instance, on gender, race, age, and kinship status. Social groups, in the minds of individuals, are almost always seen in categorical (and often binary) terms, as exemplified in statuses based on gender (male-female) and even age (young-old). Individuals attach much value and many expectations to group memberships. This often undergirds robust patterns of inequality with respect to power, honor, and material rewards (Lamont and Fournier 1992; Tilly 1998; Collins 2004).

In much of the established social science research on group boundaries, memberships are frequently unpacked without explicit reference to the national or international context in which they are situated. We call this understanding of groups *domestic*. Domestic models of groups and group boundaries contrast with alternative views that emphasize the simultaneous relevance of national-international factors.

Consider the tradition of what is called expectation-states research on gender divisions (for example, Ridgeway and Smith-Lovin 1999; Correll, Benard, and Paik 2007; Burke, Stets, and Cerven 2007). The key assumption is that individuals' beliefs about gender explain unequal outcomes with respect to power, status, and income among American women versus American men. Because these beliefs are typically well established, they operate as implicit criteria behind the behavior and decision-making of employers and other key actors. Over the life course of individuals, feedback processes will further tend to cumulatively advantage men over women. In the aggregate, historical backlashes against female gains are also probable. A host of laboratory experiments, alongside recent audit-based field experiments, provide ample evidence for the considerable and far-reaching influence of these gender beliefs and attributions.

Expectation-states scholarship yields powerful results, but ones that may simultaneously be bounded by the domestic scope of most research. The national context of the United States is held constant in this tradition of scholarship. So too is the underlying assumption that when thinking about the gender of individuals, people are assuming the targets are U.S. women and U.S. men, rather than men and women of alternative national identities. But what if individuals instead see female and male targets as having alternative national and citizenship statuses? Would these biases and beliefs be different if we were referring to foreign or immigrant men or women?

We do not yet have a good handle on the answers to these questions. Still, we can readily envision important refinements to the domestic model of group identity. What if, for instance, the substantial mother-hood penalty unearthed by Shelley Correll and her colleagues (Correll, Benard, and Paik 2007) was found to be even greater in magnitude if a female job applicant was viewed as a non-U.S. citizen relative to a male foreign national or to a female citizen? Is there, in short, an interaction between gender and national status? If so, we might even have evidence suggesting that gender effects are conditional and that the U.S. gender cleavage is about more than simply gender relations as such.[1]

A similar story could be told about much of the literature on race in America. In chapter 4, we discussed famous experimental evidence showing that white Americans are about twice as supportive of provid-ing welfare to white mothers than to black mothers, all else being equal. But what if by black mother some white respondents are thinking not just of African Americans but also black immigrants or possibly even Hispanics or other "brown skin" mothers? What if "white" connotes American and "black" connotes both African American and foreign, es-pecially non-European, which is certainly a plausible scenario given the history of whiteness in America (see Jacobson 1999)? If we describe the difference at hand as a domestic racial cleavage, we potentially misstate the true nature of the antiblack sentiment being captured in the experi-ment. These issues simply have not been explored in any systematic way, so we don't really know. But reasons are good, we think, for suspi-cion that more than just a domestic race or gender divide is driving citi-zens' responses.

The Challenge of Transnationalism

The leading alternative to domestic views of group boundaries and iden-tities is *transnationalism*. We use this term to encompass two complemen-tary yet distinct international, or between-nation, factors. The first of these is national identity as defined by citizenship, when we are consid-ering discrete groups of individuals created by national boundaries. The second is ethnic or religious identities that involve groups with connec-tions to, or locations in, multiple countries, as is common among world religions and often as well with respect to ethnic groups. Both types of transnational factors may be potentially relevant to war on terror policy attitudes, and national identity has been particularly central to critiques of domestic models of groups.

In the work of Michele Lamont and her colleagues, for instance, na-tions are viewed as central as any other potential source of influence on identity (Lamont and Fournier 1992; Lamont and Thevenot 2000; Lamont and Molnar 2002). Indeed, nations are characterized by common stocks of memory—"repertoires"—from which individuals routinely draw in thinking about phenomena as disparate as markets, aesthetics, and the deservingness of groups. Because nations tend to have quite different cultural repertoires, domestic models have difficulty grasping the inherent complexities in group boundaries. At the same time, globalization processes and international organizations have actively worked in ways that produce complicated patterns of overlap between national identities and other group memberships and attributions.

Very different in tone, but raising similar analytic challenges, is a political polemic advanced by Samuel Huntington (2004). Huntington decried what he saw as a declining salience of "Anglo-Protestant culture of the founding settlers of America" as a source of national identity. He argued that "in the 1960's . . . transnational identities began to rival and erode the pre-eminence of national identity" (xv). In doing so, Huntington presents a scenario that exemplifies Lamont's broader points concerning the rising importance of and potential overlap between domestic and transnational group memberships and identities. According to Huntington, when people think about American, they have less in mind Protestant or Anglo American than they do African American, Asian American, or even just U.S. citizen. But in what ways this is true, and how it applies to the case of policy opinions on the war on terror, remains to be seen.

What We Want to Know About Transnational Factors

We consider three empirical questions in this chapter, all of which straddle scholarly consideration of domestic and transnational group identities. The first is where we should place transnational groups with respect to hierarchies of insiders and outsiders. We measure insider and outsider hierarchies using the affect that individuals express toward specific groups. We hypothesize that insiders will elicit greater warmth and outsiders will get a cooler reception. But what these analyses will also tell us is whether established outsiders such as blacks are seen in a similar or different way when compared with outsider groups such as foreign nationals. We expect it is groups of the latter sort that have considerable relevance in the post-9/11 era because of disproportionately negative patterns of affect and emotional response.

We next examine whether national identity status itself has an impact on group affect. Here we use experiments to probe who respondents may be thinking about when they confront insider groups such as Christians, as well as outsider groups such as people from the Middle East. By using treatment effects related to U.S. citizenship status, we will also see whether national identity status has the power to reduce or increase the gaps between insider and outsider groups.

Our final question brings us back to attitude formation on the war on terror. We extend the previous chapter's results by analyzing target group cues encompassing not just national identity status but also with respect to a measure of transnational ethnicity. This tells us whether it is simply targets who are not U.S. citizens that enhance support for counterterrorism policies. Alternatively, it is possible that people are also disposed, and perhaps even more so, to support policies that target transnational ethnic minorities. As before, distinguishing these key group categories in the minds of survey respondents is critical. We rely heavily on our survey experiments to begin sorting through the effect of distinct identity cues.

Group Affect and Policy-Attitude Measures

We consider patterns of affect toward seven insider-outsider groups that deliberately straddle domestic versus transnational cleavages. These are, to be sure, hardly exhaustive of the underlying population in the U.S. context. Still, they are anchored in focal points of past scholarship (blacks, whites) and engage or extend to new and potentially important transnational conditions (foreign nationals, U.S. citizens).

Table 5.1 summarizes the group affect items and accompanying batteries of affect measures and policy-attitude experiments. The group affect items all use a 0 to 100° feeling thermometer format that is common in data collections such as the National Election Studies. For our consideration of domestic identity cleavages, we use three items for well-established groups: whites, blacks, and Christians. We present a contrast with four groups defined by transnational identities: Muslims, foreigners, people from the Middle East, and U.S. citizens.[2]

Two specific groups are the basis for our experiments into group affect formation: people from the Middle East are the first; Christians are the second. Because these are both experiments, there is a control group and then a second, treatment-effects condition. The control group version is simply the feeling thermometer item from earlier, when respondents report their degree of emotional warmth toward the group in question. But in the treatment-effects conditions, national boundaries are experimentally manipulated with respect to U.S. citizenship status. For the Middle East group affect item, the treatment-effects condition offers the reframing *people from the Middle East who are U.S. citizens*. For the Christian group affect item, the treatment is *Christians who are not U.S. citizens*.

Our new war on terror policy-attitude experiment is summarized at the bottom of table 5.1. In the military commissions experiment, respondents in the control group are asked, "Should the government move American citizens who are terrorism suspects to special military prisons and rely on military courts?"[3] In the first experimental treatment, *American citizens* is changed to *foreign nationals* to again test the candidate rel-

Table 5.1   SAPA Item Wordings and Experiments[a]

Domestic group affect
"I'd like to get your feelings toward some groups who are in the news these days. I'll read the name of a group and I'd like you to rate that group using something we call the feeling thermometer. Ratings between 50 degrees and 100 degrees mean that you feel favorable and warm toward that group. Ratings between 0 degrees and 50 degrees mean that you don't feel favorable toward that group and that you don't care too much for that group. You would rate the person at the 50 degree mark if you don't feel particularly warm or cold for the group. How about blacks . . . whites?"

Transnational group affect
"How about Muslims . . . foreign nationals . . . U.S. citizens?"

Middle East group affect [+ experiment]
"How about people from the Middle East?"
Experimental condition: "people from the Middle East" changed to "people from the Middle East who are U.S. citizens"

Christian group affect [+ experiment]
"How about Christians?"
Experimental condition: "Christians" changed to "Christians who are not U.S. citizens"

Military commissions [+ experiments]
"As you may know, Congress passed the Military Commissions Act in 2006, creating a separate set of courts and prisons in which individuals classified by the government as 'enemy combatants' can be held indefinitely. What do you think – [should the government move American citizens who are terrorism suspects to special military prisons and rely on military courts?/ Or should the government move American citizens who are terrorism suspects to regular prisons and rely on regular criminal courts?]"
Experimental condition 1: "American citizens" changed to "foreign nationals"
Experimental condition 2: "American citizens" changed to "American citizens of Middle Eastern background"

Source: Authors' compliation based on Surveys of American Policy Attitudes (Brooks and Manza, various years).
[a]Order of presentation of "people from the Middle East" and "Christians" is randomized on the feeling thermometer; for "Military commissions," order of presentation of the response options in brackets is randomized.

evance of transnational boundaries. In the second experimental treatment, *American citizens* is changed to *American citizens of Middle Eastern background* to introduce a quite different, transnational ethnic identity. In this way, we can see whether and in what ways transnational ethnic versus national boundaries overlap or instead diverge with respect to policy-attitude formation.[4]

Interaction Tests

As in chapter 4, that experimental treatments interact with layers of the population is an important possibility to consider. We do this by testing directly for interactions, considering the same half-dozen key candidates as in chapter 4. Test results are summarized in table 5.2.

In the Middle East affect experiment, there is no evidence indicating inclusion of any of the interaction candidates. But in the Christian affect experiment, the initial tests return evidence that four of the six interactions are significant. When all four candidates are considered in the same model, two of these—threat perceptions and education—dwindle in significance, as summarized in the table's note b. This leaves a pair of interactions, authoritarianism and religion, for our preferred model.[5]

In the military commissions experiment, initial evidence suggests interactions between the treatment effects and both education and authoritarianism. Considering all interactions in the same model yields evidence for just one of the threat perception interactions (see note c). We retain this single interaction in our preferred model of military commissions.[6]

Analyses and Results

Having gauged the evidence for interactions, we can now turn to our substantive questions. Where should we place transnational groups with respect to hierarchies of insiders and outsiders? Does affect toward established, domestic groups match up with the parallel range of affect toward newer, transnational groups?

Insider Versus Outsider Groups, Domestic and Transnational

We start with the results displayed in figure 5.1, where group scores are on the 0 to 100° thermometer.

Focusing on domestic groups in the figure's left side, blacks receive a lower score (67°) than whites (70°). This is a significant group difference ($t = 4.47$), and it confirms the relevance of race to group identities and boundaries for our respondents.[7] With a thermometer score of 72°, Christians as a group receive an initially higher score than whites. But the 2° difference is not significant at the .05 level.

Where things take a dramatic turn is with respect to transnational groups. Considering the remaining groups in figure 5.1, there are both impressively low scores as well as a notably high one. In the case of U.S. citizens, 75° is easily the highest group score in our analysis, and differences with both Christians and whites are significant. At the other end of the hierarchy are people from the Middle East (55°), Muslims (52°), and

Table 5.2 Experimental Treatments and Interactions[a]

	x Threat Perception	x Authoritarianism	x Partisanship	x Education	x Religion	x Race
Middle East affect	F(1) = 2.10	F(1) = 2.06	F(1) = .23	F(1) = .24	F(1) = .41	F(1) = .56
	p = .15	p = .15	p = .63	p = .62	p = .52	p = .46
β_U.S. citizens (SE)	2.28 (1.58)	.78 (.55)	.28 (.59)	.24 (.49)	1.76 (2.76)	-2.49 (3.34)
Christian affect	F(1) = 7.67[b]	F(1) = 26.47	F(1) = 1.92	F(1) = 9.93[b]	F(1) = 11.65	F(1) = .17
	p = .01	p = .00	p = .17	p = .00	p = .00	p = .68
β_U.S. citizens (SE)	-5.17 (1.87)	**-3.22** (.63)	-.97 (.70)	-10.97 (3.21)	**-.03** (.06)	-1.68 (4.07)
Military commissions	F(2) = .22	F(2) = 4.75[c]	F(2) = 1.88	F(1) = 5.09	F(2) = .69	F(2) = .25
	p = .80	p = .01	p = .15	p = .01	p = .50	p = .78
β_foreign (SE)	<-.01 (.04)	<-.02 (.01)	-.01 (.01)	.01 (.01)	-.01 (.07)	.04 (.09)
β_M.E. backgr. (SE)	-.06 (.04)	<.03 (.01)	<-.01 (.02)	**-.03** (.01)	.07 (.08)	-.02 (.09)

Source: Authors' estimates based on analysis of Surveys of American Policy Attitudes (Brooks and Manza, various years).

Note: ME backgr. = Middle Eastern background.

[a]Bolded entry indicates significance at $p < .05$.

[b]When threat and education interactions are estimated in a model with the authoritarianism and religion interactions, the threat and education interactions are not significant ($\beta_{-U.S.\ citizens\ x\ threat} = -2.71$, SE = 1.90, $p = .15$; $\beta_{-U.S.\ citizens\ x\ education} = 1.03$, SE = .62, $p = .10$).

[c]When the authoritarianism interactions are estimated in a model with the education interaction, the coefficient is not significant ($\beta_{foreign\ x\ authoritarianism} = -.02$, SE >.01, $p = .16$; $\beta_{ME\ backgr.\ x\ authoritarianism} = .01$, SE = .02, $p = .34$).

Figure 5.1   Affect Toward Insider and Outsider Groups

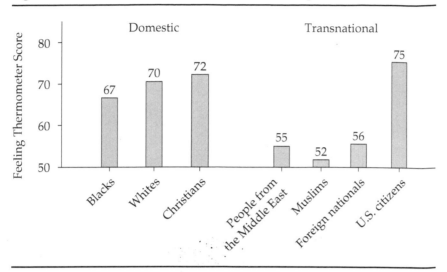

Source: Authors' calculations based on Surveys of American Policy Attitudes (Brooks and Manza, various years).

foreign nationals (56°). These are quite low scores, considerably lower than the 67° received by blacks.[8]

It is striking how we can readily identify transnationally defined groups that elicit disproportionately positive affect, in the case of U.S. citizens, and also overwhelmingly negative affect, in the case of people from the Middle East, Muslims, and foreign nationals. Evidence is strong for the relevance of transnational groups to a fuller consideration of status group hierarchies in the contemporary United States. This is a point we return to in the conclusion.

The Power of National Identity

We are now in position to look at mechanisms behind two key patterns of group affect. What we want to see is whether transnational factors, in the specific form of national identity status, can shed light on how people respond to insider versus outsider groups. Our first experiment takes the case of people from the Middle East. Results are summarized in figure 5.2.

With a score of 55°, the control group recapitulates what we already know about the cool reception that people from the Middle East receive among our survey respondents. In the experimental treatment condition, we now redescribe this group to introduce a novel identity cue: people from the Middle East who are U.S. citizens. The -4.87 *t*-score tells us that this cue has a significant impact, boosting affect by 6°. In doing so, this result suggests that part of the reason people from the Middle

Figure 5.2   Does National Identity Matter for Outsider Groups?

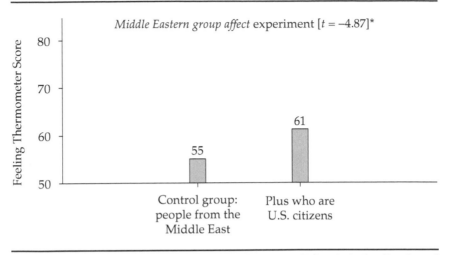

Source: Authors' calculations based on Surveys of American Policy Attitudes (Brooks and Manza, various years).
*Indicates significance at $p < .05$

East are viewed negatively is because of an underlying attribution that they are not U.S. citizens. When these attributes are decoupled in our experiment, we can see how this operates.

It is useful to put the magnitude of the U.S. citizens cue in further perspective using regression. We now treat Middle East affect as the dependent variable, where the national identity cue is a covariate, alongside the other independent variables in the analysis. Recall that as discovered earlier, there is no evidence for interactions involving the experimental U.S. citizens cue. In table 5.3, we present estimates of the magnitude of key factors on Middle East affect.[9]

The 15.30 estimate indicates that a change from the lowest to highest observed level of education is predicted to increase by over 15° affect toward people from the Middle East. Education has by far the largest effect of any measured factor, reflecting its status as a well-established mechanism behind tolerance and support for diversity. But the impact of our experimental national identity cue (6°) is also quite substantial, exceeding the parallel impact of partisanship (5°). What this means is that exposing someone to the U.S. citizens cue has a larger predicted effect on his or her feelings about people from the Middle East than if we transformed him or her from a strong Republican to a strong Democrat.

Turning to our second experiment into group affect, we now analyze a case of group affect that involves quite favorable emotional responses: Christians. As before, we want to see whether national identity boundaries, when manipulated, make a difference. We do this in figure 5.3 by

Table 5.3   Comparative Magnitude of Factors Behind Middle East Group
Affect

	Effect	| Effect |
Education	15.30	15.30
Authoritarianism	−7.27	7.27
"U.S. citizen" condition	6.25	6.25
Partisanship	−4.56	4.56

Source: Authors' estimates based on analysis of Surveys of American Policy Attitudes
(Brooks and Manza, various years).

redescribing Christians with the additional cue "who are not U.S. citizens."

The experimental treatment easily reaches statistical significance. Taking away U.S. national identity status dramatically lowers affect toward Christians by 9°. But this initial estimate does not yet take into account the two key interactions our multivariate analyses unearthed: with education and with respondents' religion. The presence of interactions contrasts with the Middle East affect experiment, and we use the calculations in figure 5.4 to properly gauge the magnitude of the national identity cue.

Estimates in this figure are range-standardized coefficients for the national identity treatment effect. But we must graph coefficients across the range of the authoritarianism and religion variables to see how the interactions play out. In the left panel, estimates connected by the dotted

Figure 5.3   Does National Identity Matter for Insider Groups?

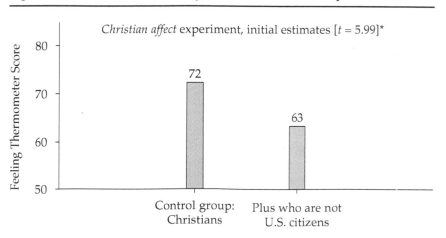

Source: Authors' estimates based on Surveys of American Policy Attitudes (Brooks and Manza, various years).
*Indicates significance at $p < .05$.

Figure 5.4   Magnitude of National Identity Effects: Affect Toward Christians

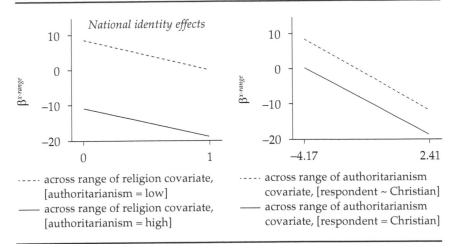

- - - - - across range of religion covariate, [authoritarianism = low]
———— across range of religion covariate, [authoritarianism = high]

- - - - - across range of authoritarianism covariate, [respondent ~ Christian]
———— across range of authoritarianism covariate, [respondent = Christian]

Source: Authors' estimates based on analysis of Surveys of American Policy Attitudes (Brooks and Manza, various years).

line are calculated while authoritarianism is held at its lowest observed level. We can see how these estimates vary across the range of the religion variable. In the second set of estimates, authoritarianism is now held constant at its highest observed level, and national identity effects vary in parallel fashion across the range of the religion variable.

The right panel shows the same type of calculations but now displays coefficient estimates for, respectively, Christian-identified respondents versus all others across the range of the authoritarianism variable. Although the difference in coefficient magnitude among Christian versus non-Christian respondents is clear, the larger source of variability is with respect to authoritarianism. Among those with more authoritarian predispositions, national identity cues have far more negative effects, tending to generate less warm feelings toward Christians as a group.

Combined with the experiment's initial results, we can again witness the power of national identity status. Overall, feelings about Christians are far less positive when they are redefined as not being U.S. citizens, and this effect is enhanced considerably by authoritarianism. The thematic point is that U.S. national identity matters enough so that when removed, the status of even a well-liked insider group rapidly plummets.

Transnational Identities and War on Terror Attitudes

How do transnational group identities influence public responses to the war on terror? We turn now to results from the military commissions

Figure 5.5 Does Transnational Ethnicity Matter?

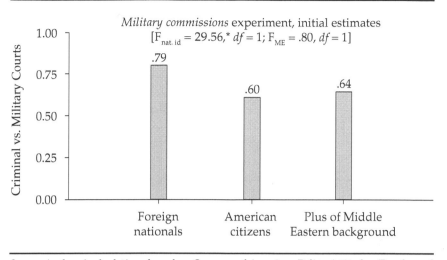

Military commissions experiment, initial estimates
$[F_{nat. id} = 29.56,^* df = 1; F_{ME} = .80, df = 1]$

Source: Authors' calculations based on Surveys of American Policy Attitudes (Brooks and Manza, various years).
Note: nat. id = national identity; ME = Middle Eastern.
*Indicates significance at $p < .05$.

experiment. There are two treatment effects for, respectively, American citizens and American citizens of Middle Eastern background. In the control group, respondents are asked about foreign nationals with respect to special military prisons/military courts. As summarized in figure 5.5, support for military commissions arrangements is high in the control group condition and appreciably lower when the target is defined as American citizens. This represents a significant effect. By contrast, the F-test for the Middle Eastern factor returns a nonsignificant result.

But consulting again the interaction test results in table 5.2, recall the evidence for a single interaction involving the Middle Eastern background factor and education. This refines our interpretation in ways we can gauge using table 5.4 estimates. These are range-standardized estimates for the largest predicted effects, including the experimental identity cues.

The largest effect is for the Middle Eastern background treatment at the lowest level of education. Although this is an impressive effect, we can also see how it declines in magnitude at higher levels of education. Indeed, for those at the highest level of education, the Middle Eastern background treatment is the smallest effect of those summarized in table 5.4. This interaction means that transnational bias is most consequential among less-educated respondents. If we round out the calculations by looking further at framing effects at the sample average for education

Table 5.4   Comparative Magnitude of Factors Behind Military Commissions Support

	Effect		Effect	
"Middle Eastern" condition, education = 5	.36	.36
Education, "Middle Eastern" condition	−.30	.30
Threat perception	.30	.30
Partisanship	.18	.18
"Foreign" condition	.16	.16
Education, "American/foreign" condition	.15	.15
"Middle Eastern" condition, education = 20	−.09	.09

Source: Authors' estimates based on analysis of Surveys of American Policy Attitudes (Brooks and Manza, various years).

(14.54 years), we obtain a resultant estimate of 0.07. For individuals at the mean level of schooling, then, the Middle Eastern background treatment has the effect of slightly raising support for military commissions.

Education also exerts considerable influence over attitudes toward military commissions. But because of the interaction, these effects also vary, depending on the target group that individuals are cued to be thinking about. When the target is defined by the Middle Eastern background cue, education has very large effects (−0.30), disposing individuals to oppose the military commissions system. But, in the other American citizens condition, and in the foreign nationals–control group condition, education has a smaller and very different impact (0.15). In these cases, higher levels of education lead to more positive attitudes toward military commissions.

The other experimental contrast to note is the comparison between the foreign nationals versus American citizens condition. Here, the 0.16 estimate tells us that the foreign nationals cue leads to higher support for military commissions than if policy targets are defined as American citizens. Because there is no interaction involving these conditions, the national identity effect is identical across all respondents.

The remaining results in table 5.4 show that threat perceptions have substantial effects. These are comparable in magnitude to the effects of education in the Middle Eastern condition. The impact of partisanship is somewhat smaller, comparable to the 0.16 national identity effect. As before, this is instructive in telling us that changing perceptions of a policy as applying to American citizens rather than foreign nationals has about the same effect as changing someone's partisanship from strong Republican to strong Democrat.

Conclusion

Target group theories receive a good deal of new support from results presented in this chapter. Results of the military commissions experiment tells us that national identity status matters, on average, more so than the earlier results in chapter 4. Counterterrorism policy support tends to be significantly lower when it is American citizens who are viewed as the target.

This chapter's experiments into attitude formation on military commissions also tell us about transnational group targets. Looking at transnational ethnic identity reveals another critical influence on counterterrorism policy attitudes. Even when U.S. citizenship status is controlled, experimental evidence indicates that transnational ethnic cues substantially shape policy-attitude formation.[10]

Our interaction effect tests show a degree of complexity as regards which specific segments of the population are most receptive to transnational ethnic cues. In the military commissions experiment, education interacts with the treatment effect. Less-educated respondents respond to the Middle Eastern background cue by giving much more support to military commissions arrangements then their more highly educated counterparts.

Stepping partly back from these results, we would emphasize an emerging and essential feature of war on terror policy attitudes. Accumulating evidence of experimental effects—relating to threat priming and target group identity characteristics—demonstrates a real degree of malleability in the opinion-formation process. Rather than a fully locked-in public that fails to respond to new information or cues, what we consistently find is a picture of counterterrorism opinion responsiveness to shifts, but shifts in the discursive and symbolic environment in which attitudes are formed. This symbolic qualification is critical. As we found in chapters 3 and 4, key political changes and even real, terrorism-related events appear to have had far less of an impact.

We also emphasize that these patterns of responsiveness show a degree of complexity among the population, with select factors such as education tending to mediate the degree to which individuals incorporate new communications into their policy reasoning. But that said, the larger message is simply that this responsiveness can be so easily found in the first place. It is particularly important because we operate within the demanding contexts of experiments. Across a range of war on terror issues, there is thus considerable room for strategically crafted messages—on the part of experts, politicians, and the media as a whole—to reach members of the public.

We know from the overall trend analyses presented in chapter 3 that our baseline attitude measures show considerable stability between 2007 and 2010. But our experiments also demonstrate that the same policy-attitude measures yield different estimates of support when target groups or threat conditions are manipulated. This means that future patterns of counterterrorism opinion stability are far from inevitable. Given that our experimental treatments involve the activation of symbolic biases, we also want to keep an eye on another emerging message: even as the comparatively low risk of international terrorism appears to decline with the passage of time, support for war on terror measures is quite easy to enhance when the public is propelled to think about target groups they dislike. Yet again, it is the presence of readily mobilized symbols, ones that are suggestive of an important degree of ethnic and national baggage, that provides the explanation.

Transnational Identity and Insider Versus Outsider Groups

Who is us, and who is them? This chapter's results speak directly to scholarly controversies concerning who are insiders versus outsiders in the current historical era. As discussed earlier, many scholars acknowledge and actively call for consideration of transnational boundaries and identities. At the same time, however, much empirical work remains steadfastly focused on within-nation domestic group boundaries. As a result, it is difficult, if not impossible, to address the impact of transnational factors without entering the realm of speculation.

Our policy-attitude and affect formation experiments produce a set of new results. Starting with our research focus on affect toward key social groups, it is transnational identity boundaries that bring out the largest gaps in affect. Such insider groups as U.S. citizens are viewed positively, even more positively than whites and Christians. Equally telling is how transnational outsiders like foreigners, Muslims, and people from the Middle East get a relatively chilly reception, even more so than well-established domestic outsider groups like blacks. Transnational outsiders appear to be at an even greater distance from domestic outsiders. Cleavages defined by transnational groups are thus potentially much larger than those defined by such established domestic cleavages as race.

Our experiments into the dynamics of group affect shed further light. Not only are transnational identity cues polarizing, they also influence patterns of affect toward established domestic groups. Consider the people from the Middle East experiment, where initially negative feelings are readily propelled in more positive directions by a simple but powerful new cue involving status as a U.S. citizen. The Christians experiment shows the parallel contribution of citizenship status to a case of positive group affect. In particular, when Christians are experimentally redefined as not U.S. citizens, they are viewed in far less positive terms, and this effect is strongest among those with lower levels of education.

It is powerful to put these two sets of results together. When we do so, what we find is that by conferring U.S. citizenship status on an outsider group and taking it away from an insider group, we can get public views of these groups to converge. The initial 17° gap between Christians and people from the Middle East shrinks down to just 2°.

All told then, our results suggest the importance of transnationalism with respect to understanding contemporary boundaries between insider versus outsider groups, and also as regards public responses to the war on terror. Looking at novel groups defined by national identity or transnational statuses extends our understanding based solely on domestic group cleavages. In the context of the contemporary United States, for instance, part of the public's positive responses to an insider group like Christians appear to be linked to a prior belief that Christians are already U.S. citizens. Ultimately, then, scholars may find it necessary to look at transnational identity characteristics even when it is domestic groups in which they are primarily interested.

Chapter 6

Policy Feedback?

O NE OF the most intriguing, if controversial, claims about policy attitudes is that they are shaped by policies themselves. That policies work in this way to feed back into the process of opinion formation is one interpretation of why policies, once adopted, often become difficult to dislodge. This dynamic is encapsulated by the expression "policies produce politics," first popularized by Paul Pierson (1993). When new laws are enacted or existing policies extended, they often create constituencies and interest groups determined to maintain them, and they may also redirect preferences on the part of citizens (Svallfors 2010).

Examples of policy feedback abound. The passage of the Social Security Act (SSA) in 1935, for example, changed the framework within which all later debates over old-age security would proceed. As the old-age insurance program linked to employment history grew and became more generous, public demands for flat old-age assistance pensions receded (Achenbaum 1983; Amenta 2006). Interest organizations, most notably the American Association of Retired Persons (AARP), formed to protect and promote old-age insurance, and the AARP eventually grew into a powerful lobby capable of mobilizing millions of citizens when significant cuts or changes to the program were proposed. Over time, the old-age insurance program of the SSA became exceptionally popular among Americans, yielding large majorities in support of the program (Campbell 2005).

Policy feedback has thus furnished analysts with a perspective from which to understand self-reproducing dynamics and the historical "stickiness" of public policies and institutions. Yet the impact of policy feedback can also become elusive when we look beyond seemingly successful instances of policy entrepreneurship. One historical case that should have been characterized by extensive patterns of policy feedback but where later analysts found virtually none was the 1996 reform of the Aid to Families with Dependent Children (AFDC) program in the United

States. Analyzing survey data before and after 1996, Joe Soss and San- ford Schram (2007) find no evidence of change in public attitudes to- ward the poor and toward specific welfare programs. Also focusing on the case of U.S. welfare reform, Joshua Dyck and Laura Hussey (2008) find that AFDC retrenchment failed to dislodge the strong impacts of racial attitudes on policy opinions. These impacts persisted even though changes in means-tested benefits were also accompanied by declining stereotypes of welfare recipients in the media (Dyck and Hussey 2008, 596).

How can we square these results with expectations from the policy feedback literature? There is a deep-seated yet largely unarticulated clash of theoretical perspectives involved. In established applications, feedback from new legislation to mass attitude formation, particularly as involving state-making or programmatic initiatives (Huber and Ste- phens 2001; Mettler and Soss 2004), is often seen as routine and unprob- lematic. This is because citizens view their interests as tied to the new regime, and policymakers often design programs with an eye to enhanc- ing perceptions of legitimacy (May 1991; Kumlin 2002). By contrast, an alternative perspective developed in the heuristics and biases tradition is that prior beliefs and biases filter how individuals reason about, and respond to, policy change (Gilovich, Griffin, and Kahneman 2002). Con- sider, for instance, the motivated reasoning scenario, in which citizens' entrenched beliefs lead to negative views of policy modification to the status quo (Ditto and Lopez 1992; Jost, Federico, and Napier 2009). In this scenario, people tend to reject or process in unexpected ways new information that is seen as inconsistent with prior belief and expectation.

The clash between the preceding views of policy feedback is impor- tant. It matters both to policy feedback scholarship and to our own pro- grammatic focus on public opinion and counterterrorism policies. Can we develop some evidence as to whether (and why) feedback processes might underlie the formation of attitudes toward counterterrorism mea- sures?

In this chapter, we engage hypotheses and competing theoretical ex- pectations drawn from debates over policy feedbacks on public opinion. What we are interested in is the possibility that the policy changes with which Presidents Bush and Obama responded to the 9/11 attacks may have propelled citizens' attitudes in new directions. To get at this com- plicated scenario, we first lay out more fully some relevant models of the mechanisms underlying policy feedback processes. We then discuss how our survey experiments allow us to test key hypotheses by, in essence, mimicking the shock of policy impacts on attitude formation.

The results of these experiments tell us something new about atti- tudes toward war on terror policies. But the feedback processes at hand also have a notably one-sided quality. In the case in which information about the passage of a new counterterrorism law is provided, opinions shift perhaps predictably toward greater support. But when information is provided about a presidential order rolling back a counterterrorism practice, opinions—rather than showing a predictable movement toward declining support—are instead unmoved. This is unexpected and important, raising again the ongoing theme of asymmetry in opinion malleability, and we flesh things out further by looking at the effects of policy change on opinions in a third and quite different domain: healthcare spending.

Two Perspectives on Policy Feedback and Public Opinion

The presumption of policy feedback scholarship is that feedback processes are common and unproblematic. This orientation owes much to the pioneering work of the economist Douglass North (1990), who demonstrated how even inefficient economic institutions tend to persist because their rules continually shape organizations and the players operating within their fields. A rupture in this path-dependent process requires the appearance of a new actor, one who would benefit from radical modifications to existing rules but at the same time have the capacity to successfully pursue implementation. Severe contradictions between economic and political institutions (North and Shirley 2008), or the intervention of an exogenous shock or organization (Boettke, Coyne, and Leeson 2008) could facilitate this type of change. But such cases are rare.[1]

State-Centered Theories and Global Feedback

Douglass North did not initially consider policy feedbacks on public opinion as such, but comparative social scientists soon became interested in applications that began to pave the way. Paul Pierson was a pioneer in this theory transfer, arguing that social welfare programs had reshaped the structure of organized interests and interest groups in developed capitalist societies (1993, 1996; see also Skocpol 1992). This same dynamic can be extended to public opinion.

Consider, for example, research on the welfare state. So dependent are most citizens on some form of government provision that alternatives to the status quo, especially in the form of spending cuts, are often vigorously resisted (Brooks and Manza 2007). Policy feedbacks can thus be seen as "ratchets," establishing "the new point of reference for discussions on further welfare state development" (Huber and Stephens 2001, 3).

Although much of the policy feedback literature has focused on political elites, interest groups, and policy coalitions, public opinion is increasingly seen as a plausible mechanism through which feedback processes unfold. For example, when governments offer job-specific training and protections, members of high-skill occupations may come to depend upon, and strongly support, such arrangements (Iversen and Soskice 2001). In social-democratic nations, a universalistic distribution of benefits and services gives working- and middle-class citizens alike a vested interest in maintaining access to government provision (Korpi and Palme 1998).

But is there more to policy effects than economic interests and incentives? What if dependence on existing institutions and attitudinal responses to policy change have an intrinsically cognitive dimension? It is here we can readily discern a second and less explicitly articulated type of mechanism.[2] Invoking classical social psychological theory, this mechanism is easily understood as cognitive dissonance reduction. It draws from a long-standing tradition of psychological research on the subject.

Cognitive dissonance involves individuals adapting to behavioral or environmental change. They do so by adjusting attitudes to reduce psychic tensions. In Leon Festinger's classic studies (1957; Festinger and Carlsmith 1959), individuals receiving minimal payment for completing a repetitive task changed their attitudes more, and in a more positive direction, than those given larger payments for the same task. Here, individuals unconsciously seek to avoid stress caused by behavioral compliance with environmental demands. The tendency is to bring attitudes in line with new realities, making policy feedback a common phenomenon. But whereas interest-centered explanations see policy change as shaping mass attitudes by giving individuals new benefits, cognitive dissonance views policy change as shaping mass opinion by instead providing little to no benefits. Both lines of thinking thus lead to global expectations of policy feedbacks as common but differ with respect to the mechanism responsible for such effects.

Festinger's results have been extended in a rich array of laboratory studies, where, for instance, individuals who read material with which they disagree are more likely to upwardly revise their opinions when receiving no tangible rewards (Aronson, Wilson, and Akert 2006; Cooper 2007; Egan, Santos, and Bloom 2007). Cognitive dissonance captures the broad class of cases in which forced compliance may lead to attitude adjustment, even in the absence of clear reward or perceived improvements to welfare. If policy change leaves citizens with little alternative to compliance, cognitive dissonance is a candidate mechanism behind feedback effects on opinion formation.

Voter Heuristics, Contingent Policy Feedback

Expectations of policy feedback in public opinion have been constructively challenged by the studies of U.S. welfare reform discussed in the introduction. These studies set us on a path toward a very different view of mechanisms behind opinion formation, especially as regards the processing of information about changes in the environment. This alternative view is best understood as emphasizing the moderating role of heuristics and biases. It leads to the expectation that policy feedback is a less common and more contingent phenomenon. Whether policy shifts reorient citizens' preferences depends on the existing biases that dispose some individuals to either welcome or instead reject the changes at hand.

In Joshua Dyck and Laura Hussey's study (2008), U.S. voters retained negative attitudes toward welfare programs and beneficiaries in the face of a transformation in the federal government's AFDC program. These enduring attitudes suggest heuristic reasoning and the influence of biases. Like partisanship or ideological identification (Sniderman, Brody, and Tetlock 1991; Bartels 2002; Jost, Federico, and Napier 2009), for instance, racial attitudes can be a powerful filter on the information that individuals are willing to accept. In the case of the 1996 welfare reform, negative views of the assumed intersection of welfare dependency and race operated as a lens through which many voters saw the issues at hand. As such, they were not easily reshaped by simply downsizing the AFDC program.

In the heuristics and biases approach, individuals rarely encounter policy and other environmental change without recourse to prior beliefs (Gilovich, Griffin, and Kahneman 2002). Of course, which particular set of beliefs is accessible is probabilistic (Iyengar 1990; Zaller 1992), varying across context as well as individual. When it comes to how policy change shapes mass opinion, the heuristics and biases approach anticipates that this influence will be mediated by which predispositions are activated. The impact of policy change interacts with prior beliefs. That leads to heterogeneous effects across the population and, again, a more contingent view of policy feedback.

Consider, for instance, our empirical focus on counterterrorism policies. It is conceivable that self-identified Republicans and Democrats will respond quite differently to information about policy change. Democrats, for instance, may be less willing to bring their attitudes toward counterterrorism in line with new counterterrorism policy realities. For their part, Republicans may likewise resist instances in which war on terror policies are pulled back. Partisan bias in response to policy change may have grown stronger in the years after the 9/11 attacks as Democratic Party politicians began to retreat from the strong positions endorsed by the Republican Party. If so, this would lead to interactions between partisanship and exposure to policy feedback stimuli, in line with the motivated reasoning scenario. This interaction would make policy feedback a contingent phenomenon.

Theoretical Expectations and Counterterrorism Policies

To summarize, what should we expect if global expectations associated with the policy feedback perspective on public opinion are met? In this case, policy influence on opinion formation should be consequential. It should operate by redefining citizens' interests or through cognitive dissonance.

But if citizens instead view policy change through the lens of prior beliefs, feedback processes will be more contingent. Policy change will not always reorient opinion, and impacts will be mediated by which heuristics and biases are activated. Democrats and Republicans may, for instance, respond quite differently when confronted with the scenario of new counterterrorism policies.

The domain of counterterrorism policy has much to offer as a context in which to consider these competing perspectives. It enables us to begin disentangling mechanisms underlying feedback effects involving interest- and incentive-related factors. In particular, the expected utility of these policies involves judgments about the threat of terrorism. Because we are able to measure individuals' self-reported threat perceptions, we can see whether this line of interest-centered explanation sheds light on policy feedback. As discussed further in the following section, additional interaction tests involving partisan heuristics help get at the main and alternative explanation of feedback mechanisms.

Policy Feedback Experiments

In this chapter, we draw on our survey experiments to get a new handle on policy feedback dynamics. Bringing experiments to bear is a novel approach to studying policy feedback. This taps into the strengths of experiments to address perennially challenging problems of omitted variables.

What distinguishes this chapter's policy feedback experiments is what the treatment effects represent. In past chapters, we cued survey respondents to think about status and identity characteristics of policy targets, or, alternatively, the prospect of terrorist attacks and associated threats. In this chapter, we prime individuals with information about a specific legislative or policy change. We are, then, using experiments to mimic the historical impact of the legislative or policy change in question.

But there is an important property of these information-centered treatment effects. Individuals may already have information about the legislative and policy change to which the survey experiment refers. If they recall this information when responding to the survey question, the experiment may find little difference between control versus treatment-effects conditions. In other words, the policy feedback experiment may tend to underestimate the true effect because policy and legislative change has also already been incorporated into baseline policy reasoning.

This is, then, a design limitation of policy feedback experiments. But because it is methodologically conservative, it makes any findings about experimental feedback effects particularly informative. This will tend to give us confidence in results that achieve statistical significance, which is good. We suspect that counterterrorism policy feedbacks after September 11 were likely. Our methodologically conservative approach makes reaching such conclusions more difficult, however.

The Feedback Experiments

We analyze three sets of experiments into policy feedback dynamics using the 2010 Surveys of American Policy Attitudes (SAPA) data. The first is an experiment into attitudes toward surveillance by the National Security Agency (NSA). It uses an item from chapter 3 and adds two new conditions. The second experiment extends chapter 3's measure of attitudes toward waterboarding into a full experiment. The third measure is new to this volume and concerns the landmark health-care reform enacted by President Obama and Congress in 2010. As we will shortly see, it provides a useful additional policy change with which to consider the feedback scenario.

Starting with NSA surveillance, the control group is asked, "Do you think that the federal government should monitor telephone conversations, banking transactions, and email between American citizens in the United States?" In one treatment-effects condition, the target is characterized as American citizens of Middle Eastern background. A second treatment prefaces the question with information about a relevant piece of counterterrorism legislation: "As you may know, the 2008 Foreign Intelligence Surveillance Amendments Act [FISA Act] gives government agencies new powers to engage in domestic surveillance of both citizens and foreign nationals without getting a court order allowing them to do so."

What makes this new experiment useful is the direct relevance of the 2008 FISA Act to the electronic surveillance issue. By giving retroactive legal status to the Bush administration's earlier illegal ("warrantless") domestic spying activities, as well as immunity to telecommunications companies for participating, the 2008 law provides a comprehensive and legitimating legal shield for new war on terror activity. Furthermore, the 2008 FISA Act is a good candidate for obscurity, given that few survey respondents can be expected to know these details off the top of their head, even when they are compelled to think about surveillance of American citizens. Of course, as discussed earlier, if survey respondents were, however, thinking about the 2008 FISA law when asked the control group question, the new experiment will return a non-significant result. We simply will not know more until we get to the results of the experiment.

Our second counterterrorism feedback experiment concerns the practice of waterboarding. In contrast to the after-the-fact legalization of domestic surveillance activity, waterboarding (as an instance of the larger category of torture) was rendered illegal by President Obama during his first week in office. We exploit this fact in the design of the waterboarding experiment. First we ask respondents, "In recent years, the government sometimes used a technique known as waterboarding on terrorist suspects in an effort to gain information about threats to the United States. Do you approve or disapprove of the use of waterboarding on terrorist suspects?" For the policy feedback experiment, we insert the following additional item of information, "As you may know, in 2009, President Obama issued an order stopping the use of coercive interrogation methods." If, indeed, feedback processes can be detected by this experiment, we expect that priming respondents with information about a presidential order will significantly reduce support for waterboarding.

The third and final experiment pursues policy feedback into the domain of social policy. This is informative because the treatment effect again involves legislation with respect to which President Obama was central (the Affordable Care Act) but also provides a comparative perspective on health care versus war on terror policies. In the control group question, we use a General Social Survey item, asking respondents, "Are we spending too much, too little, or about the right amount of money on improving the nation's health?" The policy feedback treatment is the following prefatory sentence, "As you may know, earlier this year, President Obama and Congress passed legislation that extends health insurance coverage to the large majority of Americans."

Results

We start by testing hypotheses about feedback effects. We then turn to our substantive results.

Interaction Tests and Hypotheses About Feedback Mechanisms

The results in table 6.1 provide relevant evidence concerning our interaction tests. These results are tests for interactions between experimental exposure to policy feedback and covariates measuring mechanisms of interest. Of particular relevance to the clash between global versus contingency perspectives are interactions involving, respectively, threat per-

Table 6.1 Feedback and Interaction Effects[a]

	× Threat Perception	× Authoritarianism	× Partisanship	× Education	× Religion	× Race
NSA surveillance	F(2) = 3.84	F(2) = 2.62	F(2) = .42	F(2) = 2.47	F(2) = .81	F(2) = .01
	p = .02	p = .07	p = .66	p = .09	p = .45	p = .99
$\beta_{\text{FISA Act}}$ (SE)	**.09** (.04)	.01 (.01)	.01 (.02)	.01 (.01)	.04 (.07)	<.01 (.09)
$\beta_{\text{ME backgr.}}$ (SE)	**.11** (.04)	.03 (.01)[b]	.01 (.02)	<−.02 (.01)	.09 (.07)	<.02 (.07)
Waterboarding	F(1) = 1.51	F(1) = 1.57	F(1) = .29	F(1) = .46	F(1) = 1.97	F(1) = .11
	p = .22	p = .21	p = .59	p = .50	p = .16	p = .74
$\beta_{\text{Pres. Obama}}$ (SE)	.05 (.04)	<−.02 (.01)	−.01 (.01)	<.02 (.01)	−.10 (.07)	.03 (.09)

Source: Authors' estimates based on analysis of Surveys of American Policy Attitudes (Brooks and Manza, various years).

Note: NSA = National Security Agency; FISA Act = Foreign Intelligence Surveillance Amendments Act; ME backgr. = Middle Eastern background.

[a]Bolded entry indicates significance at $p < .05$.

[b]Interaction not significant ($\beta_{\text{ME backgr.}} < .03$, SE = .01, $p = .05$) when estimated in model with interactions involving threat perceptions.

ceptions and partisanship. As in preceding chapters, we also consider several other candidates relevant to the case of counterterrorism policy attitudes.

The tests for NSA surveillance provide evidence for interactions involving threat perceptions. Initially, there is also some possible evidence for an interaction involving authoritarianism. But as summarized in table note b, this interaction coefficient falls into nonsignificance when estimated in a model including the threat perception interactions. The existence of an interaction involving threat perceptions lines up with expectations of the global, interest-centered view of feedback mechanisms, which we will discuss further.

The second set of results in table 6.1 are for the waterboarding experiment, which show no evidence for any interactions whatsoever. This indicates that when individuals are exposed to information about the presidential order banning torture, there is no selective pattern of responsiveness. The third and final experiment, for health spending, shows a similar result. As summarized in table 6.2, interaction test results are all quite far from the critical $p < .05$ threshold. In this case as well, we find little evidence for the operation of heuristic information processing, particularly as involving partisan filters among survey respondents.

Counterterrorism Policy Feedback Effects

With the interaction tests accounted for, we can now look at the evidence for policy feedback itself. Figure 6.1 summarizes the picture for the NSA surveillance experiment. The control group and both experimental conditions all make reference to the target group as being American citizens. But as summarized in the figure, but there are significant group differences involving not only the Middle Eastern background condition but also the new condition that primes respondents to think about the 2008 FISA Act. In both cases, the experimental treatments substantially raise support for surveillance of American citizens.

Although there is evidence of policy feedback effects, there is also an interaction involving respondents' threat perceptions. To extend and refine our interpretation, we present in figure 6.2 predicted effects of threat perceptions for each of the three NSA surveillance conditions. Starting with the control group, the nearly flat line connecting estimates reveals that threat perceptions have little effect in this condition. Indeed the −0.02 coefficient capturing this effect is not significant, indicating that respondents' existing perceptions of terrorism threats are not cognitively mobilized by the initial question asking about government monitoring of phone, banking, and email records among American citizens.

Asking respondents the same question, but now with experimental

Table 6.2 Feedback and Interaction Effects[a]

	× Economic Evaluations	× Partisanship	× Education	× Religion	× Race
Health spending	$\chi^2(2) = 1.72$ $p = .42$	$\chi^2(2) = 3.27$ $p = .19$	$\chi^2(2) = 1.93$ $p = .38$	$\chi^2(2) = 1.52$ $p = .47$	$\chi^2(2) = 1.96$ $p = .38$

Source: Authors' estimates based on Surveys of American Policy Attitudes (Brooks and Manza, various years).
[a]Bolded entry indicates significance at $p < .05$.

Figure 6.1   Policy Feedback and the NSA Surveillance Experiment

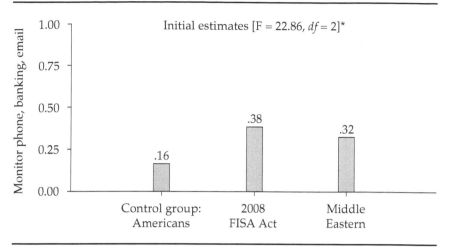

Source: Authors' calculations based on Surveys of American Policy Attitudes (Brooks and Manza, various years).
Note: NSA = National Security Agency; FISA Act = Foreign Intelligence Surveillance Amendments Act.
*Indicates significance at $p < .05$

Figure 6.2   Policy Feedback in Greater Detail[a]

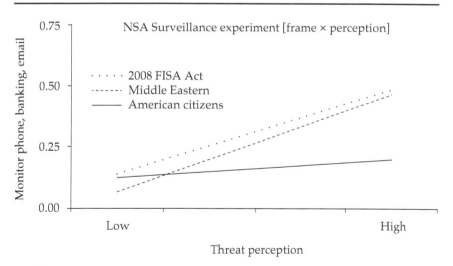

Source: Authors' estimates based on analysis of Surveys of American Policy Attitudes (Brooks and Manza, various years).
Note: NSA = National Security Agency; FISA Act = Foreign Intelligence Surveillance Amendments Act.
[a] Effect of threat perception in the "American citizens" condition is not significant ($\beta = .02$, SE = .03).

Figure 6.3   The Waterboarding Experiment

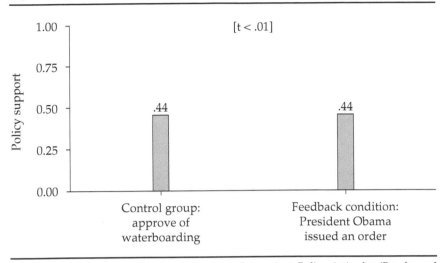

Source: Authors' estimates based on Surveys of American Policy Attitudes (Brooks and Manza, various years).

primes for the Middle Eastern background target group and for the 2008 FISA Act, changes the picture substantially. In both experimental conditions, threat perceptions now have sizeable (and fairly comparable) effects. In comparison with the control group, respondents who feel threatened in the transitional ethnicity and policy feedback conditions are disproportionately more supportive of NSA surveillance.

As illustrated in figure 6.2, the effects of the experimental treatments themselves are most substantial among individuals who are at high levels of threat perceptions. It is respondents who come into the survey worried about terrorism who are most at risk of attitude change. These individuals are susceptible to having their attitudes toward government surveillance quickly realigned by new information about counterterrorism laws or the ethnic background of policy targets.

The waterboarding experiment provides a dramatic contrast. Unlike the NSA surveillance experiment, the waterboarding experiment presents respondents with information about the ratcheting-back of a war on terror activity. As summarized in figure 6.3, the treatment is information about the presidential order prohibiting coercive interrogation techniques. Perhaps surprisingly, we find no evidence for a feedback effect. Exposure to the feedback condition does little to change respondents' attitudes toward the practice at hand.

We find the waterboarding results intriguing. Certainly they are unexpected, because we expect, if anything, the newly available information to implicitly call into question the positions that supporters endorse.

Possibly, of course, individuals in the control group are already acting on or even actively resisting information about the newly illegal status of waterboarding. But even so, that would still lead to the same notably sharp contrast with the NSA surveillance experiment. Instead, as discussed in the next section, it appears that counterterrorism policy feedbacks are asymmetrical. They propel individuals into greater policy support when new laws enable contentious practices but fail to ratchet back policy support when other laws instead rein in war on terror activities.

Health Spending as a Comparison Case

We have one experiment left, involving an important and widely debated domestic policy issue: national health policy. This comparison is instructive in that health-care reform is the domestic policy question that has received the most public attention and controversy since the election of Barack Obama in 2008. Moreover, the Obama administration's main domestic policy achievement has been the 2010 passage of the Affordable Care Act (ACA), which provided expanded coverage options for most uninsured Americans, increased subsidies for poor Americans and expanded Medicaid coverage, and mandated that everyone would have to have health insurance at rates linked to earned income.

Using the General Social Survey (GSS) spending item as our control group, respondents indicate "too little," "too much," or "about right" when asked about their preferences for health spending. The treatment is information about the recently passed ACA by the then Democrat-controlled Congress in 2010. We treat the trichotomous response items as nominal, using a chi-square test to gauge evidence for policy feedback. As summarized in figure 6.4, the test returns evidence of a significant treatment effect.

The big surprise, however, is that respondents' preferences in the feedback condition show considerably less support for health spending than those in the control group. In the control group, for instance, 49 percent of respondents choose the "too little" category, whereas 36 percent do so in the feedback condition. And whereas only 25 percent see health spending as currently "too much" in the control group, 44 percent do in the feedback condition.

In the case of health policy attitudes, then, experimental evidence indicates policy feedback effects. But these effects operate to push individuals in an explicitly contrary direction. Instead of falling in line with the new policy reality, as cognitive dissonance theory would again predict, information about the passage of a landmark new bill lowers support for health spending and perhaps activism as well. As in the waterboarding experiment, this is likely to be unwelcome news for supporters of egalitarian public policies. But, unlike both the waterboarding and

Figure 6.4   The Health Spending Experiment

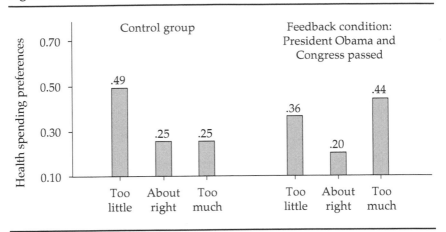

Source: Authors' estimates based on wSurveys of American Policy Attitudes (Brooks and Manza, various years).
*Spending preferences differ across control and feedback conditions: $\chi^2(2) = 23.49, p = .00$.

NSA surveillance experiments, the health spending experiment has unveiled a striking new side to policy feedback effects. Because experiments are novel for policy feedback scholarship, much remains to be done. For the current study, however, we now have a rich new array of results with which to reconsider questions concerning public opinion on counterterrorism.

Conclusion

When and why does policy feedback occur? Since the pioneering work of Douglass North (1990) and Paul Pierson (1993), an increasingly influential view among many scholars has been that policy change redirects group interests and their incentives to comply with new institutional arrangements. Although most debates over policy feedback have not involved direct investigations of public opinion, when scholars have examined the impact of policy change on public preferences, the results suggest important complications. For example, research on the 1996 reform of the AFDC program has constructively challenged this consensus (Soss and Schram 2007; Dyck and Hussey 2008), bringing to light a powerful case of nonfeedback and demonstrating the importance of grappling with conditions and processes that moderate policy feedbacks on opinion.

This has opened for consideration an important issue for scholarship on policy-attitude formation and also for research on institutional change and policymaking. This issue takes on particular relevance when it comes to the challenge of understanding public opinion on the war on terror. We consider implications for policy feedback scholarship and then for our focus on counterterrorism attitudes.

Policy Feedback

Viewed broadly, our survey experimental results lend new momentum to policy feedback scholarship. We find evidence of policy feedback effects in two of three experiments. Of course, we must caution that these experiments concern information about major instances of policy change, namely, the 2008 FISA bill providing extensive retroactive legality to domestic electronic surveillance, and the 2010 ACA restructuring U.S. health policy and ultimately extending coverage to tens of millions. Nonetheless, because our feedback experiments expose individuals to information about policy change that those in the control group may already have, the evidence at hand may, if anything, understate the strength or scope of feedback processes for major issues of this sort.

What of the clash between universal and contingency perspectives underlying scholarship on policy feedback? Initially, we might expect counterterrorism policy feedbacks to be best explicated by the literature on heuristics and biases. But our three experiments provide no instances of relevant interactions involving partisanship as a key candidate for information filtering.

Turning to mechanisms underlying more global views of how policy feedbacks operate, we do have a case—NSA surveillance—in which the dynamics at work approximate an interest-centered mechanism. In this experiment, individuals at high levels of threat perceptions are most responsive to having policy change information reorient their attitudes. Threat perceptions thus may expose individuals to having their attitudes swiftly realigned when counterterrorism policies are implemented. In this sense, they create a demand or interest on the part of those who already feel threatened.

By the same token, interest-centered explanations may not always provide the explanation in every case of feedback. This is suggested by the absence of effects of policy change in the waterboarding experiment, alongside the even more dramatic opinion reversal discovered in the health-care experiment. In both cases, we might expect new patterns of vested interests, or, alternatively, cognitive dissonance, to result in opinions falling in line with the new policy realities at hand. But this is far from what the results point to.

Health spending is particularly intriguing in this context. Remember that what we have found goes well beyond the conventional scenario in which opponents of health-care reforms oppose egalitarian reforms or more spending and are stable in these orientations. Instead, the health spending experiment suggests a more dynamic scenario: when primed to consider new information about the passage of the health-care reform bill, respondents move toward favoring much lower levels of spending.

We have observed this pattern of oppositional opinion change only in the domain of health spending. But just like the 1996 case of U.S. welfare reform, the 2010 case of health policy reform is intrinsically important. Given the nature of stakes, major players, and issues at hand, it also seems probable that health policy opinions in 2010 were formed in a set of conditions found elsewhere. In the contemporary United States, we expect that other policy domains may exhibit similar patterns of largely negative public response, even when legislation has already been passed.

Although there is clearly more to study here, the key finding we emphasize concerns the directionality of policy feedback effects. What the health spending experiment demonstrates is that rather than policy change always operating to bring opinions closer in line with reality, it may at times do the reverse, generating greater public opposition. This is an important scenario for policy feedback scholarship to consider and incorporate.[3]

What do our results say about the causes and conditions behind war on terror attitudes?

The first point is by now familiar: counterterrorism attitudes appear malleable in the face of information about policy change. But what is operating in this chapter represents a new factor beyond target group and threat priming. What is particularly surprising and informative is how counterterrorism feedbacks appear to work mainly in just one direction, toward enhanced support.

This asymmetry should be challenging for critics of the war on terrorism, and for scholars who expect counterterrorism policy support to dwindle over time. At face value, it would mean that counterterrorism policy rollback, beyond the rather singular presidential orders of January 2009, may by itself do little to bring the public back to a more nuanced position in regard to the trade-off between civil liberties and security, at least in the short term. Indeed, it may be harder to use government activism to rein in support for war on terror excesses than it is to unleash new public policies that may restrict rights yet garner citizen support.

When combined with results from previous chapters, it looks as if the historical context defined by the Obama administration may offer limited opportunity for inducing opinion change through executive orders or new legislation, at least when either liberal or egalitarian shifts in attitudes are of interest. That may be surprising to some commentators but is consistent with the over-time trends we consider in chapter 3. Recall that despite an historic presidential campaign and election outcome, attitudes related to war on terror policies showed considerable stability in the aggregate from 2007 to 2009, then onward through 2010.

Taken together, the policy feedback results make it look like counterterrorism policy support is robust when it comes to the direction of malleability. Remember that our experiments mimic policy change, and they will thus tend, if anything, to underestimate effects of the earlier shocks generated by President Bush's policy responses to the 2001 attacks. It is informative that nearly a decade after 9/11, the 2010 SAPA data found that the public responded to information about yet another controversial, new (2008) piece of counterterrorism legislation with enhanced support for domestic surveillance activities.

To be sure, in the NSA surveillance experiment respondents are moving from what are initially low levels of policy support in the control group condition. But here, as in other counterterrorism domains, the new conditions or considerations measured by our treatments buttress support for war on terror. We can now see that this degree of asymmetry in the public's reasoning and orientation helps explain support over time for many war on terror policies. In both our survey experiments and in the real world, opportunities are ample for rights-oriented or critical considerations to register. But so far, they have tended not to do so.

Conclusion

IT IS now more than a decade since the terrorist attacks of 9/11 that shocked America and set the U.S. government on a policy course that departed profoundly and unexpectedly from the liberal drift of recent decades. By most conventional measures, the war on terror is more or less over. Al-Qaeda terrorist networks around the world have been disrupted, and its leaders are mostly dead or on the run. Since 9/11, the handful of al-Qaeda plots and larger number of emulations, some homegrown, have failed in their attempts to successfully carry out a new terror attack on the United States.[1] In 2010, Central Intelligence Agency (CIA) Director Leon Panetta placed the number of al-Qaeda members in Afghanistan at "50 to 100, maybe less," suggesting that the organization had been radically diminished as a fighting force.[2] In 2011, the killing of Osama bin Laden and the postraid review of materials found in his hideaway revealed considerable degradation of al-Qaeda's remaining organizational capacity. The stated goals of the Bush administration at the beginning of the counterterrorism campaign—to keep Americans safe and to punish the perpetrators of the 9/11 attacks—have by now largely been achieved.[3]

But these successes have come at a price when areas beyond the strategic goal of fighting terrorism are considered, and they now appear to have become a permanent feature of American institutions. For several years after 9/11, the Bush administration sanctioned and deployed a program of using torture against terrorism suspects that, when it was revealed, shocked the world and shamed our allies. The ongoing, permanent detention of a large number of individuals without trial—sanctioned permanently by President Obama's executive order of March 7, 2011—departs sharply from the U.S. Constitution and the rule of law, as understood both in the Anglo American tradition and in contemporary international law. So too is the retroactively legalized, warrantless electronic surveillance of the American population, and extensive use of ethnic profiling by law enforcement and government agencies.

The new set of government surveillance institutions and coercive powers do not have clear limits. According to legal experts and commentators, these new rules and capacities potentially extend to any activist group or critic that the government labels as a national security threat.[4] Post-9/11 laws and policies have reversed rights protections sought in the wake of revelations concerning abuses by the Federal Bureau of Investigation (FBI) under J. Edgar Hoover and by the Nixon White House in the Watergate era. The new policies may establish a model for future U.S. governments, and because their reach is global, the rest of the world will likely feel their impact as well.

A fundamental empirical paradox is associated with these policies. Post-9/11 counterterrorism policies appear to be founded on an exaggerated view of the risks of terrorism. Even in the highly unusual context of 2001, the risk of dying from a terrorist attack in the U.S. was just one in 101,000 (Mueller and Stewart 2010). That contrasts with the drastically higher risks of homicide death (one in 22,000), dying in a traffic accident (one in 8,000), and cancer-related fatalities (one in 540). As we noted earlier, even bathtub drowning (one in 79,000) might be seen as posing a far greater risk to American lives in 2001 than Osama bin Laden and al-Qaeda did.

Proclamations of wartime conditions made earlier during the administration of President Bush suggest another instructive comparison. During World War II, the annual fatality risk was a sizeable one in 221. But in the years immediately after the 9/11 attacks, al-Qaeda attacks outside war zones killed virtually no Americans (Mueller 2006). Yet to date, we have spent over $700 billion on counterterrorism measures, above what federal, state, and local governments were spending on counterterrorism programs in 2001 (and not taking into account the costs of the wars in Iraq and Afghanistan) (Mueller and Stewart 2011). Evidence-based policy appears to suggest conclusions running contrary to the assumption that war on terror policies are proportional to the reality of terrorist threats. Empirically based risk assessments such as these have received surprisingly little attention in the media or, for the most part, in political and policy debates surrounding the war on terror. But they represent an important scholarly background to our investigations. So far, what the actuarial assessments tell us is that the war on terror and its accompanying policies exceed the magnitude of actual threats to American lives and welfare.[5] How did these developments affect the attitudes and beliefs of ordinary Americans?

Unleashing the Dark Side of Public Attitudes

In this book, we have called attention to a critical aspect of the war on terror that has received relatively little attention in the media or in public debate and only a modest amount of social science research. This is the activation of a "dark side" of American public opinion, in which support for coercive policies may become relatively enduring, persisting beyond the initial context in which political leaders offered their original justifications. We have emphasized the importance of both policy entrepreneurship and the role of opinion inertia in creating and sustaining the biases and beliefs underlying counterterrorism opinions. Without the new and contentious counterterrorism practices after the 9/11 attacks, the American public would have had no laws and policies to think about in the first place. But, once activated and given symbolic objects that provide key points of reference, the policy reasoning and attitudes of Americans appear to have taken hold in ways exceeding the degree of real threats and historical conditions.

This dark side of U.S. public opinion relates to previous key episodes investigated by legal scholars, historians, political psychologists, and opinion researchers over the last 100 years. The specter of popular support for rights and liberties violations, for instance, evident at the height of the McCarthy period and in later conflicts surrounding civil liberties and protest in the 1960s and 1970s, commanded widespread attention among an earlier generation of social scientists. Such episodes provided earlier evidence about what can happen when partisan entrepreneurs or social movements activate intolerant sentiments or restrictive attitudes. According to the historian Richard Hofstadter, this paranoid style has been a recurrent feature of U.S. political life, raising questions about just how extensive or easily mobilized are illiberal leanings among the American public.

In the post 9/11 period, we find evidence that Americans tended to respond rapidly, even instantaneously, to virtually any references to terrorist threats, giving greater support to many war on terror policies. We have found evidence that these processes often involve deep symbolism rather than responsiveness to real historical events. A degree of asymmetry seems apparent as well, in that the experimental cues having the largest effects tend to raise, rather than lower, counterterrorism policy support.

Through 2010, public support was notably strong for many elements of the war on terror, including especially the military commissions system, assassination, and warrantless electronic surveillance (particularly of non-Americans). In contrast, practices involving torture garnered much lower support. It is striking how precisely this maps onto the one counterterrorism practice explicitly banned by President Obama in 2009, and how counterterrorism measures receiving greater public support have persisted. Our overall evidence of continuing public support for the war on terror helps solve an important puzzle and provides foundation for considering the future of American policy in this area.

The Possibility of Path Dependence

A puzzle that the evidence presented in this book helps unravel is why counterterrorism policies have persisted even in the face of growing evidence that the risks posed by international terrorism were contained and with the passage of time since the 2001 attacks. This puzzle grew after the political sea change represented by Democratic Party's electoral victories in 2006 and 2008, and the election of President Barack Obama. It is noteworthy that Americans during the years straddling the 2008 elections could so readily be primed into feeling threatened by a hypothetical terrorist attack room but simultaneously fail to respond to the unfolding of actual events, including a number of new terrorist plots. So far at least, this insulation of the opinion formation process from the historical context may place a degree of constraint on any government committed to undoing the more popular of counterterrorism measures. So too do our experimental results showing that negative perceptions of outsider groups, when mobilized as the target of counterterrorism measures, substantially enhance support for policy.

The evidence we have presented in this book is consistent, we believe, with a path-dependent interpretation of policy change. Once the Bush administration undertook a high-intensity counterterrorism agenda, it created both organized constituencies and bureaucracies with an interest in maintaining those policies and successfully mobilized mass support for the new agenda. Not all policies or policy change affect public opinion in this way, but counterterrorism policies clearly did.

Of relevance in this context is how any mandate for a redirection in the war on terror following the 2008 election has almost entirely faded. Evidence for this proposition, reviewed more extensively in chapter 1, exists on a number of fronts. President Obama and his advisors have done little to ratchet back the "unitary executive" doctrine used by the administration of President George W. Bush to justify domestic electronic surveillance. The system of military prisons overseas, particularly the Bagram detention center in Afghanistan, alongside presidential authorization of assassination has been maintained. The Obama administration has asserted the right to conduct renditions of terrorism suspects without congressional or judicial review and has generally allowed few inquiries into misdeeds by Bush administration officials. After a few years of contentious debate and a failed attempt to try 9/11 criminal mastermind Khalid Shaikh Mohammed in a federal court in New York City, plans to close the Guantanamo Bay facility have been abandoned.

A significant part of the explanation for the persistence of these policy and legal arrangements must lie, we believe, with frequently high levels of public support and their tendencies in the face of experimental manipulation toward greater support. Connected to this is the further role of threat communication by politicians and the mass media. It is, we would emphasize, far easier to communicate threats, whatever their degree of magnitude or likelihood, than to ratchet their communication back to pre-9/11 levels. Indeed, this has been a key theme in past scholarship on the asymmetric features of media coverage and political discourse surrounding terrorism (Merolla and Zechmeister 2009; Nacos, Block-Elkon, and Shapiro 2011).

During the past decade, voters have seen the Republican Party as the preferred party for fighting terrorism (Polling Report 2012). As a result of this partisan perception, Republican politicians have had incentives to look for opportunities to portray Democrats as ineffectual on terrorism and to promote the terrorist threat, and Democrats have a real motivation not to change or substantially rethink policy for fear of being attacked for weakness. As to the media, terrorism and terror plots of all variety and often questionable magnitude continue to receive extensive media attention but little follow-up when they prove false or misleading (Mueller 2006, 2008; Nacos 2007). They also provide virtually no information or perspective with which the public can process in more realistic fashion the actual risks involved.

Taking the big picture into account, it may be instructive to ask whether some aspects of Osama bin Laden's earlier goal of sowing fear into the hearts and minds of the "infidels" of America could have gained some traction through unanticipated means. Many Americans live under the shadow of the 9/11 era, continuing to support policies and programs that have been launched and justified by reference to claims about new and "existential" conflicts. Although large expenditures on the war on terror will not, by themselves, bankrupt the United States, the diversion of resources and institutionalization of policies puts a spotlight on an unexpected and powerfully self-reinforcing feature of contemporary American politics.

Dynamics and Limits of Public Support for Counterterrorism

Our main empirical goal in this book has been to understand the underlying sources of mass attitudes toward different policy dimensions of the war on terror in a detailed and more comprehensive way than has previously been attempted. We have drawn from three national telephone surveys we conducted in 2007, 2009, and 2010. Our Surveys of American Policy Attitudes contain an array of embedded experiments into the dynamics of counterterrorism opinion formation, where experimental treatments track key ideas and levers that can shape people's largely unconscious and at times habitual thinking.

As past work in this area from which we build has demonstrated, the post-9/11 war on terror presents an analytically rich domain for understanding the formation and significance of public attitudes toward civil liberties and civil rights (see, for example, Huddy et al. 2005; Davis 2007; Hetherington and Weiler 2009). Even more so than civil liberties conflicts and controversies in the 1980s and 1990s, the past decade's sustained application of laboratory and survey opinions demonstrates something important, namely, that multiple, proximate mechanisms shape the formation of attitudes among individuals about the war on terror. Threat communication is one, as are target group cues involving national identity and transnational ethnic identity that we have investigated.

Experiments outside the laboratory give us new confidence in the strength of these cognitive factors. Taken as a whole, our results convey an important thematic lesson. Baseline counterterrorism opinion, as measured by survey items that generically reference counterterrorism laws or activities, is often readily dislodged by the communication of threats, references to policy change, and specific cues concerning the identity characteristics of groups targeted by a policy. In our policy feedback experiments, we found it easier to enhance counterterrorism support by referring to passage of war on terror laws and ratchet back support by cueing reference to executive orders banning a past practice.

Confirming Threat-Based Accounts

A theorem of classical social psychology is that the successful deployment of threats tends to generate highly illiberal and rights-restricting responses on the part of individuals. Threat is often easy to manipulate and more motivating than simple fear. A powerful accomplishment of past war on terror scholarship has been to demonstrate the partisan political relevance of threat to opinion formation (Lavine, Lodge, and Freitas 2005; Merolla and Zechmeister 2009; Hetherington and Suhay 2011).

Our experiments complement this scholarship in two ways. First, with respect to time, our results extend previous estimates with new survey data and experiments spanning the years 2007, 2009, and 2010. Second, using comparatively modest experimental cues—typically involving a single-sentence reference such as "What if the government was responding to a terrorist act that had just taken place?"—we find significant impacts on survey responses. We have been struck by the strength of the threat results on both counts. In comparison, for instance, to Merolla and Zechmeister's (2009) audiovisual treatments in laboratory settings, our own threat treatments seem relatively anemic. But they too produce rather massive impacts on counterterrorism opinion formation. As we discussed in chapter 4, threat primes are the single largest effect in experiments in which they are deployed.

We have also been surprised by the magnitude of such impacts in 2010, nearly a decade after the original 9/11 effects. Far from declining in efficacy, threat priming appears remarkably potent. This attests to the durable salience of terrorism-related issues and also to their highly symbolic construction. This symbolic dimension is important. Recall that our over-time tracking of repeated policy-attitude items found only one instance (out of ten issue domains) of opinion change during the period from 2007 to 2010. That is itself remarkable in light of tumultuous shifts in the political and policy environment during this period. But combined with the experimental results, the repeated survey analysis illustrates the point. In the aggregate, the public simply did not respond to real trends and events involving changes in government and the unfolding of a series of new terrorist plots. Yet Americans also show themselves to be more than ready to respond to experimental information about terrorist threats, even when hypothetical. These symbolic levers behind opinion formation are all the more notable in mattering in the face of the apparent non-effects of real changes in the environment.

American Nationalism and Target-Group Biases

According to historical scholarship, underlying periods of rights suppression have often seen broader mobilization of the boundaries of the American population as a whole. Nationalism and national identity is a powerful resource that partisan entrepreneurs have in their repertoire to deploy. It is one that enabled politicians and government officials to claim new authority and give priority to national security over rights protections in such episodes as the Palmer Raids following World War I, the internment of Japanese Americans in World War II, and the hunt for subversives and COINTELPRO (Counter Intelligence Program) surveillance conducted by the FBI under J. Edgar Hoover in the 1950s and 1960s. Is the post-9/11 era one in which liberal and international or humanitarian messages have been less likely to be received than nationalist-tinged and threat-accentuating ones in the competition for the American public's attention?

Complementing historical and communications scholarship in this area (Hutcheson et al. 2004; McCartney 2004; Lieven 2005), we find novel evidence for the operation of national identity as a significant lens through which Americans view policy. In our experiments, when respondents are primed to think that American citizens are the target of coercive policies, support tends to decline significantly. Similarly, an alternative cuing of policy targets as foreign nationals tends to raise support. We find the American public gives priority to their own rights and liberties but shows far less willingness to extend protections to the rest of the world's citizens. This underlying restriction is notable in its own right and parallels rather provocatively the far greater rights violations meted out to foreign nationals in the war on terror.[6]

A good deal of scholarship has considered in various ways the possibility of other, overlapping, but ultimately more powerful cleavages than national identity. We have been intrigued by this scenario and have presented a variety of experimental and statistical tests to tease out the potentially confounding roles of race and religion as leading candidates. Perhaps when people think about American citizens, particularly when they are motivated to protect the rights of Americans but not others, they are actually thinking about whites or Christians?

We find, however, little evidence for such conjectures. Experimental cues involving national identity characteristics operate the same among whites and nonwhites and among self-identified Christians versus others. Even more telling evidence comes from our experiments manipulating the national identity status of a key insider group (Christians) and a second outsider group (people from the Middle East). So powerful is the impact of U.S. citizenship status that its experimental manipulations can prompt respondents to display indistinguishable affect toward these two initially polar groups. Under experimental conditions, Christians who are not U.S. citizens now elicit the same degree of emotional warmth as people from the Middle East who are U.S. citizens. American citizenship status, in short, is remarkably important as such, and not just as a cover for other, different identity attributions.

But a second, more powerful type of dynamic cue is at hand. It is not just national identities that are relevant and operate dynamically in shaping counterterrorism attitudes. Transnational ethnic identities appear to matter a great deal. We know from our feeling thermometer experiments that groups such as Muslims and people from the Middle East elicit much cooler responses, even when we compare systematically with established domestic outsider groups such as blacks. Armed with these results, what we have looked further into is whether the novel transnational ethnic identity cues also operate when it comes to policy-attitude formation.

Our results suggest an affirmative answer. Even when holding constant American citizenship status, the ethnic cue for people from the Middle East tends to have significant effects. By itself, it increases support for counterterrorism policies and measures. As a target group, then, it is not just distinctions between U.S. citizens and others that matter. A further, potent source of symbolic bias is at work.

We should be clear that we have not directly tested a parallel, domestic target group idea, that it is blacks or perhaps Latinos as targets that are enhancing counterterrorism policy support. Following past scholarship (Kinder and Kam 2009), we think the case for using these established target groups is powerfully established as regards domestic policy. But analytically, the linkage to reasoning about the war on terror seems less clear and possibly more convoluted. We suspect that without experiments, statistical associations between domestic target group measures and counterterrorism attitude measures call for additional analyses.

Regardless, the key message of these results concerns transnational ethnic cues, which are both firmly rooted in our empirical results and of crucial relevance to war on terror attitude formation. Theoretically, these results confirm the utility of a broadened conceptualization of ethnocentrism. Insiders and outsiders are defined not only within U.S. national borders but also with reference to other nations or clusters of countries that define meaningful group identities in the war on terror.

An important footnote to these target group biases concerns the moderating effects of education. It is education, and only education, that separately channels the receptivity of individuals to the treatments in more than one of our experiments. In the military commissions experiment, for instance, the impact of transnational ethnic cues is much smaller among highly educated respondents. We know from classical scholarship that education is often associated with greater cosmopolitanism and liberalism. Our new results reveal a further side to education as a moderator of target group biases. That education may at higher levels insulate individuals from target group priming is important. It anticipates a scenario through which new contexts and events could result in the ratcheting back of public support for counterterrorism measures.

Qualifications and Possible Futures

Could things change in the near future? The education results take us to scenarios that go speculatively yet informatively beyond path dependency claims and the simple expectation that counterterrorism policy attitudes may well look the same in coming years as they do now. Three scenarios extend beyond our results.

The first possibility is that the views of the highly educated may be a harbinger of things to come. In the influential model of opinion change offered by John Zaller (1992) for instance, it is societal elites, especially as defined by education level and sometimes occupation, who respond more quickly to expert opinion shifts in the macro environment. From this perspective, the main and interaction effects of education in our study may conceivably indicate a burgeoning influence of opinion among some experts regarding the war on terror, and perhaps the rest of the population will eventually follow. That could push down policy support and in turn exert reform pressures among even the most timid of Democratic politicians as well as encourage a wider range of debate in the mass media.

A second scenario is exogenous shifts in policy positions on the part of political parties and officials. Currently, the leadership of both parties is in far less disagreement or explicit conflict than on most other policy issues. Inside the Democratic Party, antiwar and war on terror critics remain marginalized with respect to both congressional leadership and the White House. The Republican Party includes a small cadre of heterogeneous critics. As yet, however, they are also very far from the party's congressional leadership. During the 2012 presidential campaign, neither major party candidate discussed plans for downsizing counterterrorism measures.

This constellation of disparate and relatively unorganized critics would have to grow significantly for party leaders to have grounds for rethinking the magnitude and direction of the war on terror. But should intraparty opposition grow in one or both parties, new inducements to rethink policy opinions and widen the public debate would open up. The cognitive dissonance microfoundations discussed in chapter 6 might potentially translate these macro-level changes into micro-level adaptations, especially as the public hears about elite dissensus or a growing shift in direction. However distant this scenario may currently seem, the foreign policy crisis of the Vietnam War, combined with Watergate and the once-covert COINTELPRO surveillance program, prompted elite-driven policy changes of historical relevance.

Our third and final change scenario concerns the question of whose rights are at stake. Restrictive as the public's American target group biases appear, they may become a lever that undermines counterterrorism support. National identity biases are potent enough that it seems unlikely that people would readily extend equal rights sympathies to foreign nationals. But if perceptions grow that Americans' rights are being sacrificed in the name of the war on terror, opinions could shift profoundly and quite rapidly. Americans' generally positive views of rights and liberties for other Americans remain an important reality, and one central to the opinion liberalization tradition we discussed in chapter 2.[7]

A new conviction that counterterrorism policies violate Americans' liberties is unlikely to come about on the basis of autonomous reflections on the part of ordinary individuals. That is not how we know U.S. public opinion to form and be organized, at least as a general principle. By the same token, however, it is not unreasonable to envision a fuller emergence of media critics or activist entrepreneurs calling attention, with growing success, to a substantial pattern of violation of American citizens' rights. We know, for instance, that the scope of the ongoing National Security Agency (NSA) surveillance programs has led to encroachment on privacy protections and illegal searches as regards the telephone and email communication of thousands of American citizens, alongside the call records of millions of Americans as well. Should pointedly framed information about this pattern of counterterrorism activity come to the greater attention of citizens, a more critically inclined public might begin to call for surveillance policy reforms.

Final Thoughts

We emphasize three points in closing. The first concerns linkages to the macro environment of partisan political conflict, the media, and social movement organizations. We think the evidence in this book leads to the following inference: environmental changes in 2001, particularly as involving partisan entrepreneurship and very similar messages in the media, and on the part of many interest organizations, activated the public's willingness to support many of the new and intrusive counterterrorism policies.

That said, we cannot directly estimate whether a levels change in counterterrorism opinions occurred after 9/11. Such a change would indicate that measured policy attitudes had themselves shifted as a result of government officials' communication, the establishment of new policies, or the shock of the 2001 attacks. These questions will, however, gain traction with the passage of time. If, for instance, policy attitudes persist in their current levels even if government policies are modified, or, more modestly, if government officials shift their public rhetoric, it would be telling. It would be dramatic indication of the motivated reasoning scenario in which public opinion takes on substantial inertia because individuals are implicitly unwilling to question their prior beliefs, and those beliefs shape their processing of information.

Wholly separate from the issue of their historical origins and over-time trends, a second emphasis concerns the political and policy impact of contemporary counterterrorism opinions. Here, indications are clear that when it is high, public support for even contentious war on terror policies limit the "running room" for policy reform, making a rethinking of counterterrorism among political leaders a potentially costly and risky exercise. In general, we know that foreign policy and national security issues matter considerably to American voters' decision-making and behavior in elections (Aldrich et al. 2006), and evidence in the 2008 presidential election to this effect has been found (Brooks, Dodson, and Hotchkiss 2010).

Together, these points lead to our final theme, namely, the reality of mass opinion as a force to be reckoned with in scholarship on the politics of contemporary counterterrorism policy. For political psychologists and public opinion researchers, this point is well established. But for those who are in principle skeptical about the ontological or explanatory status of mass opinion, we also hope to have offered results and a broader portrait to fruitfully consider. Certain important analytical and historical puzzles cannot, we think, easily be answered without detailed consideration of the mass public. For example, what happened to voters as a result of the U.S. government's unexpected policy responses to the 9/11 attacks? Why, over time, have some challenger attempts by both activists and even entrepreneurs within the Democratic Party had such limited effects during the transition from the Bush to Obama presidencies? Whom do symbolic cues and threats propel in directions of enhanced policy support?

In all cases, we find compelling evidence that points to processes of mass opinion formation as yielding important answers. Understanding the politics of the war on terror without mass opinion may be akin to envisioning a contemporary production of Shakespeare without the possibility of an audience to which theatrical performers play, and with respect to which the tickets are purchased and the bills ultimately paid. The war on terror shows what many commentators and scholars may see as a darker side of American public opinion. Theoretical rejection of its existence, or an unwillingness to unpack its dynamics, would risk failing to engage one of the significant developments in the new millennium.

Notes

Introduction

1. According to one set of estimates, the amount spent to date on the war on terror and related wars in Iraq and Afghanistan is approximately $4 trillion (Eisenhower Study Group 2011).
2. Another little-known and potentially surprising feature of terrorism after the 9/11 attacks has involved the low representation of Muslims as perpetrators relative to population size. According to one recent study (Kurzman 2012), terrorism by Muslim Americans poses "a minuscule threat to public safety" in the United States.
3. Larry Bartels (2008, chap. 7) provides an instructive example in an analysis of the 2003 abolition of the inheritance tax. Deeply unpopular, it survived for a long period of time simply because no significant movement or policy coalition demanded its abolition. The movement against the "death tax," Bartels argues, succeeded because it activated latent beliefs and dispositions on the part of voters.

Chapter 1

1. The Hofstadter thesis has been widely debated. One key question is whether these campaigns were driven from above by political elites, threatened by the possibilities of radical mobilization from below, or whether they were populist outbursts emerging primarily from below (for example, Bell 1960; Wolfe 1973; Goldstein 2001). Similarly, the question of whether these campaigns were intertwined with rational interests or were entirely irrational generated considerable scholarly attention (for example, Rogin 1987, chap. 9). Yet Hofstadter's basic insight—that a politics of paranoia has long been an important theme in American political history—appears amply borne out by the historical record.
2. As discussed in the introduction, in 2001 the risk of homicide death (one in 22,000), dying in a traffic accident (one in 8,000), and cancer-related fatalities (one in 540) exceeded the parallel risk of dying from terrorism (Mueller and Stewart 2010).
3. The complicated maneuverings of the Iran-Contra affair in 1985 and 1986 provided the most flagrant violation of domestic and international law. Iran-

Contra was a rogue operation approved by the White House, in which arms were first sold to Iran and subsequent profits were then channeled to provide support to the Contra rebels in Nicaragua. The Iran-Contra affair nonetheless suggested to many observers just how entrenched the rights revolution had become. Senior White House officials were forced to testify before Congress, resulting in a number of resignations and criminal investigations.

4. The Geneva Conventions are a set of four international agreements (first signed in 1864, 1906, 1929, and, after World War II, amended with additional provisions added in 1949, and later packages of amendments in 1977 and 2005). The agreements specify rules for the treatment of prisoners of war, including with respect to the wounded and civilian populations. The accord establishes that prisoners of war cannot be tortured or deliberately injured; they must be treated humanely and provided adequate food, shelter, and access to medical care; and they cannot be incarcerated at the end of hostilities or indefinitely without a fair trial (if war crimes are alleged). The 1949 negotiations were chaired and led by the United States, and the United States closely followed the guidelines during the Korean and Vietnam Wars.

5. Other discussions of 24 and its impact can be found in Mayer (2008) and Sands (2008). The show appeared to exert so much influence it was feared by some officials to be encouraging excessive enthusiasm among U.S. military personnel for harsh interrogation and the show's producers were urged to revise the tone accordingly (Buncombe 2007; Mayer 2007). The implications of the ticking time bomb have been invoked in many contexts; for example, philosophical debates over morality versus torture (compare Allhof 2005; Zizek 2006), or by the prominent legal scholar Alan Dershowitz (2002), who surprised many in offering a cautious defense of torture (albeit requiring prior court warrant), citing the scenario of the ticking time bomb in his justification. Supreme Court Justice Antonin Scalia even declared at an international jurist conference that "Jack Bauer saved Los Angeles. . . . He saved hundreds of thousands of lives . . . Are you going to convict Jack Bauer? . . . Say that criminal law is against him? 'You have the right to a jury trial?' Is any jury going to convict Jack Bauer? "I don't think so. . . . So the question is really whether we believe in these absolutes. And ought we believe in these absolutes" (quoted in Lattman 2007).

6. The presence of John Yoo at the Office of Legal Counsel when the 9/11 attacks happened was, in the words of journalist Jane Mayer (2008, 65–66), "like having a personal friend who could write medical prescriptions." For Yoo's own account, see his memoir of this period (Yoo 2006). It is important to note that there were other influential advocates of extreme antiterror measures, centering primarily in the Office of Vice President Dick Cheney but with allies throughout the rest of the Bush administration.

7. One dramatic example is the case of Maher Arar, a Canadian citizen and engineer who was arrested in September 2002 at JFK airport and later flown to a black prison in Syria. There, Arar was incarcerated for a full year during which time he was interrogated and tortured by Syrian intelligence. Arar's case is well known because of a full-scale investigation by the Canadian government into the conditions of his confinement, which ultimately led to a

$11.5 billion compensatory award to Arar. Ironically, the Canadian edition of *Time* magazine named Arar as its "newsmaker of the year" during the same time that the American edition conferred the same honor on President George Bush. A summary of the Arar case is presented by his American lawyers, David Cole and Jules Lobel (2007, 22–24). The 2007 Gavin Hood film *Rendition* draws on some of the facts of the Arar case, melded together with that of another mistakenly arrested and tortured German national named Khalid el-Masri.

8. "Guantanamo Bay History," *CBC News Online*, May 21, 2009; Nicholas Kulish and Scott Shane, "Flight Data Show Rendition Planes Landed in Poland," *New York Times*, February 23, 2010; "Guantanamo Bay Naval Base (Cuba)," *New York Times*, September 19, 2010.

9. Peter Finn and Anne Kornblut, "Obama Creates Indefinite Detention System for Prisoners at Guantanamo Bay," *Washington Post*, March 8, 2011.

10. In an historical study, Christopher Pyle (2001) notes that over time the United States has become more willing to return people seeking political refuge and has generally loosened its commitment to being a welcoming environment for dissidents of all stripes.

11. Another dimension of international policymaking involved numerous European countries (including Austria, Belgium, Denmark, Germany, Greece, Ireland, Italy, Portugal, Spain, Sweden, and the United Kingdom) allowing the passage of CIA rendition flights, in violation of European Union (and in many cases, national) laws.

12. Eliot Spitzer, the former governor of New York, was caught in a scandal involving payments to a prostitution ring triggered by a large wire transfer that, under tightened banking regulations designed to reduce transfers to terrorist organizations, became the subject of an investigation. No criminal charges were filed against Spitzer, but his political career effectively ended.

13. Scott Shane and Mark Mazzetti, "Interrogation Methods Are Criticized," *New York Times*, May 30, 2007, A1; Jane Mayer, "Counterfactual: A Curious History of the CIA's Secret Interrogation Program," *The New Yorker*, March 29, 2010.

14. An instructive further example is provided by the case of Faisal Shahzad, a naturalized American citizen who attempted in May 2010 to set off a bomb in New York City's Times Square. After the discovery of smoke coming out of a parked car, law enforcement agents took only fifty-three hours to track down and arrest Shahzad. Subsequent questioning by agents returned information about Shahzad's overseas training with the Pakistani Taliban, and a guilty plea resulted in a sentence of life in prison in October 2010.

15. In June 2010, the Obama administration officially announced it was abandoning plans to close the Guantanamo facility by the originally intended date of 2013 (Charlie Savage, "Obama Team Is Divided on Anti-Terror Tactics," *New York Times*, March 28, 2010).

16. Jane Mayer, "The Predator War: What Are the Risks of the C.I.A.'s Covert Drone Program," *The New Yorker*, October 26, 2009; Peter Bergen and Katherine Tiedemann, "No Secrets in the Sky," *New York Times*, April 26, 2010.

17. Manning's confinement has been the subject of numerous protests, includ-

ing a recent letter from 250 leading legal scholars signed by a couple of former administration appointees (including Lawrence Tribe of Harvard University, Obama's teacher and former advisor to the Justice Department; see Ed Pilkington, "Bradley Manning: Top U.S. Scholars Voice Outrage at 'Torture,'" *The Guardian*, April 10, 2011).

Chapter 2

1. Davis's surveys included five measures of public attitudes toward government policy activities associated with the war on terror: identification cards, detentions, ethnic profiling, law enforcement searches, and wiretapping. Two of these five items show a clear majority of respondents supporting the activity in question (Davis 2007, 119), attitudes changing little between 2001 and 2004.
2. In this scenario, individuals selectively accept new stimuli, filtering out those items perceived as inconsistent with prior beliefs or expectations (Kunda 1990; Ditto and Lopez 1992; Jost, Banaji, and Nosek 2004). This often leads to perplexing, even suboptimal outcomes.
3. Despite considerable debate about the precise interrelationship between partisanship and voters' domestic policy evaluations (for example, MacKuen, Erikson, and Stimson 1988; Green, Palmquist, and Schickler 1998), there is little doubt that partisanship matters considerably to voting behavior and that the measurement of partisanship shows a good deal of reliability (Bartels 2000; see also Krosnick and Berent 1993).

Chapter 3

1. The appendix discusses additional details concerning sampling, interview procedures and protocols, and response rates.
2. Jon Krosnick's and Matthew Berent's (1993) experiments with alternative formats returned compelling evidence that the branching design substantially enhances the reliability of attitude items in surveys. Our use of this design format does have a consequence of limiting direct comparison with past versions of our questions that were fielded in earlier surveys. On par, however, the goal of better measurement in the SAPA surveys outweighed the consideration of over-time replication and comparisons with surveys conducted before 2007.
3. As long as the intervals are equal, the numerical values given to the strongly agree-support through strongly disagree-oppose response categories will yield identical statistical results with respect to t-tests and p-values (and coefficients and standard errors will differ solely by a constant). We follow a common convention by using a 0 to 1 range, where the five response categories are scored 0, 0.25, 0.50, 0.75, and 1.
4. Self-identified Democrats went from a score of 0.49 in 2007 to 0.38 in 2009 and 0.34 in 2010.

Chapter 4

1. SAPA's policy-attitude items all use a two-part, branching format, where after the initial question respondents are probed as to the intensity of their opinions. For the airport security items, respondents who choose favor after the initial question are then asked, "Would that be strongly or slightly favor?" Respondents who instead choose oppose after the initial question are asked, "Would that be strongly or slightly oppose?" Together, the two-part format yields five-point response scales in which the middle category is reserved for don't-know and no-opinion responses.

2. As indicated in the table 4.1 note, the order of presentation is randomized: 50 percent of respondents are asked, "The government should take all steps necessary to prevent additional acts of terrorism in the United States even if it means foreign nationals' individual rights and liberties might be violated"; the other 50 percent are asked, "Even if it means foreign nationals' individual rights and liberties might be violated, the government should take all steps necessary to prevent additional acts of terrorism in the United States."

3. In our SAPA surveys, the threat perceptions item is placed near the end of the interviews so as to avoid priming respondents when probing opinions on counterterrorism policies.

4. There are four response options for this item: <1> *not concerned at all*, <2> *not very concerned*, <3> *somewhat concerned*, and <4> *very concerned*.

5. The order of presentation is randomized for all pairs of traits in the SAPA survey.

6. Using Tukey's HSD (honestly significant difference) test, assuming equal variances, and Tamhane's T2 test, which does not assume equal variances, the resultant p-values for this comparison are, respectively, .36 and .35. Both of these are comfortably above a conventional threshold of .05.

7. As summarized in the third row of table 4.2 estimates, the interaction between education and the second treatment effect (reference to real terrorism threats) is not significant ($t = 1.57$, $p = .12$); deleting this interaction from the model results in no significant change in fit.

8. In this experiment (and in all other experiments in this chapter), we conducted additional tests for interactions involving categorical measures of party identification (that is, Democratic identifier = 1, Republican identifier = 1) as well as an additional interaction involving ideological identification. In all cases test results returned nonsignificant effects.

9. The predicted .14 effect of the treatment at the mean level of education can thus be considered an estimate of overall or average effect. But recall again that because of the nature of the interaction, that estimate is best conjoined with parallel estimates at the highest (and lowest) levels of education as well (see again table 4.3).

10. For this test, the F-statistic is .17, $p = .68$.

11. When there are interactions between assignment to experimental framing conditions and education, it is necessary to present estimates of the magnitude of relevant effects at specific levels of the education covariate (as in table 4.3 estimates). For table 4.4 estimates, however, it is not necessary to do

so because the main effects of education ($\beta = -0.03$) and the two interactions with experimental condition ($\beta_{\text{education} \times \text{foreign/-threat}} = 0.03$; $\beta_{\text{education} \times \text{American/-threat}} = 0.03$) cancel each other out.

Chapter 5

1. An innovative study conducted by Matthew Brashears (2008) offers results suggesting the utility of bringing in international comparisons. Analyzing cross-national survey data from the International Social Survey Program (ISSP), Brashears found evidence linking a measure of gender status expectations to the proportion of women in supervisory positions at the country level. But how gender attitudes are influenced by the national identity of the target of attitudes is not possible to investigate in ISSP or other existing cross-national survey data.

2. As shown in table 5.1, several group feeling thermometers are the control group in subsequent experiments into affect formation.

3. As before, we use Krosnick and Berent's (1993) branching format for the policy-attitude items, where respondents answer first an agree-disagree question and then a second question probing opinion strength.

4. Two factors underlie the Military Commissions Act experiment, and as discussed in the results section, we can thus test for the candidate relevance of each.

5. We note coefficient, standard error estimate, and associated p-values for the authoritarianism ($\beta_{-\text{U.S. citizens} \times \text{authoritarianism}} = -2.90$, SE = 0.64, $p = .00$) and religion ($\beta_{-\text{U.S. citizens} \times \text{Christian}} = -8.00$, SE = 3.24, $p = .01$) interactions, discussing and interpreting their respective magnitudes in detail.

6. The coefficient, standard error estimate, and associated p-value for this interaction are as follows: $\beta_{\text{ME background} \times \text{education}} = -.03$, SE = 0.01, $p = .00$. We discuss and interpret the magnitude of this interaction in detail.

7. Note that excluding black respondents from these calculations yields new thermometer scores of 66° for blacks and 71° for whites (the t-score for this comparison is 5.11).

8. Although we are primarily interested in relative differences between group feeling thermometer's scores, it bears noting that all scores tend to be pushed upward because of social desirability and related biases. This cautions against viewing scores in the 50° degree range as suggesting an absolute degree of warmth.

9. To enable comparison between categorical and continuous covariates, estimates use a range standardization. As in the chapter 4 estimates, coefficients for categorical covariates reflect a change from 0 to 1, and coefficients for continuous covariates reflect a change from the lowest to the highest observed score.

10. It also bears emphasizing that our results in this chapter suggest the greater relevance of transnational over domestic ethnic biases. Both can, in principle, be usefully considered as part of an encompassing theory of ethnocentrism (Kinder and Kam 2009). But, like John Sides and Kimberly Gross (2011), we view nondomestic groups as having the most direct relevance to attitudes toward the war on terror.

Chapter 6

1. "Wars, revolutions, conquest, and natural disasters are sources of discontinuous institutional change. . . . But the single most important point about institutional change, which must be grasped if we are to begin to get a handle on the subject, is that institutional change is overwhelmingly incremental" (North 1990, 89).

2. Interestingly, North's later work (2006) calls for greater consideration of cognitive processes that link individuals to institutions and institutional change, offering a sharp distinction between interests and (nonrational) processes of belief formation.

3. This pattern of public opposition to policy change is, we would emphasize, very much at the center of the thermostatic model of opinion formation (see, for example, Wlezien 1995; Stimson, Mackuen, and Erikson 1995), where aggregate opinion is viewed as constantly adjusting to economic and political change. In contrast to policy feedback, however, the thermostatic model predicts that the public will respond negatively toward any rising trend involving public policy, thus reversing a preference for liberal policies when government implements liberal pieces of legislation, and also moving away from conservative preferences when the government tacks in a conservative direction.

Conclusion

1. A conceivable exception is the 2009 shooting rampage of Major Nidal Hasan that left thirteen dead and twenty-nine injured on an army base in Fort Hood, Texas. Radically disenchanted with U.S. military policy, Hasan had electronically communicated with and sought "spiritual guidance" from anti-American cleric Anwar Al-Awlaki. But Hasan appears to have been acting alone, and whether his killing spree qualifies as international terrorism appears debatable at best.

2. A sign of this degraded capacity was the bizarre attempt to reband the organization through the possible use of a new name, a move contemplated by its leader, Osama bin Laden, before his death (Burke 2011).

3. One sign of the possibly expanding imbalance between counterterrorism activities and the more limited presence of large-scale terrorism is the growing practice by the FBI of offering bombs for sale to individuals (Shipler 2012). On purchase of the (deactivated) devices, the individuals in question are arrested and charged with plotting terrorism.

4. For example, the domestic surveillance arm of the CIA was used against the University of Michigan political scientist Juan Cole, who publishes an influential blog that had been highly critical of U.S. policy in the Middle East and Afghanistan. Top CIA officials are alleged to have ordered an investigation of Cole to seek derogatory information on him, evidently at the request of the Bush administration (James Risen, "Ex-Spy Alleges Bush White House Sought to Discredit Critic," *New York Times*, June 11 2011). In chapter 1, we noted other examples of activist groups that have been caught in the new domestic surveillance net.

5. Massive federal government budget deficits in recent years give these issues another important dimension (Eisenhower Study Group 2011). Total expenditures to date for America's two wars in Afghanistan and Iraq alone are approaching $1.5 trillion (Belasco 2011), alongside future health-care costs for veterans, the costs of rebuilding the two countries, and the maintenance of a greatly enlarged surveillance bureaucracy whose large annual budgets are a state secret. The economist Joseph Stiglietz has estimated the full cost of these wars at more than $3 trillion (Stiglitz and Blimes 2008).

6. David Cole, "Their Liberties, Our Security," *Boston Review*, vol. 27, no 6, December 2002/January 2003.

7. In this context, we would emphasize the relevance of our results concerning the absence of evidence that authoritarian values or personality traits moderate the impact of threat and target group processes. It is here that the American public's dark side, we believe, falls well short of a less malleable and considerably more restrictive foundation provided by authoritarianism.

References

Achenbaum, W. Andrew. 1983. *Shades of Gray: Old Age, American Values and Federal Policies Since 1920*. Boston: Little Brown.

Adorno, Theodor, Else Frenkel-Brunswik, Daniel Levinson, and Nevitt Sanford. 1950. *The Authoritarian Personality*. New York: Harper and Row.

Aldrich, John, Christopher Gelpi, Peter Feaver, Jason Reifler, and Kristen Thompson Sharp. 2006. "Foreign Policy and the Electoral Connection." *Annual Review of Political Science* 9(June): 477–502.

Alexander, Matthew, and John Bruning. 2008. *How to Break a Terrorist: The U.S. Interrogators Who Used Brains, Not Brutality, to Take Down the Deadliest Man in Iraq*. New York: Free Press.

Allhof, Fritz. 2005. "A Defense of Torture: Separation of Cases, Ticking Time Bombs, and Moral Justification." *International Journal of Applied Philosophy* 19(2): 243–64.

Altemeyer, Bob. 1996. *The Authoritarian Specter*. Cambridge, Mass.: Harvard University Press.

Amenta, Edwin. 2006. *When Movements Matter: The Townsend Plan and the Rise of Social Security*. Princeton, N.J.: Princeton University Press.

American Bar Association. 2003. *Task Force on the Treatment of Enemy Combatants Revised Report*. Chicago: American Bar Association.

American Civil Liberties Union. 2001. "ACLU Responds to Senate Passage of Anti-Terrorism Bill, Ashcroft Speech; Promises to Monitor Implementation of Sweeping New Powers." *ACLU Online*, October 25, 2001. http://www.aclu.org/national-security/aclu-responds-senate-passage-anti-terrorism-bill-ashcroft-speech-promises-monitor- (accessed July 24, 2012).

———. 2010. "Bagram FOIA." *ACLU Online*, February 10, 2012. http://www.aclu.org/national-security/bagram-foia (accessed July 24, 2012).

Aronson, Elliot, Timothy Wilson, and Robin Akert. 2006. *Social Psychology*, 6th ed. Upper Saddle River, N.J.: Pearson Prentice Hall.

Bafumi, Joseph, and Robert Shapiro. 2009. "A New Partisan Voter." *Journal of Politics* 71(1): 1–24.

Baldassarri, Delia, and Andrew Gelman. 2008. "Partisans Without Constraint: Political Polarization and Trends in American Public Opinion." *American Journal of Sociology*, 114(2): 408–46.

Balkin, Jack. 2008. "The Constitution and the National Surveillance State." *University of Minnesota Law Review* 93(1): 1–25.

Bamford, James. 2008. *The Shadow Factory: The Ultra-Secret NSA from 9/11 to the Eavesdropping on America*. New York: Doubleday.

Bartels, Larry. 2000. "Partisanship and Voting Behavior, 1952–1996." *American Journal of Political Science* 44(1): 35–50.

———. 2002. "Beyond the Running Tally: Partisan Bias in Political Perceptions." *Political Behavior* 24(2): 117–50.

———. 2008. *Unequal Democracy: The Political Economy of the New Gilded Age*. Princeton, N.J.: Princeton University Press.

Beckfield, Jason. 2003. "Inequality in the World Polity: The Structure of International Organization." *American Sociological Review* 68(2): 401–24.

Belasco, Amy. 2011. "The Cost of Iraq, Afghanistan, and Other Global War on Terror Operations Since 9/11." CRS Report RL33110. Washington, D.C.: Congressional Research Service. http://www.fas.org/sgp/crs/natsec/RL33110 .pdf (accessed July 2, 2011).

Bell, Daniel. 1960. *The End of Ideology*. Glencoe, Ill.: The Free Press.

Bergen, Peter, and Katherine Tiedemann. 2010. "No Secrets in the Sky," *New York Times*, April 26.

Best, Samuel, Brian Krueger, and Jeffrey Ladewig. 2006. "The Polls-Trends: Privacy in the Information Age." *Public Opinion Quarterly* 78(3): 375–401.

Bobo, Lawrence, and Frederick Licari. 1989. "Education and Political Tolerance: Testing the Effects of Cognitive Sophistication and Target Group Affect." *Public Opinion Quarterly* 53(3): 285–308.

Boettke, Peter, Christopher Coyne, and Peter Leeson. 2008. "Institutional Stickiness and the New Development Economics." *American Journal of Economics and Sociology* 67(2): 331–58.

Boli, John, and George M. Thomas. 1997. "World Culture in the World Polity: A Century of International Non-Governmental Organization." *American Sociological Review* 62(2): 171–90.

———. 1999. *Constructing World Culture: International Nongovernmental Organizations Since 1875*. Palo Alto, Calif.: Stanford University Press.

Bowles, Samuel, and Herbert Gintis. 1986. *Capitalism and Democracy*. New York: Basic Books.

Brashears, Matthew. 2008. "Sex, Society, and Association: A Cross-National Examination of Status Construction Theory." *Social Psychology Quarterly* 71(1): 72–82.

Brinkley, Alan. 2003. "A Familiar Story: Lessons from Past Assaults on Freedoms." In *The War on Our Freedoms: Civil Liberties in an Age of Terrorism*, edited by Richard Leone and Greg Rick Jr. New York: Century Foundation.

Brody, Richard A. 1991. *Assessing the President: The Media, Elite Opinion, and Public Support*. Palo Alto, Calif.: Stanford University Press.

Brooks, Clem, Kyle Dodson, and Nikole Hotchkiss. 2010. "National Security Issues and U.S. Presidential Elections, 1992–2008." *Social Science Research* 39(4): 518–26.

Brooks, Clem, and Jeff Manza. 2007. *Why Welfare States Persist: The Importance of Mass Opinion in Democracies*. Chicago: University of Chicago Press.

———. Various years. *Surveys of American Policy Attitudes, 2007, 2009, 2010*. Bloomington: Center for Survey Research, Indiana University.

Buncombe, Andrew. 2007. "U.S. Military Tells 24 to Cut Out the Torture Scenes . . . Or Else!" *The Independent,* February 13.

Burke, Jason. 2011. *The 9/11 Wars.* New York: Penguin.

Burke, Peter, Jan Stets, and Christine Cerven. 2007. "Gender, Legitimation, and Identity Verification in Groups." *Social Psychology Quarterly* 70(1): 27–40.

Burstein, Paul. 1998. "Bringing the Public Back In: Should Sociologists Consider the Impact of Public Opinion on Public Policy?" *Social Forces* 77(1): 27–62.

———. 2003. "The Impact of Public Opinion on Public Policy: A Review, and an Agenda." *Political Research Quarterly* 56(1): 29–40.

Cainkar, Louise. 2004. "The Impact of the September 11 Attacks and their Aftermath on Arab and Muslim Communities in United States." *Global Security and Cooperation Quarterly* 13(Summer/Fall): 1–24.

Campbell, James. 2005. "Why Bush Won the Presidential Election of 2004: Incumbency, Ideology, Terrorism, and Turnout." *Political Science Quarterly* 120(2): 219–41.

CBC News. 2009. "Guantanamo Bay History," *CBC News Online,* May 21.

Chang, Nancy. 2002. *Silencing Political Dissent.* New York: Seven Stories Press.

Chong, Dennis, and James Druckman. 2007. "Framing Theory." *Annual Review of Political Science* 10(June): 103–26.

Cole, David. 2002/2003. "Their Liberties, Our Security." *Boston Globe,* December/January.

———. 2011. "Guantanamo: The New Challenge to Obama." *New York Review of Books,* June 11.

Cole, David, and James Dempsey. 2006. *Terrorism and the Constitution: Sacrificing Civil Liberties in the Name of National Security,* 3rd ed. New York: New Press.

Cole, David, and Jules Lobel. 2007. *Less Safe, Less Free: Why America Is Losing the War on Terror.* New York: New Press.

Collins, Randall. 2004. *Interaction Ritual Chains.* Princeton, N.J.: Princeton University Press.

Cook, Fay Lomax, and Edith Barrett. 1988. "Public Support for Social Security." *Journal of Aging Studies* 2(4): 339–56.

Cooper, Joel. 2007. *Cognitive Dissonance: 50 Years of a Classic Theory.* London: Sage Publications.

Correll, Shelley, Stephen Benard, and In Paik. 2007. "Getting a Job: Is There a Motherhood Penalty?" *American Journal of Sociology* 112(5): 1297–1338.

Coryn, Chris, James Beale, and Krista Myers. 2004. "Response to September 11th: Anxiety, Patriotism, and Prejudice in the Aftermath of Terror." *Current Research in Social Psychology* 9(12): 165–83.

Cutler, Stephen, and Robert Kaufman. 1975. "Cohort Changes in Political Attitudes: Tolerance of Ideological Nonconformity." *Public Opinion Quarterly* 39(1): 69–81.

David, Paul. 1985. "Clio and the Economics of QWERTY." *American Economic Review* 75(2): 332–37.

Davis, Darren. 2007. *Negative Liberty: Public Opinion and the Terrorist Attacks on America.* New York: Russell Sage Foundation.

Davis, Darren, and Brian Silver. 2004. "Civil Liberties vs. Security: Public Opinion in the Context of the Terrorist Attacks on America." *American Journal of Political Science* 48(1): 28–46.

Davis, David Brion. 1971. *Fear of Conspiracy: Images of Un-American Subversion from the Revolution to the Present.* Ithaca, N.Y.: Cornell University Press.

Davis, James A. 1975. "Communism, Conformity, Cohorts, and Categories: American Tolerance in 1954 and 1972–73." *American Journal of Sociology* 81(3): 491–513.

Dershowitz, Alan. 2002. *Shouting Fire: Civil Liberties in a Turbulent Age.* Boston: Little, Brown.

Ditto, Peter, and David Lopez. 1992. "Motivated Skepticism: Use of Differential Decision Criteria for Preferred and Nonpreferred Conclusions." *Journal of Personality and Social Psychology* 63(4): 568–84.

Dyck, Joshua, and Laura Hussey. 2008. "The End of Welfare as We Know It? Durable Attitudes in a Changing Information Environment." *Public Opinion Quarterly* 72(4): 589–618.

Editorial. 2011. "A Conflict Without End." *New York Times,* May 26. Available at: http://www.nytimes.com/2011/05/17/opinion/17tue1.html

Egan, Louisa, Laurie Santos, and Paul Bloom. 2007. "The Origins of Cognitive Dissonance: Evidence from Children and Monkeys." *Psychological Science* 18(11): 978–83.

Eisenhower Study Group. 2011. "Executive Summary: The Cost of War." Providence, R.I.: Watson Institute, Brown University.

Epp, Charles. 1998. *The Rights Revolution: Lawyers, Activists, and Supreme Courts in Comparative Perspective.* Chicago: University of Chicago Press.

Ernst, Daniel. 1995. *Lawyers Against Labor.* Champaign: University of Illinois Press.

Evans, Jennifer. 2001. "Hijacking Civil Liberties: The USA PATRIOT Act of 2001." *Loyola University Chicago Law Journal* 33(Summer): 933–90.

Fazio, Russell, and Michael Olson. 2003. "Implicit Measures in Social Cognition Research: Their Meaning, and Use." *Annual Review of Psychology* 54: 297–327.

Festinger, Leon. 1957. *A Theory of Cognitive Dissonance.* Palo Alto, Calif.: Stanford University Press.

Festinger, Leon, and James M. Carlsmith. 1959. "Cognitive Consequences of Forced Compliance." *Journal of Abnormal and Social Psychology* 58(2): 203–10.

Finn, Peter, and Anne Kornblut. 2011. "Obama Creates Indefinite Detention System for Prisoners at Guantanamo Bay," *Washington Post,* March 8.

Fisher, Louis. 2005. *Presidential Power and Military Tribunals.* Lawrence: University Press of Kansas.

Foner, Eric. 1999. *The History of American Freedom.* New York: W. W. Norton.

Forbath, William. 1992. *Law and the Shaping of the American Labor Movement.* Cambridge, Mass.: Harvard University Press.

Foyle, Douglas. 1999. *Counting the Public In: Presidents, Public Opinion, and Foreign Policy.* New York: Oxford University Press.

Frank, David John, Bayliss Camp, and Steven Boutcher. 2010. "Worldwide Trends in the Criminal Regulation of Sex, 1945 to 2005." *American Sociological Review* 75(6): 867–93.

Frank, David John, Ann Hironaka, and Evan Schofer. 2000. "The Nation-State, and the Natural Environment over the Twentieth Century." *American Sociological Review* 65(1): 96–116.

Frank, David John, and Elizabeth McEneaney. 1999. "The Individualization of Society and the Liberalization of State Policies on Same-Sex Sexual Relations, 1984–1995." *Social Forces* 77(4): 911–44.

Frum, David, and Richard Perle. 2004. *An End to Evil: How to Win the War on Terror*. New York: Random House.

Gaines, Brian, James H. Kuklinski, Paul J. Quirk, Buddy Peyton, and Jay Verkuilen. 2007. "Same Facts, Different Interpretations: Partisan Motivation and Opinion on Iraq." *Journal of Politics* 69(4): 957–74.

Gilens, Martin. 1999. *Why Americans Hate Welfare*. Chicago: University of Chicago Press.

Gilovich, Thomas, Dale Griffin, and Daniel Kahneman. 2002. *Heuristics and Biases: The Psychology of Intuitive Judgment*. New York: Cambridge University Press.

Goldstein, Robert J. 2001. *Political Repression in Modern America, 1870 to 1976*. Urbana: University of Illinois Press.

Goodwin, Jeff. Forthcoming. *The Logics of Terrorism*. New York: Russell Sage Foundation.

Goux, Darshan, Patrick Egan, and Jack Citrin. 2008. "The War on Terror, and Civil Liberties." In *Public Opinion and Constitutional Controversy*, edited by Nathanael Persily, Jack Citrin, and Patrick Egan. New York: Oxford University Press.

Green, Donald, Bradley Palmquist, and Eric Schickler. 1998. "Macropartisanship: A Replication, and Critique." *American Political Science Review* 92(4): 883–99.

———. 2002. *Partisan Hearts and Minds: Political Parties and the Social Identities of Voters*. New Haven, Conn.: Yale University Press.

Greenwald, Anthony, Debbie McGhee, and Jordan Schwartz. 1998. "Measuring Individual Differences in Implicit Cognition: The Implicit Association Test." *Journal of Personality and Social Psychology* 74(6): 1464–80.

Groves, Robert M. 2006. "Nonresponse Rate, and Nonresponse Bias in Household Surveys." *Public Opinion Quarterly* 70(5): 646–75.

Hagan, John. 2003. *Justice in the Balkans: Prosecuting War Crimes in the Hague Tribunal*. Chicago: University of Chicago Press.

Hersh, Seymour. 2005. "The Coming Wars: What the Pentagon Can Now Do in Secret." *The New Yorker,* January 24.

Hetherington, Marc. 1998. "The Political Relevance of Political Trust." *American Political Science Review* 92(4): 791–808.

Hetherington, Marc, and Elisabeth Suhay. 2011. "Authoritarianism, Threat, and Americans' Support for the War on Terror." *American Journal of Political Science* 55(3): 546–60.

Hetherington, Marc, and Jonathan Weiler. 2009. *Authoritarianism and Polarization in American Politics*. New York: Cambridge University Press.

Higham, John. 2002. *Strangers in the Land: Patterns of American Nativism, 1860–1925*, 2nd ed. Rutgers, N.J.: Rutgers University Press.

Hofstadter, Richard. 1965. *The Paranoid Style in American Politics, and Other Essays*. New York: Alfred A. Knopf.

Horowitz, Morton. 1992. *The Transformation of American Law, 1870–1960*. New York: Oxford University Press.

Huber, Evelyne, and John Stephens. 2001. *Development and Crisis of the Welfare State: Parties and Policies in Global Markets*. Chicago: University of Chicago Press.

Huddy, Leonie, Stanley Feldman, Gallya Lahav, and Charles Taber. 2003. "Fear, and Terror: Psychological Reactions to 9/11." In *Framing Terrorism: The News*

Media, the Government and the Public, edited by Pippa Norris, Montague Kern, and Mary Just. New York: Routledge.

Huddy, Leonie, Stanley Feldman, Charles Taber, and Gallya Lahav. 2005. "Threat, Anxiety, and Support of Antiterrorism Policies." *American Journal of Political Science* 49(3): 593–608.

Huddy, Leonie, Nadia Khatib, and Theresa Capelos. 2002. "The Polls-Trends: Reactions Terrorist Attacks of September 11, 2001." *Public Opinion Quarterly* 66(3): 418–450.

Huntington, Samuel. 2004. *Who Are We? The Challenges to America's National Identity.* New York: Simon & Schuster.

Hutcheson, John, David Domke, Andre Billeadeaux, and Philip Garland. 2004. "U.S. National Identity, Political Elites, and a Patriotic Press Following September 11." *Political Communication* 21(1): 27–50.

Ignatieff, Michael. 2007. *The Rights Revolution,* 2nd ed. Toronto: House of Anansi Press.

Iversen, Torben, and David Soskice. 2001. "An Asset Theory of Social Policy Preferences." *American Political Science Review* 95(4): 875–93.

Iyengar, Shanto. 1990. "The Accessibility Bias in Politics: Television News, and Public Opinion." *International Journal of Public Opinion Research* 2(1): 1–15.

Jacobson, Matthew F. 1999. *Whiteness of a Different Color: European Immigrants and the Alchemy of Race.* Cambridge, MA: Harvard University Press.

Jacoby, Jeff. 2007. "War on Terror Is Working." *Boston Globe,* September 9.

James, Randy. 2009. "A History of Military Commissions." *Time Magazine,* May 18.

Jenkins-Smith, Hank, and Kerry Herron. 2005. "United States Public Response to Terrorism: Full Lines or Bedrock?" *Review of Policy Research* 22(5): 599–623.

Johnson, Lock. 1988. *A Season of Inquiry: Congress and Intelligence.* Chicago: Dorsey Press.

Jost, John, Mahzarin Banaji, and Brian Nosek. 2004. "A Decade of System Justification Theory: Accumulated Evidence of Conscious, and Unconscious Bolstering of the Status Quo." *Political Psychology* 25(6): 881–919.

Jost, John, Christopher Federico, and Jaime Napier. 2009. "Political Ideology: Its Structure, Functions, and Elective Affinities." *Annual Review of Psychology* 60(2009): 307–33.

Kahneman, Daniel. 2011. *Thinking Fast and Slow.* New York: Farrar, Strauss and Giroux.

Kahneman, Daniel, Paul Slovic, and Amos Tversky. 1982. *Judgment Under Uncertainty: Heuristics and Biases.* New York: Cambridge University Press.

Kam, Cindy, and Donald Kinder. 2007. "Terror and Ethnocentrism: Foundations of American Support for the War on Terrorism." *Journal of Politics* 69(2): 320–38.

Keeter, Scott, Courtney Kennedy, Michael Dimock, Jonathan Best, and Peyton Craighill. 2006. "Gauging the Impact of Growing Nonresponse on Estimates from a National RDD Telephone Survey." *Public Opinion Quarterly* 70(5): 759–79.

Key, V. O., Jr. 1964. *Politics, Parties, and Pressure Groups,* 5th ed. New York: Crowell.

Keyssar, Alexander. 2000. *The Right to Vote.* New York: Basic Books.

Kimeldorf, Howard. 1992. *Reds or Rackets.* Berkeley: University of California Press.

Kinder, Donald, and Cindy Kam. 2009. *Us Against Them: Ethnocentric Foundations of American Opinion*. Chicago: University of Chicago Press.

Kinder, Donald, and Lynn Sanders. 1996. *Divided by Color*. Chicago: University of Chicago Press.

Korpi, Walter, and Joakim Palme. 1998. "The Paradox of Redistribution, and Strategies of Equality: Welfare State Institutions, Inequality, and Poverty in the Western Countries." *American Sociological Review* 63(October): 661–87.

Krosnick, Jon, and Matthew Berent. 1993. "Comparisons of Party Identification, and Policy Preferences the Impact of Survey Question Format." *American Journal of Political Science* 37(3): 941–64.

Kulish, Nicholas, and Scott Shane. 2010a. "Flight Data Show Rendition Planes Landed in Poland," *New York Times*, February 23.

———. 2010b. "Guantanamo Bay Naval Base (Cuba)," *New York Times*, September 19.

Kumlin, Staffan. 2002. "Institutions-Experiences-Preferences: How Welfare State Design Affects Political Trust, and Ideology." In *Restructuring the Welfare State: Political Institutions and Policy Change*, edited by Bo Rothstein and Sven Steinmo. New York: Palgrave Macmillan.

Kunda, Ziva. 1990. "The Case for Motivated Reasoning." *Psychological Bulletin* 108(3): 480–98.

Kurzman, Charles. 2012. *Muslim-Americans Terrorism in the Decade Since 9/11*. Durham, N.C.: Triangle Center on Terrorism, and Homeland Security.

Lamont, Michele, and Marcel Fournier, eds. 1992. *Cultivating Differences: Symbolic Boundaries and the Making of Inequality*. Chicago: University of Chicago Press.

Lamont, Michele, and Virag Molnar. 2002. "The Study of Boundaries in the Social Sciences." *Annual Review of Sociology* 28(August): 167–95.

Lamont, Michele, and Laurent Thevenot, eds. 2000. *Rethinking Comparative Cultural Sociology: Repertoires of Evaluation in France and the United States*. New York: Cambridge University Press.

Lattman, Peter. 2011. "Justice Scalia Hearts Jack Bauer." *Wall Street Journal Law Blog*, June 20. http://blogs.wsj.com/law/2007/06/20/justice-scalia-hearts-jack-bauer (accessed July 5, 2011).

Lavine, Howard, Milton Lodge, and Kate Freitas. 2005. "Threat, Authoritarianism, and Selective Exposure to Information." *Political Psychology* 26(2): 219–44.

Lichtblau, Eric. 2008. *Bush's Law: The Remaking of American Justice*. New York: Pantheon Books.

Lichtenstein, Nelson. 2003. *State of the Union: A Century of American Labor*. Princeton, N.J.: Princeton University Press.

Lieven, Anatol. 2005. *America Right or Wrong: An Anatomy of American Nationalism*. New York: Oxford University Press.

Lippmann, Walter. (1922) 1997. *Public Opinion*. New York: Free Press.

Lipset, Seymour Martin. 1996. *American Exceptionalism: A Double-Edged Sword*. New York: W. W. Norton.

Litwack, Dahlia. 2008. "The Fiction Behind Torture Policy." *The Daily Beast*, July 25.

Lord, Charles, Lee Ross, and Mark Lepper. 1979. "Biased Assimilation and Attitude Polarization: The Effects of Prior Theories on Subsequently Considered Evidence." *Journal of Personality and Social Psychology* 37(8): 2098–109.

Lupia, Arthur, Mathew McCubbins, Samuel Popkin, James Kuklinski, and Dennis Chong. 2000. *Elements of Reason: Cognition, Choice, and the Bounds of Rationality*. New York: Cambridge University Press.

MacKuen, Michael, Robert Erikson, and James Stimson. 1988. "Macropartisanship." *American Political Science Review* 83(4): 1125–42.

Mahler, Jonathan. 2007. *The Challenge: Hamden v. Bush and the Fight Over Presidential Power*. New York: Farrar, Straus and Giroux.

Manza, Jeff, and Clem Brooks. 2012. "How Sociology Lost Public Opinion: A Genealogy of a Missing Concept in the Study of the Political." *Sociological Theory* 30(2): 89–113.

Manza, Jeff, Clem Brooks, and Christopher Uggen. 2004. "Public Attitudes Toward Felon Disenfranchisement in the U.S." *Public Opinion Quarterly* 68(2): 276–87.

Manza, Jeff, and Fay Lomax Cook. 2002. "A Democratic Polity? Three Views of Policy Responsiveness in the United States." *American Politics Quarterly* 30(4): 630–67.

Marcus, George, John Sullivan, Elizabeth Theiss-Morse, and Sandra Wood. 1995. *With Malice Toward Some: Help People Make Civil Liberties Judgments*. New York: Cambridge University Press.

Marshall, T. H. 1950. *Citizenship and Social Class*. Cambridge: Cambridge University Press.

May, Peter. 1991. "Reconsidering Policy Design: Policies and Publics." *Journal of Public Policy* 11(2): 187–206.

Mayer, Jane. 2007. "Whatever It Takes: The Politics of the Man Behind 24." *The New Yorker*, February 22.

———. 2008. *The Dark Side: The Inside Story of How the War on Terror Turned into a War on American Ideals*. New York: Doubleday.

———. 2009. "The Predatory War: What Are the Risks of the C.I.A.'s Covert Drone Program," *The New Yorker*, October 26.

———. 2010. "Counterfactual: A Curious History of the CIA's Secret Interrogation Program." *The New Yorker*, March 29.

———. 2011. "A Deal in the N.S.A. Case." *The New Yorker*, June 9.

McCartney, Paul. 2004. "American Nationalism, and U.S. Foreign Policy from September 11 to the Iraq War." *Political Science Quarterly* 119(3): 399–423.

McCarty, Nolan, Keith Poole, and Howard Rosenthal. 2006. *Polarized America: The Dance of Ideology and Unequal Riches*. Cambridge, Mass.: MIT Press.

Mell, Patricia. 2002. "Big Brother at the Door: Balancing National Security with Privacy Under the USA PATRIOT Act." *Denver University Law Review* 80(2): 375–428.

Merolla, Jennifer, and Elizabeth Zechmeister. 2009. *Democracy at Risk: How Terrorist Threats Affect the Public*. Chicago: University of Chicago Press.

Mettler, Suzanne, and Joe Soss. 2004. "The Consequences of Public Policy for Democratic Citizenship: Bridging Policy Studies, and Mass Politics." *Perspectives on Politics* 2(1): 55–73.

Meyer, John. 2000. "Globalization: Sources, and Effects on National States, and Societies." *International Sociology* 15(2): 233–48.

———. 2001. "Reflections: The Worldwide Commitment to Educational Equality." *Sociology of Education* 74(Extra Issue): 154–58.

Meyer, John, John Boli, George Thomas, and Francisco Ramirez. 1997. "World Society, and the Nation-State." *American Journal of Sociology* 103(1): 144–81.

Moynihan, Colin, and Scott Shane. 2011a. "For Anarchist, Details of Life as an FBI Target." *New York Tiimes,* May 28.

———. 2011b. "The Phony Tough-on-Terror Crowd." *New York Times,* June 26.

Mueller, John. 1970. "Presidential Popularity from Truman to Johnson." *American Political Science Review* 64(1): 18–34.

———. 1994. *Policy and Opinion in the Gulf War.* Chicago: University of Chicago Press.

———. 2005. "The Iraq Syndrome." *Foreign Affairs* 84(1): 44–54.

———. 2006. *Overblown: How Politicians, the Terrorism Industry and Others Stoke National Security Fears.* New York: Free Press.

———. 2008. "Terrorphobia: Our False Sense of Insecurity." *American Interest* 3(5)(May/June): 6–13.

Mueller, John, and Mark Stewart. 2010. "Hardly Existential: Thinking Rationally About Terrorism." *ForeignAffairs.com,* April 2, 2010. http://www.foreign affairs.com/articles/66186/john-mueller-and-mark-g-stewart/hardly-existen tial (accessed July 25, 2012).

———. 2011. *Terror, Security, and Money: Balancing the Risks, Benefits, and Costs of Homeland Security.* New York: Oxford University Press.

Nacos, Brigitte. 2007. *Mass-Mediated Terrorism: The Central Role of the Media in Terrorism and Counterterrorism.* Lanham, Md.: Rowman & Littlefield.

Nacos, Brigitte, Yaeli Block-Elkon, and Robert Shapiro. 2011. *Selling Fear: Counterterrorism, the Media, and Public Opinion.* Chicago: University of Chicago Press.

National Commission on Terrorist Attacks upon the United States (National Commission). 2004. *The 9/11 Commission Report.* New York: W. W. Norton.

North, Douglass. 1990. *Institutions, Institutional Change and Economic Performance.* Cambridge: Cambridge University Press.

———. 2006. *Understanding the Process of Economic Change.* Princeton, N.J.: Princeton University Press.

North, Douglass, and Mary Shirley. 2008. "Conclusion: Economics, Political Institutions, and Financial Markets." In *Political Institutions and Financial Development,* edited by Stephen Haber, Douglass North, and Barry Weingast. Palo Alto, Calif.: Stanford University Press.

Nosek, Brian, Anthony Greenwald, and Mahzarin Banaji. 2007. "The Implicit Association Test at Age 7: A Methodological, and Conceptual Review." In *Automatic Processes in Social Thinking and Behavior,* edited by John Bargh. New York: Psychology Press.

Nunn, Clyde Z., Harry J. Crockett Jr., and J. Allen Williams Jr. 1978. *Tolerance for Nonconformity: A National Survey of Americans' Changing Commitment to Civil Liberties.* San Francisco: Jossey-Bass Publishers.

Odum, Howard. 1943. *Rumors of Race.* Chicago: University of Chicago Press.

Oorschot, Wim van. 2008. "Who Should Get What, and Why?" In *Welfare States: Construction, Deconstruction, Reconstruction,* edited by Stephan Leibfried and Steffen Mau. London: Edward Elgar.

Page, Benjamin, and Robert Shapiro. 1992. *The Rational Public: Fifty Years of Trends in Americans' Policy Preference.* Chicago: University of Chicago Press.

Panagopoulos, Costas. 2006. "The Polls-Trends: Arab, and Muslim Americans, and Islam in the Aftermath of 9/11." *Public Opinion Quarterly* 70(4): 608–24.

Pierson, Paul. 1993. "When Effect Becomes Cause: Policy Feedback, and Political Change." *World Politics* 45(4): 595–628.

———. 1996. "The New Politics of the Welfare State." *World Politics* 48(January): 143–79.

———. 2000. "Path Dependence, Increasing Returns, and the Study of Politics." *American Political Science Review* 94(2): 251–67.

Pilkington, Ed. 2011. "Bradley Manning: Top U.S. Scholars Voice Outrage at 'Torture,'" *The Guardian,* April 10.

Polling Report. 2007. "Terrorism, p. 3 (2006–2007)." *PollingReport.com.* http://www.pollingreport.com/terror3.htm (accessed August 31, 2008).

———. 2009. "Terrorism, p. 2 (2007–2009)." *PollingReport.com.* http://www.pollingreport.com/terror2.htm (accessed August 31, 2008).

———. 2012. "Terrorism (2010–2012)." *PollingReport.com.* http://www.pollingreport.com/terror.htm (accessed April 8, 2011).

Putnam, Robert. 2002. "Bowling Together." *The American Prospect* 13(1): 20–22.

Pyle, Christopher. 2001. *Extradition Politics and Human Rights.* Philadelphia, Pa.: Temple University Press.

Pyszczynski, Tom, Sheldon Solomon, and Jeff Greenberg. 2003. *In the Wake of 9/11: The Psychology of Terror.* Washington, D.C.: American Psychological Association.

Rasinski, Kenneth, Jennifer Bertold, Tom W. Smith, and Bethany Albertson. 2002. "America Recovers: A Follow-Up to a National Study of Public Response to the September 11th Terrorist Attacks." Chicago: NORC.

Ridgeway, Cecilia, and Lynn Smith-Lovin. 1999. "The Gender System, and Interaction." *Annual Review of Sociology* 25(August): 191–216.

Risen, James. 2011. "Ex-Spy Alleges Bush White House Sought to Discredit Critic," *New York Times,* June 11.

Risen, James, and Eric Lichtblau. 2009. "E-mail Surveillance Renews Concerns in Congress." *New York Times* online edition, June 17. http://www.nytimes.com/2009/06/17/us/17nsa.html?pagewanted=all&_r=0.

Rogin Michael. 1987. *Ronald Reagan, the Movie: And Other Episodes in Political Demonology.* Berkeley: University of California Press.

Rousseau, David. 2006. *Identifying Threats and Threatening Identities: The Social Construction of Realism and Liberalism.* Palo Alto, Calif.: Stanford University Press.

Saad, Lydia. 2006. "Anti-Muslim Sentiments Fairly Commonplace: Four in Ten Americans Admit Feeling Prejudice against Muslims." *Gallup.com,* August 10, 2006. http://www.gallup.com/poll/24073/AntiMuslim-Sentiments-Fairly-Commonplace.aspx (accessed August 31, 2008).

Sands, Philippe. 2008. *Torture Team: Rumsfield's Memo and the Betrayal of American Values.* London: Palgrave-McMillan.

Savage, Charlie. 2007. "Barack Obama's Q&A." *Boston Globe,* December 20.

———. 2009. "Obama Upholds Detainee Policy in Afghanistan." *New York Times,* February 22.

———. 2010a. "Obama Team Is Divided on Anti-Terror Tactics," *New York Times,* March 28.

———. 2010b. "Officials Push to Bolster Law on Wiretapping," *New York Times,* October 19. Available at http://query.nytimes.com/gst/fullpage.html?res

=9C04E2D61339F93AA25753C1A9669D8B63&n=Top%2fReference%2fTimes%20Topics%2fSubjects%2fT%2fTerrorism.

———. 2011. "Two Senators Say Patriot Act is Being Misinterpreted. *New York Tiimes*, May 26.

Schanzer, David, Charles Kurzman, and Ebrahim Moosa. 2010. "Anti-Terror Lessons of Muslim Americans." Washington, D.C.: National Institute of Justice.

Schmierbach, Mike, Michael Boyle, and Douglas McLeod. 2005. "Civic Attachment in the Aftermath of September 11th." *Mass Communication & Society* 8(4): 323–46.

Schofer, Evan, and Ann Hironaka. 2005. "The Effects of World Society on Environmental Protection Outcomes." *Social Forces* 84(1): 25–47.

Schrecker, Ellen. 1986. *No Ivory Tower: McCarthyism and the Universities*. New York: Oxford University Press.

Schubert, James, Patrick Stewart, and Mary Ann Curran. 2002. "A Defining Presidential Moment: 9/11, and the Rally Effect." *Political Psychology* 23(3): 559–83.

Schuman, Howard, Charlotte Steeh, Lawrence Bobo, and Maria Krysan. 1997. *Racial Attitudes in America: Trends and Interpretations*, rev. ed. Cambridge, Mass.: Harvard University Press.

Shane, Scott. 2010a. "Terrorism Fight Creates Battle over Prosecution." *New York Times*, February 12.

———. 2010b. "U.S. Approves Targeted Killing of American Cleric." *New York Times*, April 6.

———. 2012. "Shifting Mood May End Blank Check for U.S. Security Efforts," *New York Times,* October 24.

Shane, Scott, and Mark Mazzetti. 2007. "Interrogation Methods Are Criticized," *New York Times,* May 30.

Shipler, David. 2012. *Rights at Risk: The Limits of Liberty in Modern America*. New York: Knopf.

Sides, John, and Kimberly Gross. 2011. "Stereotypes of Muslims, and Support for the War on Terror." Unpublished manuscript, Department of Political Science, George Washington University.

Skocpol, Theda. 1992. *Protecting Soldiers and Mothers: The Political Origins of Social Policy in the United States*. Cambridge, Mass.: Harvard University Press.

Skrentny, John. 2002. *The Minority Rights Revolution*. Cambridge, Mass.: Harvard University Press.

Smist, Frank. 1990. *Congress Overseas the U.S. Intelligence Community, 1957–1989*. Knoxville: University of Tennessee Press.

Smith, Rogers M. 1997. *Civic Ideals: Conflicting Visions of Citizenship in U.S. History*. New Haven, Conn.: Yale University Press.

Smith, Tom W. 1990. "Liberal, and Conservative Trends in the United States Since World War II." *Public Opinion Quarterly* 54(4): 479–507.

———. 2012. "Trends in Confidence in Institutions, 1973–2006." Unpublished manuscript, National Opinion Research Center, Chicago, IL.

Sniderman, Paul, Henry Brody, and Philip Tetlock. 1991. *Reasoning and Choice: Explorations in Political Psychology*. New York: Cambridge University Press.

Sniderman, Paul, Joseph Fletcher, Peter Russell, and Philip Tetlock. 1996. *The Clash of Rights: Liberty, Equality, and Legitimacy in Pluralist Democracy*. New Haven, Conn.: Yale University Press.

Sniderman, Paul, and Douglas Grob. 1996. "Innovations in Experimental Design in General Population Attitude Surveys." *Annual Review of Sociology* 22 (August): 377–99.

Sobel, Richard. 2001. *The Impact of Public Opinion on U.S. Foreign Policy.* New York: Oxford University Press.

Soss, Joe, and Sanford Schram. 2007. "A Public Transformed? Welfare Reform as Policy Feedback." *American Political Science Review* 101(1): 111–27.

Starr, Paul. 2007. *Freedom's Power.* New York: Perseus Books.

Steensland, Brian. 2006. "Cultural Categories, and the American Welfare State: The Case of Guaranteed Income Policy." *American Journal of Sociology* 111(5): 1273–326.

Steensland, Brian, Jerry Park, Mark Regnerus, Lynn Robinson, Bradford Wilcox, and Robert Woodberry. 2000. "The Measure of American Religion: Toward Improving the State of the Art." *Social Forces* 79(1): 291–318.

Stiglitz, Joseph, and Lauren Blimes. 2008. *The Three Trillion Dollar War: The True Cost of the Iraq Conflict.* New York: Norton.

Stimson, James A., Michael B. Mackuen, and Robert S. Erikson. 1995. "Dynamic Representation." *American Political Science Review* 89(3): 543–65.

Stouffer, Samuel. (1955) 1992. *Communism, Conformity, and Civil Liberties,* 2nd ed. New Brunswick, N.J.: Transaction Publishers.

Strossen, Nadine. 2003. "Maintaining Human Rights in a Time of Terrorism: A Case Study in the Value of Legal Scholarship in Shaping Law, and Public Policy." *New York Law School Law Review* 46(3-4): 373–93.

Sullivan, John L., James Piereson, and George E. Marcus. 1982. *Political Tolerance and American Democracy.* Chicago: University of Chicago Press.

Svallfors, Stefan. 2010. "Policy Feedback, Generational Replacement, and Attitudes to State Intervention: Eastern, and Western Germany, 1990–2006." *European Political Science Review* 2(1): 119–35.

Thiessen, Marc. 2010. *Courting Disaster: How the CIA Kept America Safe and How Barack Obama Is Inviting the Next Attack.* Washington, D.C.: Regnery Publishing.

Tilghman, Andrew. 2012. "Official: U.S. Misjudged al-Qaida Capabilities." *Army Times,* February 7.

Tilly, Charles. 1998. *Durable Inequality.* Berkeley: University of California Press.

Tyler, Tom. 2006. *Why People Obey the Law.* Princeton, N.J.: Princeton University Press.

U.S. Congress. Senate. Committee on Judiciary, Subcommittee on Civil Rights. 1974. *Hearings on Military Surveillance.* 74th Congress, April 9–10. Washington: Government Printing Office.

U.S. Congress. Senate. Select Committee to Study Governmental Operations with Respect to Intelligence Activites. 1976. *Final Report, Book III: Supplementary Detailed Staff Reports on Intelligence Activities and the Rights of Americans.* Washington: Government Printing Office. http://www.icdc.com/~paulwolf/cointelpro/churchfinalreportIIIb.htm (accessed July 3, 2011).

Vaisey, Stephen. 2009. "Motivation, and Justification: A Dual-Process Model of Culture in Action." *American Journal of Sociology* 114(6): 1675–715.

Vallely, Richard. 2004. *The Two Reconstructions: The Struggle for Black Enfranchisement.* Chicago: University of Chicago Press.

Voss, Kim. 1994. *The Making of American Exceptionalism*. Ithaca, N.Y.: Cornell University Press.

Wilson, Thomas. 1994. "Trends in Tolerance Toward Rightist, and Leftist Groups, 1976–1988: Effects of Attitude Change, and Cohort Succession." *Public Opinion Quarterly* 58(4): 539–56.

Wlezien, Christopher. 1995. "The Public as Thermostat: Dynamics of Preferences for Spending." *American Journal of Political Science* 39(4): 981–1000.

Wlezien, Christopher, and Stuart Soroka. 2010. *Degrees of Democracy*. New York: Cambridge University Press.

Wolfe, Alan. 1973. *The Seamy Side of Democracy: Repression in America*. New York: David McKay.

———. 2008. *The Future of Liberalism*. New York: Vintage.

Wu, Frank. 2004. "Profiling in the Wake of September 11: The Precedent of the Japanese American internment." In *Civil Liberties vs. National Security in a Post-9/11 World*, edited by M. Catherine Darmer, Robert Baird, and Stuart Rosenbaum. Amherst: Prometheus Books.

Yoo, John. 2006. *War by Other Means: An Insider's Account of the War on Terror*. New York: Atlantic Monthly Press.

Zaller, John. 1992. *The Nature and Origin of Mass Opinion*. New York: Cambridge University Press.

Zimmer, Brendon, ed. 2011. *Extradition and Rendition: Background and Issues*. Hauppauge, N.Y.: Nova Science Publishers.

Zizek, Slavoj. 2006. "The Depraved Heros of 24 Are the Himmlers of Hollywood." *The Guardian*, January 10.

Index

Boldface numbers refer to figures and tables.

179